Jack Lewis and His American Cousin, Nat Hawthorne

Jack Lewis and His American Cousin, Nat Hawthorne

A Study of Instructive Affinities

D. G. Kehl

WIPF & STOCK · Eugene, Oregon

JACK LEWIS AND HIS AMERICAN COUSIN, NAT HAWTHORNE
A Study of Instructive Affinities

Copyright © 2013 D. G. Kehl. All rights reserved. Except for brief quotations in critical publications or reviews, no part of this book may be reproduced in any manner without prior written permission from the publisher. Write: Permissions, Wipf and Stock Publishers, 199 W. 8th Ave., Suite 3, Eugene, OR 97401.

Wipf&Stock
An Imprint of Wipf and Stock Publishers
199 W. 8th Ave., Suite 3
Eugene, OR 97401

www.wipfandstock.com

ISBN 13:978-1-61097-836-1

Manufactured in the U.S.A.

For Wanda,
my constant source of inspiration,
For Kevin and Kathie, Kenyon and Josette,
along with Emily, Aidan, Owen, Bennett, and Brynn,
all avid Lewis aficionados,
For my colleagues on the editorial board of *Sehnsucht: The
C. S. Lewis Journal*,
who offered encouragement and helpful suggestions,
And for the students in my class on Lewis and Hawthorne
at Arizona State University

Special thanks are due to the Emeritus College at Arizona State University
for the generous grant in support of this project.

"The heart, the heart,—there was the little yet boundless sphere wherein existed the original wrong of which the crime and misery of this outward world were merely types. Purify that inward sphere, and the many shapes of evil that haunt the outward... will turn to shadowy phantoms and vanish of their own accord..."

NATHANIEL HAWTHORNE, "EARTH'S HOLOCAUST"

"... The instrument through which you see God is your whole self. And if a man's self is not kept clean and bright, his glimpse of God will be blurred—like the Moon seen through a dirty telescope. That is why horrible nations have horrible religions: they have been looking at God through a dirty lens."

C. S. LEWIS, *MERE CHRISTIANITY*

Contents

Introduction: Instructive Affinities | ix

Part I Personal Backgrounds and Worldviews
1. Pondering "the Ultimates," "Things That Lie Beyond Human Ken" | 3
2. Worldviews: *Sub Specie Aeternitatis* | 16
3. Backgrounds and Lifestyles | 30

Part II Mutual Themes
4. Myths Retold and Myths Made | 47
5. Scientists and Scientism | 64
6. "The Great Power of Blackness": Sin—Original, Besetting, Unpardonable | 81

Part III Characterization
7. Perpetuators and Victims of the Power of Blackness | 103
8. Counteractors and Ambivalents in the Power of Blackness | 123

Part IV Companion Pieces
9. *Culpa*—Happy or Sad? *Perelandra* and *The Marble Faun (Transformation)* | 151
10. The Black Veil and the White: "The Minister's Black Veil," *The Blithedale Romance, Till We Have Faces* | 167
11. Allegories to the 3rd Power: "The Celestial Railroad" and *The Pilgrim's Regress* | 183
12. Four Loves and Seven Gables: *The Four Loves* and *The House of the Seven Gables* | 198

Conclusion: Baptized Imaginations | 212
Bibliography | 219
Index | 227

Introduction: Instructive Affinities

SOUTHERN POET AND CRITIC Allen Tate delivered a major address titled "Our Cousin, Mr. Poe" before the Poe Society of Baltimore on October 7, 1949, and later repeated the address as a Bergen Lecture at Yale University. In this seminal essay, Tate discussed "the recognition of a relationship, almost of the blood, which we must in honor acknowledge," concluding that "we may 'place' him [Poe] but we may not exclude him from our board... He is so close to me that I am sometimes tempted to enter the mists of pre-American genealogy to find out whether he may not actually be my cousin."[1] The same could be said of Jack Lewis in relation to his American "cousin," Nat Hawthorne. Surprisingly, no one has acknowledged and discussed this relationship, almost of blood, thus unwittingly excluding him from the English board.

The basis for what may initially seem a fantastic claim of cousinage can be found in Lewis's early letters to his friend Arthur Greeves. Lewis expressed great admiration for Hawthorne's work, particularly for *The House of the Seven Gables*, which he called "the most glorious (almost) novel that I have ever read... I really think I have never enjoyed a novel more... I intend to read all Hawthorne after this," though Lewis is quick to add, praising with a not-so-faint damn, "What a pity such a genius should be a beastly American!"[2] Similarly, eleven years later, in a letter to his brother Warnie, Lewis wrote: "Hawthorn [sic] I admire beyond words." Then, drawing a contrast to Longfellow, for whom he admits only "a sneaking affection," Lewis adds: "Hawthorne takes some old building dating from the New England times and weaves out of the very few centuries at his

---

1. Tate, "Our Cousin, Mr. Poe," in Robert Regan, Editor, *Poe: A Collection of Critical Essays*, 40, 50. Cf. Hyatt H. Waggoner, who refers to Hawthorne as "first cousin to William Faulkner and Robert Penn Warren (*The Presence of Hawthorne*, 13).

2. Lewis, Letter of 15 November 1910 and Letter of 29 November 1919, 152–53.

Introduction: Instructive Affinities

disposal an air of antiquity which is not often attained even in Europe where we have so much *arithmetically* greater a past to conjure with."[3]

Lewis seemed especially to admire the Gothic horror of Hawthorne's novel, noting: "I love the idea of a house with a curse! And although there is nothing supernatural in the story itself there is a brooding sense of mystery and fate over the whole thing: Have you read it?"[4] A week later he writes,

> Although by experience I am somewhat shy of recommending books to other people I think I am quite safe in earnestly advising you to make 'the Gables' your next purchase. By the way I shouldn't have said 'mystery', there is really no mystery in the proper sense of the word, but a sort of feeling of fate & inevitable horror as in 'Wuthering Heights'. . . There is one lovely scene where the villain—Judge Phycheon [sic]—has suddenly died in his chair, all alone in the old house, and it describes the corpse sitting there as the day wears on and the room grows darker—darker—and the ticking of his watch. But that sort of bald description is no use! I must leave you to read that wonderful chapter to yourself.[5]

The following year, 1917, Lewis again mentions that he is reading Hawthorne: "At present I am engaged on Hawthorne's 'Transformation' [the English title of *The Marble Faun*]." Then he chides his friend for apparently not heeding his advice to read Hawthorne: "In spite of repeated advice from me I don't think you have ever read this man. This one is very good indeed & has a lot about painting in it & some fine descriptions of Italian scenery." Surprisingly, he adds, "It is better than 'The Scarlet Letter', but, of course, not so good as 'The House with [sic] the Seven Gables.'"[6]

Of the eight American writers Lewis mentions to Greeves,[7] what was it about this "beastly" American's work that struck such a responsive chord in Lewis, what specifically did he admire about Hawthorne's work, and how does exploration of affinities between the two writers illuminate the beliefs and art of each?

---

3. Lewis, Letter of 12 December 1927, *The Collected Letters of C. S. Lewis*, I, 743.

4. Lewis, Letter of 22 November 1916, *They Stand Together: The Letters of C. S. Lewis to Arthur Greeves*, 152.

5. Ibid., Letter of 10 November 1916, 153.

6. Ibid., Letter of 28 October 1917, 200.

7. The eight are Hawthorne, Melville, Irving, Poe, Emerson, Longfellow, James, and London.

Introduction: Instructive Affinities

The life and work of C. S. Lewis has been much discussed in relation to various other writers and their work, such as George MacDonald, G. K. Chesterton, J. R. R. Tolkien (along with other Inklings, such as Charles Williams and Owen Barfield) and, more recently, Francis Schaeffer and even Sigmund Freud.[8] Thomas L. Martin's *Reading the Classics with C. S. Lewis*, predicated on Lewis as a literary touchstone, has offered brief essays on major periods of English literature and various genres, with the intent of providing new insights into both Lewis's work and the literature he so cherished. The essay on "Modern Literature" devotes just four pages to American writers (though the author remarks that "Lewis read a number of American authors"[9]) and briefly discusses only Henry James and T. S. Eliot. Similarly, John Stuart Bell's *From the Library of C. S. Lewis: Selections from Writers Who Influenced His Spiritual Journey*[10] includes only brief selections from just three American writers (John Woolman, T. S. Eliot, and not surprisingly Joy Davidman). The omissions seem especially surprising in view of the fact that Lewis's library, housed at the Marion E. Wade Center at Wheaton College, includes numerous volumes by more than forty different American writers.

The attempt to trace "influence," the supposed impact that a writer or literary work has on other writers or works, was quite common in the early twentieth century, but because it was often tenuous and far-fetched

---

8. See, for example, Jeff McInnis, *Shadows and Chivalry: Pain, Suffering, Evil and Goodness in the Works of George MacDonald and C. S. Lewis* (Eugene, OR, 2008); Michael H. Macdonald and Andrew A. Tadie, Eds. *G. K. Chesterton and C. S. Lewis: The Riddle of Joy* (Grand Rapids, 1989); R. J. Reilly, *Romantic Religion: A Study of Barfield, Lewis, Williams, and Tolkien* (Athens, GA, 1971); Humphrey Carpenter, *The Inklings: J. R. R. Tolkien, C. S. Lewis, Charles Williams, and Their Friends* (New York, 1981); Harry Lee Poe and James Ray Veneman, *The Inklings of Oxford: C. S. Lewis, J. R. R. Tolkien, and Their Friends* (Grand Rapids, 2009); Gareth Knight, *The Magical World of the Inklings: J. R. R.. Tolkien, C. S. Lewis, Charles Williams, Owen Barfield* (Element, 1991); Colin Duriez, *Tolkien and C. S. Lewis: The Gift of Friendship* (Mahwah, NJ, 2003); Diana Pavlac Glyer, *The Company They Keep: C. S. Lewis and J. R. R. Tolkien as Writers in Community* (Kent, OH, 2007); Martha C. Sammons, *War of the Fantasy Worlds: C. S. Lewis and J. R. R. Tolkien on Art and Imagination* (Santa Barbara, 2010); Lionel Adey, *C. S. Lewis' 'Great War' with Owen Barfield* (Cumbria, UK, 2002); Scott R. Burson and Jerry L. Walls, *C. S. Lewis and Francis Schaeffer* (Downers Grove, 1998); Armand M. Nicholl Jr., *The Question of God: C. S. Lewis and Sigmund Freud Debate God, Love, Sex, and the Meaning of Life* (New York, 2002);

9. Christopher, "Modern Literature," 257.

10. Bell, *From the Library of C. S. Lewis: Selections from Writers Who Influenced His Spiritual Journey.*

Introduction: Instructive Affinities

the practice fell into some disrepute.[11] Rather than "influence," this study explores what might be called instructive affinities[12]—that is, parallels, connections, relationships, commonalities, or consanguinities between Lewis and Hawthorne, for the purpose of mutual illumination. Striking parallels between the two writers include their spiritual beliefs, their personal backgrounds and lifestyles, their worldviews, the central motifs in their writings, their major characters, and various works that can be examined as companion pieces for mutual illumination. The parallels are so uncanny, or so preternaturally pervasive, to borrow a favorite term of Hawthorne's, that Nat and Jack might be called kindred spirits. A careful examination of the parallels can provide mutual illumination of each writer.

---

11. Harold Bloom in *The Anxiety of Influence: A Theory of Poetry* (New York: Oxford, 1973) posits a theory involving misprision (misreading), one trope being *kenosis* ("emptying," the Greek term borrowed from Paul in Philippians 2:7), whereby the writer "empties" the original text and "fills" the subsequent text with, ordinarily, a lower meaning. For application of this theory to fiction see D.G. Kehl, "*Kenosis* of Biblical Texts: Method and Meaning in Zora Neale Hurston's *Their Eyes Were Watching God*," MAWA, *The Middle-Atlantic Writers Association Review*, Vol. 16, December, 2001, 40–51.

12. The phrase is derivative of Goethe's *Elective Affinities*, the title of his third novel (*Die Wahlvenwandstschaften*, 1809), a scientific phrase once used to describe the tendency of certain chemical species to combine with certain substances or species in preference to others, compounds that only interacted with each other under certain circumstances. (For use of the phrase as an organizing metaphor, see Rene Magritte's 1933 painting "Elective Affinities," Tom Stoppard's 1993 play *Arcadia*, and Paolo Taviani's 1996 film *The Elective Affinities*.)

Hawthorne's familiarity with the writings of Goethe has been well documented (e.g., see Roy R. Male, *Hawthorne's Tragic Vision*, 33; Hubert H. Hoeltje, *Inward Sky: The Mind and Heart of Nathaniel Hawthorne*, 391, 511, 515 et al.), as has Lewis's (e.g., *The Collected Letters of C. S. Lewis*, Vol. I, 97, Vol. II, 441, 737, Vol. III, 597).

Part I

Personal Backgrounds and Worldviews

1

Pondering "the Ultimates," "Things That Lie Beyond Human Ken"

Scholars have drawn a multiplicity of differing conclusions about Hawthorne's religious beliefs, and few seem to agree.[1] Was he a quasi-Calvinist or Calvin's ironic stepchild? Was he a rebellious Puritan or a bastardly Puritan *malgre lui*? Was he a faux-Unitarian or a semi-orthodox Trinitarian? Was he a qualified Transcendentalist or a Transcendental Symbolist? The uncertainty, the disagreement, the ambivalence indicate the impossibility and undesirability of summarily labeling either Hawthorne or Lewis—or any great artist.

Hawthorne was more reticent than Lewis about his personal beliefs, but, at least in the minds of some, he seemed to think of himself, and inspired others to think of him, as a devoted, if not devout Christian. His son, Julian, wrote that his father "believed in God, but never sought to define him."[2] The choice of the word "define" seems especially pertinent etymologically, from the Latin verb *definire*, "to set a limit to, to delimit, to set bounds or boundaries." Would it not be presumptuous to set limits on the Almighty? Several years after Hawthorne's death, "his wife Sophia wrote about her husband's belief in Christ: 'I remember my husband

---

1. See, for example, such works as Randall Stewart's *Nathaniel Hawthorne: A Biography*, Hyatt H. Waggoner's *The Presence of Hawthorne* and *Hawthorne: A Critical Study*, Hubert H. Hoeltje's *Inward Sky: The Mind and Heart of Nathaniel Hawthorne*, Leonard J. Fick's *The Light Beyond: A Study of Hawthorne's Theology*, Agnes McNeill Donohue's *Hawthorne: Calvin's Ironic Stepchild*, Darrel Abel's *The Moral Picturesque: Studies in Hawthorne's Fiction*, Michael J. Colacurcio's *The Province of Piety: Moral History in Hawthorne's Early Tales*.

2. Moore, *The Salem World of Nathaniel Hawthorne*, 121.

saying once that he could not do without the warmth of his best image of His Father.'" Further, when Emerson is reported to have told Hawthorne that they must get rid of Christ, Hawthorne replied, "No, Mr. Emerson, we cannot do without Christ."[3] Though Hawthorne never asserted his beliefs in a systematic way, he did, as did Lewis, ponder, discuss, and write about the four great storylines or major motifs, along with variations and ramifications thereof: Divine Providence, the diabolic adversary, human mutiny and fall, and potential redemption and restoration, or, expressed another way: creation, fall, redemption, restoration.

One of the few attempts to summarize Hawthorne's beliefs specifies two of the storylines and implies the others: "His own religious beliefs were limited to a few points, never systematically stated. He had a sure faith in Providence, in a Providence that knows better than man. He thought of Jesus as the Redeemer of mankind, though in what sense explicitly he seems not to have recorded . . . He had, finally an unwavering belief in the immortality of the soul."[4] Another critic has this to say: "The philosophy of Hawthorne is a broadly Christian scheme which contains heaven, earth, and hell. Whether heaven and hell are realities or only subjective states of mind is one of Hawthorne's crucial ambiguities. I do not call him a Christian humanist, as do some excellent critics, for it seems to me that heaven and hell *are* real to him and play too large a part in his fiction to be relegated to the background."[5]

While Hawthorne was serving as U.S. consul in Liverpool (1853–1857), Herman Melville visited, and the two took a long walk along the shore in Southport, settling in to talk in a hollow among the dunes. Hawthorne later recorded their discussion in his *English Notebooks*, perhaps revealing as much about himself and his beliefs as about Melville and his:

> Melville, as he always does, began to reason about Providence and futurity, and of everything that lies beyond human ken, and informed me that he had "pretty much made up his mind to be annihilated"; but still he does not seem to rest in that anticipation; and, I think, will never rest until he gets hold of a definite belief. It is strange how he persists—and has persisted ever since I knew him, and probably long before—in wandering to and fro over these deserts, as dismal and monotonous as the sand hills amid which we were sitting. He can neither believe, nor be comfortable

---

3. Ibid., 121.
4. Hoeltje, *Inward Sky: The Mind and Heart of Nathaniel Hawthorne*, 460–61.
5. Fogle, *Hawthorne's Fiction: The Light and the Dark*, 5–6.

in his unbelief, and he is too honest and courageous not to try to do one or the other. If he were a religious man, he would be one of the most truly religious and reverential; he has a very high and noble nature, and better worth immortality than most of us.[6]

Here Hawthorne implies the desirability, even the need, for "a definite belief," which can bring rest and comfort, as well as his admiration for religiosity and reverence, his own belief in immortality, and his disagreement with the idea of annihilation hereafter. Further, his metaphoric reference to the monotonous and dismal experience of reasoning about "everything that lies beyond human ken," likening it to continuous wandering in a desolate wasteland, suggests much about his view of spiritual epistemology, about reason and revelation, about reasoning and imagining, about head and heart.

In a strikingly similar instance, Lewis, writing in 1922 (before his conversion, even to Theism), recorded having a long conversation with Owen Barfield: "We then drifted into a long talk about ultimates. Like me, he has no belief in immortality etc., and always feels the materialistic pessimism at his elbow. He is most miserable. He said however that the 'hard facts' which worried us, might to posterity appear mere prejudices de siecle, as the 'facts' of Dante do to us. Our disease, I said, was really a Victorian one. The conversation ranged over many topics and finally died because it was impossible to hold a court between two devil's advocates."[7] As with the Hawthorne-Melville duologue, this one reveals a similar, if not identical,

---

6. Hawthorne, *The English Notebooks*, 163. Several years earlier, when Melville visited Hawthorne in Lenox, Massachusetts, Hawthorne noted that "after supper, Melville and I had a talk about time and eternity, things of this world and of the next," a talk "that lasted pretty deep into the night" (*The American Notebooks*, 448).

7. Lewis, *All My Road Before Me: The Diary of C. S. Lewis*, 40. The "hard facts" apparently refer to the difficulty of reconciling what seem to be scientific "facts" with the existence and goodness of God. Lewis, who was to become a member of the Oxford Dante Society, later remarks in various letters that he spent several stays with Barfield, during which they had "splendid talks and reading of Dante," on one night staying up till four. In another letter Lewis tells a correspondent that he is pleased to hear that he has "the Dantesque mood and [has] begun to doubt," for "'blind faith' is indeed unsuitable for us who are alive now: we know too much and see life too widely and it is culpable not to make use of our widened landscape. The comfortable little universe with heaven above and hell beneath, an absolute up and down and a bare six thousand years of recorded history, could furnish you well enough with a world-view that a man could write in his pocket book and have done. But we haven't got that now, and I feel that we ought to use our own data even if they lead only to destruction," Letter of 25 February 1922, *The Collected Letters of C. S. Lewis*, I, 520.

Part I: Personal Backgrounds and Worldviews

subject being discussed—"the ultimates," including immortality, a range of "many topics," the unspecified "etc." Writing at this time as an unbeliever, recorder Lewis, unlike recorder Hawthorne, reveals his concurrence in unbelief and even skepticism, but, like Hawthorne, he notes his friend's lack of rest and comfort, saying that "he is most miserable," apparently due to "materialistic pessimism." He refers to their unbelief, their struggle with the "hard facts," as their "disease," even a siecle pandemic, part of the zeitgeist. Whereas there seems to be no evidence that either party in the first duologue is playing devil's advocate—perversely or merely for sake of argument upholding the opposing side or supporting an indefensible cause—, in the second duologue the diabolic advocacy strategy is said to be mutual but the topics and tactics are not specified.

Although he apparently never explicitly attested to a personal conversion as Lewis did, Hawthorne wrote of redemption not through some utopian meliorism (like Brook Farm, the cooperative community, established by the Transcendental Club near West Roxbury, MA, 1841–1847, which Hawthorne wrote about in *The Blithedale Romance*) but through a changed heart: "The heart, the heart, —there was the little yet boundless sphere wherein existed the original wrong of which the crime and misery of this outward world were merely types. Purify that inward sphere, and the many shapes of evil that haunt the outward . . . will turn to shadowy phantoms and vanish of their own accord; but if we go no deeper than the intellect, and strive, with merely that feeble instrument, to discern and rectify what is wrong, our whole accomplishment will be a dream."[8] Randall Stewart has suggested that Hawthorne may have remembered these thoughts from Jonathan Edwards's treatise on "Religious Affections": "Hawthorne and Edwards were agreed that regeneration must come from within; that it was an affair of the heart, the religious affections, and not of the intellect merely; that the inward sphere must be purified."[9] Hawthorne believed redemption is necessary because one of "the old verities and truths of the heart," to borrow William Faulkner's phrase, [10]

---

8. Hawthorne, "Earth's Holocaust," *The Complete Short Stories of Nathaniel Hawthorne*, 412.

9. Stewart, *Nathaniel Hawthorne: A Biography*, 247.

10. Faulkner, "Nobel Prize Acceptance Speech," *The Portable Faulkner*, Edited by Malcolm Cowley, 723–24. Faulkner stated further that young writers have forgotten "the problems of the human heart in conflict with itself, which alone can make good writing . . . , the old universal truths lacking which any story is ephemeral and doomed—love and honor and pity and pride and compassion and sacrifice."

Pondering "the Ultimates," "Things That Lie Beyond Human Ken"

is that the heart is depraved, as the Old Testament prophet attests: "The heart is deceitful above all things and desperately wicked. Who can know it?" (Jeremiah 17:9). Accordingly, in *The American Notebooks* Hawthorne included the following idea for a possible future work: "The human Heart to be allegorized as a cavern; at the entrance there is sunshine, and flowers growing about it. You step within, but a short distance, and begin to find yourself surrounded with a terrible gloom, and monsters of divers kinds; it seems like Hell itself. You are bewildered, and wander long without hope." Unmistakably, this metaphor of the heart conveys the idea of horrific gloominess, frightening denizens, and chthonian hopelessness. But further down and further into the cavern of the human heart, a light suddenly shines, reproducing the flowers and sunny beauty of the entrance. Hawthorne concludes: "the gloom and terror may lie deep; but deeper still is this eternal beauty."[11] What, then, is one to conclude about Hawthorne's view of human depravity? He was seemingly haunted by the Puritan/Calvinistic doctrine of total depravity, which provided a pervasive tension in his fiction and prompted the creation of such depraved monsters as Roger Chillingworth, Mistress Hibbins, Ethan Brand, Giacomo Rappaccini, Judge Pyncheon, and others, but his inveterate ambivalence and Romantic idealism are evident here, as elsewhere.

Lewis is less equivocal in his view of total depravity, stating in his discussion of "Human Wickedness" in *The Problem of Pain*: "This chapter will have been misunderstood if anyone describes it as a reinstatement of the doctrine of Total Depravity. I disbelieve that doctrine, partly on the logical ground that if our depravity were total we should not know ourselves to be depraved, and partly because experience shows us much goodness in human nature."[12] Hawthorne would almost certainly concur with Lewis's assessment of human nature, for the light shining deep within the metaphoric cavern renders it bright, peaceful, and eternally beautiful. Perhaps it is the same radiance, a sacramental expression of nature, which illuminates the interior of the church which Robin Molineux visits, a beam hovering around the pulpit and resting upon the open page of the great Bible, causing

11. Hawthorne, *The American Notebooks*, 237.

12. Lewis, *The Problem of Pain*, 66–67. Note Lewis's further discussion in his essay "The Poison of Subjectivism": ". . . The general tenor of scripture does not encourage us to believe that our knowledge of the Law has been depraved in the same degree as our power to fulfil it . . . Our righteousness may be filthy and ragged [cf. Isaiah 64:6]; but Christianity gives us no ground for holding that our perceptions of right are in the same condition. They may, no doubt, be impaired; but there is a difference between imperfect sight and blindness," *Christian Reflections*, 79.

Part I: Personal Backgrounds and Worldviews

Robin's heart to shiver with an intense feeling of loneliness and nostalgia for home.[13] What Lewis states explicitly, Hawthorne illustrates implicitly with allegorical, or sometimes symbolic, word pictures.

If human nature is depraved but not "totally," in the sense that a light-beam of truth is retained in the heart, enabling humans to perceive right, "the Law's goodness," and to "rejoice in it according to the inward man,"[14] how do these two writers view the solution to the problem of human depravity? The concluding paragraph of Hawthorne's "Fancy's Show Box" provides evidence of his belief in the need of repentance for mercy and redemption: "Man must not disclaim his brotherhood, even with the guiltiest, since, though his hand be clean, his heart has surely been polluted by the flitting phantoms of iniquity. He must feel that, when he shall knock at the gate of heaven, no semblance of an unspotted life can entitle him to entrance there. Patience must kneel, and Mercy come from the footstool of the throne, or that golden gate will never open!"[15] Hyatt H. Waggoner has well said of this passage: "Repent and ask God's mercy: If this is 'Puritan,' it is also Pauline, and orthodox . . . [epitomized in] a single short prayer, the 'Jesus Prayer': 'Lord Jesus Christ, have mercy upon me, a sinner' . . . Hawthorne inclined toward the orthodox formulation derived from St. Paul, 'justification by grace through faith.'"[16]

Though he apparently believed in their necessity, Hawthorne only hinted at his own repentance and redemption. For example, in a letter to Sophia Peabody, his future wife, he wrote: "We are all but shadows—we are not endowed with real life, and all that seems most real about us is but the thinnest substance of a dream—till the heart is touched. That touch creates us—then we begin to be—thereby we are beings of reality, and inheritors of eternity."[17] It is not clear if Hawthorne is attributing this essential creative "touch" of the heart, a prerequisite to real life and

---

13. Hawthorne, "My Kinsman, Major Molineux," *The Complete Short Stories of Nathaniel Hawthorne*, 525.

14. Lewis, "The Poison of Subjectivism," *Christian Reflections*, 79.

15. *The Complete Short Stories of Nathaniel Hawthorne*, 113. In his *American Notebooks* he includes the following entry for a possible future work: "To sit at the gate of Heaven, and watch persons, as they apply for admittance, some gaining it, others being thrust away" (Edited by Claude M. Simpson, 236).

16. Waggoner, *Hawthorne: A Critical Study*, 13.

17. Hawthorne, Letter of 4 October 1840, *Selected Letters of Nathaniel Hawthorne*, 80.

Pondering "the Ultimates," "Things That Lie Beyond Human Ken"

inheritance of eternity, to the Almighty or to Sophia, to both, or most likely, to the former through the instrumentality of the latter.

Lewis was much more explicit about his conversion, recounting it first in the often cited passage from *Surprised by Joy*: "In the Trinity Term of 1929 I gave in, and admitted that God was God, and knelt and prayed: Perhaps, that night, the most dejected and reluctant convert in all England . . . Really, a young Atheist cannot guard his faith too carefully. Dangers lie in wait for him on every side. You must not do, you must not even try to do, the will of the Father unless you are prepared to 'know of the doctrine.'"[18] This was his conversion to Theism, belief in the existence of one infinite, personal God conceived as Ruler of the universe, as evidenced through general revelation (nature) and special revelation (God's Word). Two years later, on September 28, 1931, as Lewis rode to Whipsnade Zoo in the sidecar of his brother Warnie's motorcycle, he took what he called "the final step." "When we set out," he said, "I did not believe that Jesus Christ is the Son of God, and when we reached the zoo I did."[19] In a letter to Arthur Greeves, written on October 1, 1931, Lewis spoke of his "first step in far deeper mysteries" and stated, "How deep I am just now beginning to see: for I have just passed on from believing in God to definitely believing in Christ—in Christianity." He promised to try explaining it further another time, acknowledging that his "long night talk with [Hugo] Dyson and [J. R. R.] Tolkien had a great deal to do with it."[20]

There is abundant evidence that Lewis pondered the meaning and implications of conversion, regeneration, salvation—and wrote explicitly of these doctrines, whereas Hawthorne depicted them implicitly in his tales, which shall be discussed subsequently. For example, Lewis spoke

---

18. Lewis, *Surprised by Joy*, 182, 180–81. The phrase "Conversion Story" was to appear on the back of the dust jacket. Lewis is citing John 7:17, where Jesus says, "If anyone wills to do His will, he shall know concerning the doctrine, whether it is from God or whether I speak on My own authority." Cf. David C. Downing's book *C. S. Lewis's Journey to Faith: The Most Reluctant Convert*, Downers Grove: InterVarsity Press, 2002.

19. Lewis, *Surprised by Joy*, 189.

20. Lewis, *They Stand Together: Letters of C. S. Lewis to Arthur Greeves*, 425. In a letter of 21 December 1941, Lewis said, "Dyson and Tolkien were the immediate human causes of my own conversion. Is any pleasure on earth as great as a circle of Christian friends by a good fire?" *The Collected Letters of C. S. Lewis*, II, 501. Henry Victor Dyson, "Hugo," was an Inkling, lecturer and tutor in English at the University of Reading, also Fellow and Tutor at Oxford. John Ronald Reuel Tolkien was an Inkling, close friend of Lewis, and Professor of Anglo-Saxon at Oxford, best known as the author of *The Hobbit* and *The Lord of the Rings*.

Part I: Personal Backgrounds and Worldviews

of the "stages" of regeneration: "As Charles Williams says there are three stages: (1.) The Old Self on the Old Way. (2.) The Old Self on the new [sic] Way. (3.) The New Self on the New Way,"[21] but he never elaborated on the stages. In another letter he stresses the grace and sovereignty of God in conversion: "Everyone looking back on *his own* conversion must feel—and I am sure the feeling is in some sense true—'It is not I who have done this. I did not choose Christ: He chose me. It is all free grace, wh. I have done nothing to earn.' That is the Pauline account; and I am sure it is the only true account of every conversion *from the inside*. Very well. It then seems to us logical & natural to turn this personal experience into a general rule 'All conversions depend on God's choice.'"[22]

How might Lewis have responded to Hawthorne's reticence in attesting to a conversion experience? Perhaps these comments in a 1955 letter are pertinent: Some Protestants "have a whole programme of 'conviction', 'conversion' etc. marked out, the same for everyone, & will not believe that anyone can be saved who doesn't go through it 'just so'. But . . . God has His own unique way with each soul. There is no evidence that St. John even underwent the same kind of 'conversion' as St. Paul." Lewis concludes by echoing a statement from George MacDonald's *Sir Gibbie* (1879): "The time for speaking comes rarely, the time for being never departs."[23]

Just as Hawthorne spoke, as noted above, of the need for "the inward sphere," the heart, to be purified, Lewis has meister-devil Screwtape describe the human as a series of concentric circles, with the heart and will at the real center, the intellect coming next, followed by fantasy on the outside.[24] Lewis emphasizes the necessity of engaging the whole self,

---

21. Letter of 15 October 1951, *The Collected Letters of C. S. Lewis*, Vol. III, 141. Charles Walter Stansby Williams was an Inkling, editor at Oxford University Press, and author of numerous works, including "supernatural thrillers," such as *The Place of the Lion*.

22. Lewis, Letter of 3 August 1953, *The Collected Letters of C. S. Lewis*, III, 354–55. It should be noted that Lewis goes on in the letter to qualify the issue, obviously struggling with the tension between predestination and free will. He concludes, "The real inter-relation between God's omnipotence and Man's freedom is something we can't find out."

23. Ibid., Letter of 2 March 1955, 576. George MacDonald (1824–1905) was an essayist, critic, lecturer, poet, and novelist, author of over fifty books, including twenty-five novels, the best known being *Lilith* and *Phantastes*, which, Lewis said, was to "convert, even to baptize," his imagination. Lewis acknowledged MacDonald as his "master," asserting, "I fancy I have never written a book in which I did not quote from him" (Preface, *George MacDonald: 365 Readings*, xxxiii).

24. Lewis, *The Screwtape Letters*, 28.

Pondering "the Ultimates," "Things That Lie Beyond Human Ken"

which must be cleansed, in one's relationship with God: ". . . the instrument through which you see God is your whole self. And if a man's self is not kept clean and bright, his glimpse of God will be blurred—like the Moon seen through a dirty telescope. That is why horrible nations have horrible religions: they have been looking at God through a dirty lens."[25] Significantly, both authors emphasize the need for cleansing—*from the inside out*. In another letter Hawthorne wrote that "no man is safe from sin and disgrace till by divine assistance he has thoroughly cleansed his heart—which few of us take the pains to do, though many satisfy themselves with a shallow and imperfect performance of that duty."[26] Hawthorne seems to suggest that the cleansing is a joint effort of humans and God—human effort assisted by the Divine—whereas Lewis states more explicitly that "the guilt is washed out not by time but by repentance and the blood of Christ . . ."[27]

Both authors seem to agree that the only solution to human depravity requires a radical change of the heart, not mere external reformation, perhaps what Hawthorne meant by "a shallow and imperfect performance." Again, Lewis states explicitly, "We must not suppose that even if we succeeded in making everyone nice we should have saved their souls. A world of nice people, content in their own niceness, looking no further, turned away from God, would be just as desperately in need of salvation as a miserable world and might even be more difficult to save. For mere improvement is not redemption . . . God became man to turn creatures into sons: not simply to produce better men of the old kind but to produce a new kind of man."[28] Hawthorne illustrates and dramatizes these truths in various works, such as "The Celestial Railroad" (to be discussed in chapter 11).

Relative to the redemption and restoration storyline/motif, what are the two writers' views and practices of church attendance? This question could be answered with more certitude if Lewis had critiqued Hawthorne's sketch "Sunday at Home," collected in *Twice-Told Tales* (1837, enlarged in 1842). Of course, Hawthorne, after his Unitarian upbringing, is reported to have ordinarily stayed away from all churches.[29] The sketch,

---

25. Lewis, *Mere Christianity*, 164–65.

26. Hawthorne, Letter of 6 November 1863, *Selected Letters of Nathaniel Hawthorne*, 256.

27. Lewis, *The Problem of Pain*, 61.

28. Lewis, *Mere Christianity*, 167.

29. Waggoner, "Art and Belief," *The Presence of Hawthorne*, 40. According to Margaret B. Moore, "It is clear that Hawthorne did not attend church in Salem after

Part I: Personal Backgrounds and Worldviews

which is generally overlooked or summarily dismissed as simply an ironic narrative mocking staid Sunday Christians, merits a closer examination, perhaps to be enhanced by consideration in relation to what Lewis said about church attendance.

The narrator of Hawthorne's sketch is a first-person persona and participant, apparently the author himself, peeking on a Sabbath morning from his chamber window on Herbert Street in Salem, observing the adjacent East (or Second) Church as the sunshine steals downward from the steeple's weathercock to the street below. He is gladdened when he spies scores of little girls and boys decked out in colorful array, an old woman in black and an old man with "darksome brow," two long lines of people streaming into the church, followed by the slow and solemn clergyman. When the gray sexton closes the door, the chambered spy imagines the congregants standing to pray and questions whether he can bring his own heart into unison "with a fervor of supplication, but no distinct request," perhaps "the safest kind of prayer," that is, one so indistinct that it anticipates no definite answer and therefore cannot disappoint if / when none comes. Surely, there is some cogent irony at work here and elsewhere in the sketch. The narrator's imagined prayer, "Lord, look down upon me in mercy!" is undercut by the language in the following reference to "that *sentiment gushing* from my soul." He hears the hymn but says he can enjoy it better in his solitary chamber than in the church, where "the full choir and the *massive* melody of the organ would *fall with a weight upon me*," and he concludes that reading the printed sermons is preferable to hearing them declaimed. Though he has *imagined* that the earth is hallowed by the Sabbath sunshine, assuring that his soul can never lose the instinct of its faith, in the final paragraph he questions if it was really "worth while to rear this massive edifice, to be a desert in the heart of the town, and populous only for a few hours of each seventh day," then invokes a consecration: "May its site, which was consecrated on the day when the first tree was felled, be kept holy forever, a spot of solitude and peace, amid the trouble and vanity of our week-day world!"[30] Is this simply ironic, subtly captious, derisive?

---

college." She notes that Hawthorne's sister Elizabeth told of a friend who "once . . . came to him crying because somebody had told her that he was an infidel—he must be, as he never went to church. Hawthorne denied being an 'infidel,' and told her that 'he did go to church whenever he happened to be elsewhere than in Salem, on a Sunday.' He did not go often elsewhere either," Moore concludes (*The Salem World of Nathaniel Hawthorne*, 120).

30. Hawthorne, "Sunday at Home," *Twice-Told Tales*, 25.

Pondering "the Ultimates," "Things That Lie Beyond Human Ken"

Michael J. Colacurcio has well said that "to propose that 'Sunday at Home' was conceived in irony . . . is not to deny its biographical relevance altogether. It is merely to recommend a certain critical caution. As the sketch reveals attitudes which are widely shared rather than intimately personal, it may actually serve us best as a reminder of all that it is not telling; of all that we, perhaps, should yet like to know, in spite of Hawthorne's own systematic reticence."[31]

Longing to know more than Hawthorne's reticence has revealed but taking care to observe the "certain caution" which Colacurcio justifiably recommends, might one at least raise the question: is the persona being merely ironic when he says: ". . . though my form be absent, my inner man goes constantly to church, while man, whose bodily presence fills the accustomed seats, have left their souls at home . . ." or later when he says, ". . . a feeling of loneliness comes over me, and brings also an uneasy sense of neglected privileges and duties. O, I ought to have gone to church!"?[32] Perhaps a response most apropos comes from another reticent Massachusetts nonconformist, just twenty-three years hence, from a village just 106 miles west of Salem: "Some keep the Sabbath going to Church— / I keep it staying at home . . . / God preaches, a noted Clergyman— / And the sermon is never long, / So instead of getting to Heaven at last— / I'm going all along."[33]

What were Lewis's views and practices of church attendance? Did he spend his Sundays at home peeking from behind a window curtain or "with a bobolink for a chorister and an orchard for a dome"? His remarks in *Surprised by Joy* sound even more anti-ecclesiastical than Hawthorne's! "The idea of churchmanship was to me wholly unattractive," he writes, though he adds that after he became a Theist he started attending his parish church on Sundays and his college chapel on weekdays because he "thought one ought to 'fly one's flag' by some unmistakable overt sign." Hawthorne would surely have smiled at Lewis's statement: "I was not in the least anti-clerical, but I was deeply anti-ecclesiastical . . . Though I liked clergymen

---

31. Colacurcio, *The Province of Piety: Moral History in Hawthorne's Early Tales*, 494–95.

32. Hawthorne, "Sunday at Home," 18, 20.

33. The lines, of course, are by Emily Dickinson (1830–1886), who lived a reclusive life in her parents' home in the western Massachusetts village of Amherst. From a comment in a letter, it is clear that Lewis read and relished Dickinson's poetry: "What I am reveling in at present is Emily Dickinson" (Letter of 24 October 1960, *The Collected Letters of C. S. Lewis*, III, 1200).

Part I: Personal Backgrounds and Worldviews

as I like bears, I had as little wish to be in the Church as in the zoo." Surely Lewis's American cousin would have understood the reasons Lewis gives:

> It was to begin with, a kind of collective, wearisome 'get-together' affair. I couldn't yet see how a concern of that sort should have anything to do with one's spiritual life. To me, religion ought to have been a matter of good men praying alone and meeting by twos and threes to talk of spiritual matters. And then the fussy, time-wasting botheration of it all! The bells, the crowds, the umbrellas, the notices, the bustle, the perpetual arranging and organizing. . . . Thus my churchgoing was a merely symbolical and provisional practice. If it in fact helped to move me in the Christian direction, I was and am unaware of this.[34]

Lewis refers negatively to the bells as part of the "botheration" and says, "the hymns were (and are) extremely disagreeable to me," whereas Hawthorne's persona speaks, perhaps ironically, of "the music of the bell" and of the hymn, which he feels he can enjoy better from a distance than if he sat within the church's walls.

Lewis's next known remarks about churchmanship came in 1944, when he agreed to respond to questions about Christianity at the head office of Electric and Musical Industries Ltd. at Hayes, Middlesex. Question 16 was: "Is attendance at a place of worship or membership with a Christian community necessary to a Christian way of life?" Lewis responded as follows: "That's a question which I cannot answer. My own experience is that when I first became a Christian, about fourteen years ago, I thought that I could do it on my own, by retiring to my rooms and reading theology, and I wouldn't go to the churches and Gospel halls; and then later I found that it was the only way of flying your flag; and, of course, I found that this meant being a target." By "being a target" he meant that getting up early to go to church was not only inconvenient but also selfishly upsetting to the household. He says further that he very much disliked the hymns, which he considered "fifth-rate poems set to sixth-rate music." But later he began to see the merits of church attendance: "I came up against different people of quite different outlooks and different education, and then gradually my conceit just began peeling off. I realized that the hymns (which were just sixth-rate music) were, nevertheless, being sung with devotion and benefit by an old saint in elastic-side boots in the opposite pew, and then you realize that you aren't fit to clean those

---

34. Lewis, *Surprised by Joy*, 186–87.

boots. It gets you out of your solitary conceit."[35] There is no evidence that Hawthorne's solitary conceit, if it was in fact such, ever peeled off. Or is Lewis now being ironic?

All the evidence makes it clear that Lewis is not being ironic at all. In a letter written in December of 1950, Lewis writes: "The New Testament does not envisage solitary religion: some kind of regular assembly for worship and instruction is everywhere taken for granted in the Epistles. So we must be regular practicing members of the Church." But then he adds, almost as if he has his American cousin in mind: "Of course we differ in temperament. Some . . . find it more natural to approach God in solitude; but we must go to church as well. Others find it easier to approach Him thro' the services: but they must practice private prayer & reading as well. For the Church is not a human society of people united by their natural affinities but the Body of Christ in which all members however different . . . must share the common life, complementing and helping and receiving one another precisely by the differences." His summary seems especially applicable not only to Hawthorne's nineteenth and his own twentieth century but to our twenty-first as well: "If people like you and me find much that we don't naturally like in the public & corporate side of Christianity all the better for us: it will teach us humility and charity towards simple low-brow people who may be better Christians than ourselves. I naturally *loathe* nearly all hymns: the face, and life, of the charwoman in the next pew who revels in them, teach me that good taste in poetry or music are *not* necessary to salvation."[36]

The two writers shared many views regarding God, human depravity, redemption, and churchmanship. Whereas Hawthorne was much more reticent and restrained, often couching his views in allegorical or symbolic word-pictures or irony, Lewis was much more open and candid, expressing his views not only in fiction but also in expository essays and personal letters. Surely one cannot read much of the work of these two writers without concluding that they shared similar worldviews.

---

35. Lewis, "Answers to Questions on Christianity," *God in the Dock*, 61–62.

36. Lewis, Letter of 7 December 1950, *The Collected Letters of C. S. Lewis*, III, 68–69. For a fuller discussion of Lewis's view of church music, see "On Church Music," *Christian Reflections*, 94–99.

2

Worldviews: *Sub Specie Aeternitatis*

HAWTHORNE AND LEWIS PONDERED similar concepts—the "ultimates," "the things that lie beyond human ken." Further, they apparently drew some of the same conclusions and developed comparable worldviews, that is, the set of basic assumptions or presuppositions which they held, consciously or subconsciously, about the basic nature of life and the world, or to put it metaphorically, the lens through which they viewed and depicted human existence. They both seemed to view mortal life *sub specie aeternitatis*, under the aspect or from the standpoint of eternity.

In neither case, however, were their worldviews monolithic or static; rather each evolved or developed progressively through several different views before each reached its predominant form. Growing up in Salem, Hawthorne was early influenced by the Congregationalist First Church, where he reportedly "drank in the lilting cadence of Scripture and stored up its parables" for their intriguing stories and plagued his family with various theological questions.[1] This influence continued during his four years at Bowdoin College, with the stern discipline and strict Calvinist doctrines of its president, and where Hawthorne chafed under the compulsory religious services.[2]

Growing up on the outskirts of Belfast, Ireland, Lewis seems to have been little influenced either by the Sunday services to which his parents took him or by the set prayers he was taught. He apparently did pray seriously and read the Bible during his stay at Wynyard, one of the English

---

1. Wineapple, *Hawthorne: A Life*, 23–24. He was obviously fascinated with the parable genre, which is how he labeled "The Minister's Black Veil" on the title page and "Earth's Holocaust" in its concluding statement.

2. Mellow, *Nathaniel Hawthorne in His Times*, 29.

boarding schools he attended, and reportedly "talked about religion with other boys in an entirely healthy and profitable way."[3] Like Hawthorne at Bowdoin College, Lewis at Malvern College was something of a rebel and came to regard himself as an atheist, a worldview he held until that momentous Trinity Term of 1929 at Oxford, when he was converted, albeit reluctantly, to Theism, belief in a Higher Power outside himself, and, two years later, to belief in Christ. In the words of his brother Warren, Lewis's conversion "was no sudden plunge into a new life but rather a slow steady convalescence from a deep-seated spiritual illness of long standing."[4]

There is no substantive evidence that Hawthorne ever held an a-Theistic worldview, but at times he seems to have experienced doubts, though not "a-gnostic" in the sense of Thomas Henry Huxley's coinage, denoting the *impossibility* of knowing if there is a God, but rather simply "not knowing," from the Greek *a + ginosko*. "Doubts may flit about me, or seem to close their evil wings, and settle down," Hawthorne says in his essay "Sunday at Home," "but, so long as I imagine that the earth is hallowed . . . while that blessed sunshine lives within me—never can my soul have lost the instinct of its faith."[5] His use of the word "instinct" suggests a natural, unlearned, inborn tendency to believe. Almost as a corrective rejoinder to Hawthorne's comments, Lewis, in a letter offering a critique of an article about himself, stated: "*Instinct* again dangerous. Neither you nor I believe this gift to be a merely biological phenomenon."[6]

Both Hawthorne and Lewis acknowledged the mysteries of the spiritual, the divine. In a letter to Sophia, Hawthorne assured her that his views were caused by "no want of faith in mysteries, but from a deep reverence of the soul, and of the mysteries which it knows within itself, but never transmits to the earthly eye or ear."[7] Similarly, Lewis, writing of the resurrection of the body, said, "The best is perhaps what we understand least."[8]

During Hawthorne's youth, a heated battle raged between the Trinitarianism and Unitarianism, the latter reacting against the resurgence of orthodox Calvinism following the Great Awakening, heightened by William Ellery Channing's controversial sermon of 1819 titled "Unitarian

---

3. Sayer, *Jack: C. S. Lewis and His Times*, 27.
4. Ibid., 129.
5. Hawthorne, *Twice-Told Tales*, 17.
6. Lewis, Letter of 4 July 1955, *The Collected Letters of C. S. Lewis*, III, 628.
7. Hawthorne, *Selected Letters of Nathaniel Hawthorne*, edited by Myerson, 96.
8. Lewis, *A Grief Observed*, 59.

Part I: Personal Backgrounds and Worldviews

Christianity." Unitarianism is the belief that God is one unity in both nature and person, denying the full deity of Christ and of the Holy Spirit as well as such doctrines as original sin, depravity, inherited guilt, loss of free will, eternal retribution, vicarious atonement et al. Lewis, for his part, surely speaking for Hawthorne, indicted Unitarianism in no uncertain terms and, alluding to its denial of Christ's divinity and other such doctrines, asks Arthur Greeves, "Don't you think we shd. allow *any* weight to the fruits of these doctrines? Where are the shining examples of human holiness wh. ought to come from Unitarianism if it is true? Where are the Unitarian 'opposite numbers' to St. Francis, George Herbert, Bunyan, Geo. Macdonald, and even burly old Dr Johnson? Where are the great Unitarian books of devotion? Where among them shall I find 'the words of life'? Where have they helped, comforted, & strengthened us?"[9] Hawthorne might have replied: "Yes, where indeed?"

Unitarianism, in turn, prepared the way for Transcendentalism, the philosophic and literary movement which flourished from about 1836 to 1860. Reacting against orthodox Calvinism and eighteenth century rationalism, this eclectic movement stressed philosophical idealism, intuition, individualism and self-reliance, the immanence of God in the natural world, and social reform. The name was apparently derived from Kant, who called all knowledge "transcendental," in the sense that it is concerned not with objects but with the mode of knowing objects. Ralph Waldo Emerson, undoubtedly the central figure, was the author of the 1836 seminal essay "Nature," sometimes called "the Transcendentalist Bible." Though Hawthorne shared some ideas of Transcendentalism and in 1841 spent six months at Brook Farm, the utopian community established by the Transcendental Club, and though Sophia was drawn to the Transcendental group, Hawthorne did not, would not, could not share, among other ideas, belief in human nature free of latent evil. One of his most caustically satirical representations is Giant Transcendentalism: "as to his form, his features, his substance, and his nature generally, it is the chief peculiarity of this huge miscreant that neither he nor himself, nor anybody for him, has ever been able to describe them."[10]

Hawthorne clearly repudiates Emerson's philosophy, for example, in his essay "The Old Manse," where he notes that people often flocked to

---

9. Lewis, Letter of 11 December 1944, *They Stand Together: The Letters of C. S. Lewis to Arthur Greeves*, 503.

10. Hawthorne, "The Celestial Railroad," *The Complete Short Stories of Nathaniel Hawthorne*, 301.

Worldviews: Sub Specie Aeternitatis

Emerson "as the finder of a glittering gem hastens to a lapidary, to ascertain its quality and value," but he, though he "might have asked of this prophet the master word that should solve me the riddle of the universe," concludes that though he has "admired Emerson as a poet of deep beauty and austere tenderness, [he has] sought nothing from him as a philosopher."[11]

Whereas Lewis temporarily found attractive, only later to learn their inadequacy, "hard-boiled atheism," "popular realism," Philosophical Idealism,[12] Pantheism, progressing then to Theism and ultimately to orthodox Christianity, Hawthorne's worldview developed from elements of Trinitarian Calvinistic Congregationalism to influence of Unitarianism to some shared beliefs but ultimate repudiation of Transcendentalism to what might be called, lacking an explicit attestation of conversion, a quasi-Christian ("seeming" or "as it were") worldview, *au fond* ("at bottom" or "basically"), putative or assumptive Christianity.

The two writers shared similar or comparable worldviews, each viewing time and mortal life *sub specie aeternitatis*, both often pondering what Lewis called *tempus et aeternitas*. "We dwell in the shadow cast by Time, which is itself the shadow of Eternity,"[13] Hawthorne wrote, seemingly echoing Plato, as Lewis did as well: "Time is the moving image of eternity. All visible things exist just in so far as they succeed in imitating the Forms."[14]

---

11. Hawthorne, *Mosses from an Old Manse*, 41–42. Surprisingly, Lewis seemed to admire Emerson even more than did Hawthorne. For example, when asked if he cared for American writers, he responded, "Robert Frost and Ralph Waldo Emerson." (Griffin, *Clive Staples Lewis: A Dramatic Life*, 322). In a letter to Arthur Greeves, he wrote: "You are quite right about Emerson. I often pick him up here for an odd quarter of an hour, and go away full of new ideas. Every sentence is weighty: he puts into paragraphs what others, seeking charm, expand into whole essays or chapters. At the same time his tense concentration makes him painful reading, he gives you no rest. I don't know why you object to his style—it seems to me admirable. Quel dommage that such a man should be an American." (Letter of 12 September 1918, *They Stand Together: The Letters of C. S. Lewis to Arthur Greeves*, 231). Lewis's fascination for Emerson is further demonstrated by the various comments written in the margins of his seven books by Emerson housed in the Marion E. Wade Center at Wheaton College.

12. Note Hyatt H. Waggoner's comment that "Hawthorne was an idealist who wrote in the age of Philosophical Idealism," concluding that he was something of an idealist as his opposition to materialism suggests ("Art and Belief," *The Presence of Hawthorne*, 63–64).

13. Hawthorne, *The American Notebooks*, Edited by Randall Stewart, 197.

14. Lewis, *The Allegory of Love: A Study in Medieval Tradition*, 45–46. Possible influence of Plato on the two writers is another study in itself. "It's all in Plato, all in Plato," Lord Digory emotes in *The Last Battle*, 170. "Open your Plato," Lewis writes in "Bluspels and Flalansferes," "and you will find yourself among the great creators of

Part I: Personal Backgrounds and Worldviews

To both writers, time and the natural world bespeak eternity and the supernatural world; the eternal is shadowed in things of the earth. The narrator of Hawthorne's "Earth's Holocaust" tells the desperate bookworm whose precious books have been burned, "The great book of Time is still spread wide open before us; and, if we read it aright, it will be to us a volume of eternal truth."[15] The criterion for eternal truth, it is to be noted, is a correct reading of the great book of Time, along with a recognition that the necessary condition for a better world is not social reformation but purification of individual hearts. Similarly, Lewis, also using a book analogy, approvingly cites a line from the seventeenth century poet Thomas Traherne: "The world . . . is the beautiful frontispiece to Eternity."[16] In a subsequent letter he borrows the same metaphor, writing that he desires death not when this world seems harshest but when there seems to be most of Heaven already here, causing him to long for the *patria*: "It is the bright frontispiece [which] whets one to read the story itself . . . Our best havings are wantings."[17]

One of the great lessons read in the book of Time, and perhaps an illustration of a correct reading thereof, is the transforming nature of love, a theme Hawthorne would develop in *The House of the Seven Gables*. In a letter to his wife Sophia, Hawthorne tells her that hitherto he has been walking all his life in the dream of time, among shadows, but now there is something that has taken him out of that dream—above time, apart from time, even while in the midst of time—their mutual affection, which "diffuses eternity round about us." Thus, he concludes, "the grosser life [temporal] is a dream and the spiritual life [eternal] a reality."[18] Images of time in Hawthorne are often associated with death and are "grosser" in the sense of being "unpleasant," "offensive," "lacking in fineness or refinement." Clifford, in *The House of the Seven Gables*, comes to realize "that no great mistake, whether acted or endured, in our

---

metaphor, and therefore among the masters of meaning," *Selected Essays*, 265. "The natural world is, for Plato, a world of shadows," Lewis wrote in *English Literature in the Sixteenth Century*, 386. Hawthorne, however, was clearly skeptical of Concord Platonism, perhaps, as Randall Stewart notes, because it "did less justice to the solid satisfactions of this life," perhaps because he was resisting "a state in which the Idea shall be all in all" (*Nathaniel Hawthorne: A Biography*, 73).

15. Hawthorne, *The Complete Short Stories of Nathaniel Hawthorne*, 409.

16. Lewis, Letter of 8 July 1930, *The Collected Letters of C. S. Lewis*, I, 914.

17. Lewis, Letter of 5 November 1954, *The Collected Letters of C. S. Lewis*, III, 522–23.

18. Hawthorne, Letter of 1 January 1840, *Selected Letters of Nathaniel Hawthorne*, 71.

mortal sphere, is ever really set right [because] Time, the continual vicissitude of circumstances, and the invariable inopportunity of death render it impossible."[19] This truth, the narrator adds, "would be a very sad one but for the higher hopes which it suggests." These "higher hopes" are the belief in immortality and Eternal Reality.

Perhaps part of the putative grossness of temporal life is the real and ever-present danger that time's physicality can be delusional and distract from the reality of eternity. For example, Hawthorne warned his wife Sophie that no "delusion can be more lamentable and mischievous than to mistake the physical and material for the spiritual. What [is] so miserable as to lose the soul's true, though hidden, knowledge and consciousness of heaven, in the mist of an earth-born vision?"[20] Accordingly, Aylmer, his idealistic scientist in "The Birthmark," in attempting to eradicate earthly imperfection, missed the essence of the perfect: "he failed to look beyond the shadowy scope of time, and, living once for all in eternity, to find the perfect future in the present."[21]

If time according to Hawthorne is dreamlike, shadowy, and "grosser," to Lewis it is defective because of its transience, its vicissitude. "Time is a defect of reality since by its v. nature any temporal being loses each moment of its life to get the next—the moments run through us as if we were sieves!"[22] He adds that God's life is non temporal, for He dwells in "the eternal Now." Again he stresses the transcendence of God, who "is not in Time and therefore does not *foresee* your future actions but *sees* them. He is *already* in tomorrow and *still* in yesterday."[23] He reiterates the point further in "Time and Beyond Time" in *Mere Christianity*: "Almost certainly God is not in Time. His life does not consist of moments following one another. If a million people are praying to Him at ten-thirty tonight, He need not listen to them all in that one little snippet which we call ten-thirty. Ten-thirty—and every other moment from the beginning

19. Hawthorne, *The House of the Seven Gables*, 272.

20. Hawthorne, Letter of 18 October 1841, *Selected Letters of Nathaniel Hawthorne*, 96.

21. Hawthorne, "The Birthmark," *The Complete Short Stories of Nathaniel Hawthorne*, 238.

22. Lewis, Letter of 4 February 1949, *The Collected Letters of C. S. Lewis*, II, 915. In another letter he speaks of "the nature of time—there being no real *present*, every moment already past however quickly you try to grab it. How rich we shall be when we get off this single railway-line into the rich green country left and right" (Letter of 2 February, 1956, *The Collected Letters of C. S. Lewis*, III, 701).

23. Lewis, Letter of 22 January 1959, *The Collected Letters of C. S. Lewis*, III, 1014.

of the world—is always the Present for Him. If you like to put it that way, He has all eternity in which to listen to the split second of prayer put up by a pilot as his plane crashes in flames."[24] Lewis then uses several analogies, one being that of a novelist who is not hurried along, time-bound, in the imaginary time of his novel.[25] In another he notes that if time were pictured as a straight line along which humans travel, then God is the whole page on which the line is drawn, being above, outside, and all around, therefore containing the whole line and seeing it all.

Lewis uses yet another analogy in referring to what he calls one of the "mysteries" of the New Testament, "a sort of double vision. A. Into our salvation as eternal fact, as it (and all else) is in the timeless vision of God. B. Into the same thing as a process worked out in time. Both must be true in some sense but it is beyond our capacity to envisage both together. Can one get a faint idea of it by thinking of A. A musical score as it is written down with all the notes there at once. B. The same thing *played* as a process in time."[26]

Lewis's Screwtape says, "The humans live in time but our Enemy destines them to eternity . . . [and] wants them to attend chiefly to two things, to eternity itself, and to that point of time which they call the Present. For the Present is the point at which time touches eternity . . .; in it freedom and actuality are offered."[27] Similarly, in his essay "Historicism," Lewis asks: "Where except in the present, can the Eternal be met?"[28] He refers to this present moment as the Eternal Now. Consequently, Screwtape tells Wormwood that their diabolical business is to get humans away from the Eternal and from the Present, always drawing their attention to the future, which, he says, is least like Eternity, because the past is frozen and no longer flowing, the Present being "all lit up with eternal rays." Similarly, the narrator in Hawthorne's *The Marble Faun*, says: "How wonderful, that this our narrow foothold of the Present

---

24. Lewis, *Mere Christianity*, 166–67.

25. Lewis, whether consciously or not, reverses the analogy used by James Joyce in *A Portrait of the Artist as a Young Man*: "The artist, like the God of the creation, remains within or behind or beyond or above his handiwork, invisible, refined out of existence, indifferent, paring his fingernails" (215). Joyce compares the artist with God, whereas Lewis compares God with the artist.

26. Lewis, Letter of 6 May 1962, *The Collected Letters of C. S. Lewis*, III, 1336. See also Lewis's discussion of time in relation to prayer and "Special Providences" in Appendix B of *Miracles*, 174–81.

27. Lewis, *The Screwtape Letters*, 75.

28. Lewis, *Christian Reflections*, 113.

should hold its own so constantly, and, while every moment changing, should still be like a rock betwixt the encountering ties of the long Past and the infinite To-come!"[29]

Hawthorne expressed the core belief that both human misery and happiness constitute a claim for eternal life: "God himself cannot compensate us for being born, in any period short of eternity. All the misery endured here constitutes a claim for another life;—and, still more, all the happiness, because all true happiness involves something more than the earth owns, and [needs] something more than a mortal capacity for the enjoyment of it."[30] Because this finite, temporal existence is too transient for all the misery and injustice to be rectified and humans compensated, accordingly, it lays claim for the infinite, eternal existence; because the capacity of this mortal existence is inadequate to fulfill the longings for happiness and joy, it lays claim for an immortal, eternal existence.

Lewis expressed essentially the same idea in various places: "If I find in myself a desire which no experience in this world can satisfy, the most probable explanation is that I was made for another world . . . Probably earthly pleasures were never meant to satisfy it, but only to arouse it, to suggest the real thing . . . I must keep alive in myself the desire for my true country, which I shall not find till after death."[31] Again he wrote: ". . . we remain conscious of a desire which no natural happiness will satisfy. . . ."[32] Further, he states: ". . . the human soul was made to enjoy some object that is never fully given—nay, cannot even be imagined as given—in our present mode of subjective and spatio-temporal experience."[33]

The natural world, both writers say, points to the supernatural world. For example, on an especially beautiful autumn day in 1843, Hawthorne wrote: "There is a pervading blessing diffused over all the world. I look out of the window and think, 'O perfect day! O beautiful world! O good God!' And such a day is the promise of a blissful eternity. Our Creator would never have made such weather, and given us the deep heart to enjoy it, above and beyond all thought, if he had not meant us to be immortal. It opens the gates of heaven and gives us glimpses far

---

29. Hawthorne, *The Marble Faun*, 411.
30. Hawthorne, *The English Notebooks*, 101.
31. Lewis, *Mere Christianity*, 136–37.
32. Lewis, *The Weight of Glory*, 6.
33. Lewis, *The Pilgrim's Regress*, xii.

inward."³⁴ He exults in being alive and thanks God for breath. Another time he writes: "God does not let us live any where or any how on earth, without placing some thing of Heaven close at hand, by rightly using and considering which, the earthly darkness or trouble will vanish, and all be Heaven—."³⁵

Walter Hooper has well said that Lewis was always at his best while writing about Heaven. He devotes an entire chapter to Heaven in *The Problem of Pain*, describing the longing for heaven as "the signature of each soul . . . There have been times when I think we do not desire heaven but more often I find myself wondering whether, in our heart of hearts, we have ever desired anything else."³⁶ Further, in his chapter on "Hope" in *Mere Christianity*, he writes that "our whole education tends to fix our minds on this world . . . [and] when the real want for Heaven is present in us, we do not recognize it. Most people, if they had really learned to look into their own hearts, would know that they do want, and want acutely, something that cannot be had in this world. There are all sorts of things in this world that offer to give it to you, but they never quite keep their promise."³⁷

Both writers spoke of the joys of heaven. For example, Hawthorne commented that "a man will undergo great toil and hardship for ends that must be many years distant, —as wealth or fame, —but none for an end that may be close at hand, —as the joys of heaven."³⁸ Lewis, who said that "Joy is the serious business of Heaven,"³⁹ commented that "the joys of Heaven are, for most of us in our present condition, 'an acquired taste'— and certain ways of life may render the taste impossible of acquisition."⁴⁰ For Hawthorne the joys of heaven seem ironically more immanent (and imminent) and accessible than the earthly pseudo-joys of wealth and prestige, whereas for Lewis the joys of Heaven are perhaps impossible to acquire because of "our present condition" and "certain ways of life," that is, guilt and human wickedness.

In another letter Lewis suggests that the perfect joy of Heaven is attributable to perfect obedience, for "what indeed can we imagine Heaven

---

34. Hawthorne, *The American Note-Books*, 453.
35. Hawthorne, *The American Notebooks*, 237.
36. Lewis, *The Problem of Pain*, 146, 145.
37. Lewis, *Mere Christianity*, 135.
38. Hawthorne, *The American Note-Books*, 121.
39. Lewis, *Letters to Malcolm: Chiefly on Prayer*, 93.
40. Lewis, *The Problem of Pain*, 61.

Worldviews: Sub Specie Aeternitatis

to be but unimpeded obedience."[41] He goes on to observe that one of the causes of our love of inanimate nature is that we see the will of the Creator being carried out unequivocally, thus rendering nature completely beautiful. Heaven's joy is also attributable to perpetual worship: "the perpetual worship *is* the perpetual vision, the perfect exercise of all one's faculties on the perfect Object."[42]

Perhaps no single work deals more with and reveals more about Hawthorne's belief in Heaven vis-à-vis earth, faith and doubt, light and darkness, reality and dream, truth and illusion than his much-neglected "Night Sketches: Beneath an Umbrella." The narrator ventures out to walk on a rainy winter's night, encountering a dark, black, impenetrable nothingness, "as though heaven and all its lights were blotted from the system of the universe."[43] He sees, sequentially, seven different lights—a dim light casting a reddened gleam, shop lights casting a red glitter, red, blue, and yellow meteors in an apothecary's window, a gleam from a family's lighted window, illumination from a stately mansion, light from a final lamp struggling feebly with the darkness, and finally light from a tin lantern. He also observes six sets of figures: a poor woman struggling to keep her umbrella right-side-out, a retired sea-captain, a slipshod gentleman seeking a doctor, a young couple who slip and fall on a patch of ice, a family circle by their fireside, and a solitary figure carrying a tin lantern. The narrator witnesses the various delusive gleams, the dark night keeping splendor from diffusing the darkness, the obscurity able to be dispelled only by radiance from above. The narrator concludes with the "moral"—that "we, all night wanderers through a stormy and dismal world, if we bear the lamp of Faith, enkindled at a celestial fire, it will surely lead us home to that heaven whence its radiance was borrowed."[44] The darkness of the natural, temporal world is total and unremitting, punctuated here and there only with false, illusory lights. This void, the narrator learns, can be illuminated only by the lamp of Faith, which has been kindled at a celestial fire, and only this light can lead us home to Heaven, from whence its radiance came.

Sounding almost like a brief commentary on Hawthorne's allegorical sketch are the following statements in Lewis's discussion of the

41. Lewis, Letter of 8 January 1936, *The Collected Letters of C. S. Lewis*, II, 177.
42. Ibid., Letter of 17 August 1949, 971.
43. Hawthorne, "Night Sketches: Beneath an Umbrella," *Twice-Told Tales*, Vol. II, 268.
44. Ibid., 275.

Part I: Personal Backgrounds and Worldviews

Incarnation: "'He came down from Heaven' can almost be transposed into 'Heaven drew earth up into it'... The pure light walks the earth; the darkness, received into the heart of Deity, is there swallowed up. Where, except in uncreated light, can the darkness be drowned?"[45] Hawthorne and Lewis seem to agree that only the celestial light of Faith can diffuse, dispel, swallow up the darkness of despair.

Lewis spoke much more explicitly of Heaven and Hell than did Hawthorne, who depicted the latter in his fiction. In *The Problem of Pain* Lewis devoted an entire chapter each to Heaven (chapter 10) and to Hell (chapter 8). The eternal dance, he says, "makes heaven drowsy with the harmony." "All the pains and pleasures we have known on earth are early initiations in the movement of that dance: but the dance itself is strictly incomparable with the sufferings of this present time. As we draw nearer to its uncreated rhythm, pain and pleasure sink almost out of sight. There is joy in the dance, but it does not exist for the sake of joy. It does not even exist for the sake of good, or of love. It is Love Himself, and God Himself, and therefore happy." To enter heaven, he says further, "is to become more human than you ever succeeded in being in earth; to enter hell is to be banished from humanity. What is cast (or casts itself) into hell is not a man: it is 'remains.'"[46] Only "remains" are left of Hawthorne's Ethan Brand, who first invokes and then casts himself into the "deadly element of Fire" in the lime kiln, which functions as microcosm and symbol of hellfire.[47]

Brand also dramatizes other points Lewis makes, such as the three symbols of Hell—punishment, destruction, and privation or banishment, with the recurring image of fire combining the ideas of torment and destruction[48]—and the "irrevocableness" of both Heaven and Hell.[49] Clearly, Lewis pondered much about the horror of Hell, noting in a letter: "About Hell: how do we get over Mt. VII 13, 14? But I agree we *must* get

---

45. Lewis, *Letters to Malcolm: Chiefly on Prayer*, 70–71.

46. Lewis, *The Problem of Pain*, 153, 125. See also the Letter of 18 January 1941, *The Collected Letters of C. S. Lewis*, II, 465: "You will remember that in the parable, the saved go to a place prepared for *them*, while the damned go to a place never made for men at all." Cf. Matthew 25: 34, 41—"Then shall the King say unto them on his right hand, Come, ye blessed of my Father, inherit the kingdom prepared for you from the foundation of the world ... Then shall he say also unto them on the left hand, Depart from me, ye cursed, into everlasting fire, prepared for the devil and his angels."

47. Hawthorne, "Ethan Brand," *The Complete Short Stories of Nathaniel Hawthorne*, 483.

48. Lewis, *The Problem of Pain*, 124–25.

49. Lewis, Letter of 20 July 1943, *The Collected Letters of C. S. Lewis*, II, 585.

over that one somehow or go mad. And leaving that one out, perhaps we can accept your argument that tho' Hell exists we are not absolutely forced to hold that anyone will reach it. But wouldn't the same, in logic, on the same grounds, hold of Heaven?"[50] Hawthorne dramatizes one way of "getting over" the horror of Hell and thereby avoiding madness—to deny its existence as Mr. Smooth-it-away and others do in "The Celestial Railroad," also denying the reality of Tophet, the place near Jerusalem where human sacrifices were made to Molech,[51] thus a microcosm or symbol of Hell. The train on which the contemporary pilgrim-narrator is riding passes a door in the hillside, reputed to be "a byway to hell," and pauses in "a smoky and lurid cavern," at "the mouth of the infernal region" from which "darted huge tongues of dusky flame" and in which could be seen "strange, half-shaped monsters and visions of faces horribly grotesque . . ." and from which could be heard "awful murmurs, and shrieks, and deep, shuddering whispers of the blast, sometimes forming themselves into words almost articulate . . . The inhabitants of the cavern . . . were unlovely personages, dark, smoke-begrimed, generally deformed, with misshapen feet, and a glow of dusky redness in their eyes as if their hearts had caught fire and were blazing out . . ."[52] The flames are "lurid," a favorite adjective of Hawthorne's and Poe's, meaning ghastly, deathly pale, glowing through a haze, and the noise is loudly cacophonous, harsh-sounding, jarring, dissonant, with echoing cachinnation, that is, loud, grotesque, derisive laughter. Such, according to Hawthorne, are the sights and sounds of Hell.

Similarly, Lewis's Screwtape exults in the unmitigated noise of hell: "Noise—Noise, the great dynamism, the audible expression of all that is exultant, ruthless, and virile—Noise which alone defends us from silly qualms, despairing scruples and impossible desires. We will make the whole universe a noise in the end. We have already made great strides in this direction as regards the Earth. The melodies and silences of Heaven

50. Ibid., Letter of 24 October 1940, 450–51. Matthew 7:13–14 says: "Enter in at the narrow gate: for wide is the gate, and broad is the way, that leadeth to destruction, and many there be who go in that way; Because narrow is the gate, and hard is the way, which leadeth unto life, and few there be that find it."

51. Cf. II Kings 23:10—"And he [Josiah, king of Judah] defiled Tophet, which is in the valley of the children of Hinnom, that no man might make his son or his daughter to pass through the fire to Molech [ancient Phoenician and Ammonite god, to whom children were sacrificed by burning]."

52. Hawthorne, "The Celestial Railroad," *The Complete Short Stories of Nathaniel Hawthorne*, 299–300.

will be shouted down in the end . . . Music and silence—how I detest them both!" This pathetic fiend then quotes "the description one human writer made of heaven: 'the regions where there is only life and therefore all that is not music is silence.'"[53] Hell is all noise, the result of internecine conflict between death and life, whereas Heaven is all music and silence because the risen Prince of Peace reigns where there is only life.

Screwtape also expresses what he calls "the whole philosophy of Hell [which] rests on the axiom that one thing is not another thing, and, specially, that one self is not another self. My good is my good and your good is yours. What one gains another loses . . . ; it means the sucking of will and freedom out of a weaker self into a stronger. 'To be' *means* 'to be in competition.'"[54] Lewis writes in *The Problem of Pain* that a characteristic of the lost soul is the rejection of everything that is not himself, finally achieving his wish—"to live wholly in the self and to make the best of what he finds there. And what he finds there is Hell."[55]

Several figures in Hawthorne's fiction dramatize these competitive, self-aggrandizing characteristics. One such is Roger Chillingworth, who "strove to go deep into his patient's [Dimmesdale's] bosom, delving among his principles, prying into his recollections, and probing everything with a cautious touch, like a treasure-seeker in a dark cavern . . . ; at some inevitable moment, will the soul of the sufferer be dissolved, and flow forth in a dark, but transparent stream . . ."[56] Similarly, Ethan Brand, who, like Chillingworth, turns into a very fiend, has, with "cold and remorseless purpose," diabolically "wasted, absorbed, and perhaps annihilated [Esther's] soul, in the process."[57] The language emphasizes the diabolical violation: delving, prying, probing, dissolving, wasting, absorbing, perhaps annihilating.

Lewis makes further points about both Heaven and Hell in *The Great Divorce: A Dream*. For example, in his dialogue with George MacDonald, his teacher explains that both are retrospective: ". . . Heaven,

---

53. Lewis, *The Screwtape Letters*, 120, 119. The human writer is George MacDonald: ". . . and he [the resurrected Christ] entered the regions where there is only life, and therefore all that is not music is silence, (for all noise comes of the conflict of Life and Death) . . . " ("The Hands of the Father," *Unspoken Sermons*, 188).

54. Lewis, *The Screwtape Letters*, 94.

55. Lewis, *The Problem of Pain*, 123.

56. Hawthorne, *The Scarlet Letter*, 114.

57. Hawthorne, "Ethan Brand," *The Complete Short Stories of Nathaniel Hawthorne*, 480.

Worldviews: Sub Specie Aeternitatis

once attained, will work backwards and turn even that agony into a glory . . . ," a process beginning, he says, even before death. "The good man's past begins to change so that his forgiven sins and remembered sorrows take on the quality of Heaven: the bad man's past already conforms to his badness and is filled only with dreariness. And that is why, at the end of all things, when the sun rises here and the twilight turns to blackness down there, the Blessed will say, 'We have never lived anywhere except in Heaven, ' and the Lost, 'We were always in Hell.' And both will speak truly."[58] MacDonald says further that "the whole difficulty of understanding hell is that the thing to be understood is so nearly Nothing." "All Hell," he says further, "is smaller than one pebble of your earthly world: but it is smaller than one atom of *this* world, the Real world . . . [whereas] Heaven is reality itself. All that is fully real is Heavenly."[59]

Heaven, then, is what Lewis called "the ultimate Fact, the fountain of all other facthood, the burning and undimensioned depth of the Divine Life. Most certainly also, to be united with that Life in the eternal Sonship of Christ is, strictly speaking, the only thing worth a moment's consideration."[60] In *The Chronicles of Narnia* this ultimate Fact is Aslan's country, believed in and sought steadfastly by—a mouse! Reepicheep expresses his determination to reach Aslan's country: "My own plans are made. While I can, I sail east in the *Dawn Treader*. When she fails me, I paddle east in my coracle. When she sinks, I shall swim east with my four paws. And when I can swim no longer, if I have not reached Aslan's country . . . I shall sink with my nose to the sunrise . . ."[61] In a letter to a fifth grade class in Maryland, Lewis said that Reepicheep did get to Aslan's country, and that "anyone in our world who devotes his entire life to seeking Heaven will be *like* Reepicheep."[62] No character in the work of the master from New England and none in the work from the master of old England seeks the ultimate reality of Heaven more earnestly than this exemplary mouse! Which of us has not been outdone by this diminutive, courageous rodent?

---

58. Lewis, *The Great Divorce: A Dream*, 69. Note that Lewis repeats this passage in a letter of 25 May, 1944, written while he was working on the novel (*The Collected Letters of C. S. Lewis*, II, 617).

59. Lewis, *The Great Divorce*, 77, 138, 70.

60. Lewis, *Miracles: A Preliminary Study*, 160–61.

61. Lewis, *The Voyage of the 'Dawn Treader'*, 184.

62. Lewis, Letter of 29 May 1954, *C. S. Lewis Letters to Children*, 45.

3

Backgrounds and Lifestyles

THESE TWO WRITERS, ONE from old England and one from New England, separated by space and time, not only pondered similar ideas and held similar worldviews but also shared markedly similar tastes and loves, antipathies and aversions, experiences and trials.

It should come as no surprise that the two writers shared a love for many of the same authors and books, especially during their early, formative years. Various Hawthorne biographers point out that his two favorite books in his earlier years were Spenser's *Faerie Queene* and Bunyan's *The Pilgrim's Progress*, which he read and reread (and frequently alluded to) throughout his life. Similarly, according to George Sayer, Lewis read Spenser's *Faerie Queene* in one sitting at Great Bookham, regretting that it was not longer, and he read *The Pilgrim's Progress* twice[1] and mentioned to his friend Arthur Greeves that he was "awfully bucked" by it.[2]

Hawthorne's reading has been described variously as "avid," "prodigious" and "voracious," this latter adjective used also by Austin Warren in his essay "Hawthorne's Reading": "He gradually became a voracious reader as the records of withdrawals from Salem lending library show. His early favorites were Spenser, Bunyan, and Shakespeare. The first two particularly affected his maturing allegorical mind and led him to see the spiritual

---

1. Sayer, *Jack: C. S. Lewis and His Times*, 58. Sayer mentions that by and large, Lewis formed his literary tastes in his early years and hardly altered them. Apparently, the same could be said of Hawthorne.

2. Letter of 15 November 1916, *They Stand Together: The Letters of C. S. Lewis to Arthur Greeves*, 150. According to the *Random House Dictionary of the English Language*, "bucked" is informal English slang for "elated," "happy."

significance in natural events."³ His sister Elizabeth reportedly remembered Nathaniel sitting half an afternoon in a large chair, quietly enveloped in reading *The Pilgrim's Progress* and Spenser's *Faerie Queene*, which was an early favorite and one of the first books he was to purchase. In addition to works of the Puritanesque Bunyan, Spenser, and Milton, other favorites were Addison and Steele's *The Spectator*, Samuel Johnson's *Idler*, Alexander Pope's satires, and Byron's *Childe Harold's Pilgrimage*. Other favorites of both writers were, of course, Dante, Milton, and Chaucer, along with Wordsworth and the younger Romantic poets—Shelley, Keats, and Byron.⁴ They also shared great admiration for the romantic novels of Sir Walter Scott, Lewis mentioning at least fifteen of Scott's works to his friend Arthur Greeves and Hawthorne mentioning at least eighteen of Scott's works in his *English Notebooks* and admiring Scott's works so much that he reportedly expressed a wish that he had not read them so he might have the pleasure of reading them again for the first time!

Austin Warren's assessment of Hawthorne's reading applies to a somewhat lesser degree to Lewis's. Hawthorne, he says, "read without the desire to exhibit his knowledge and taste or to sharpen his critical wits by dissecting the talents and tomes of others. That he was a keen and detached critic of his own work, with a clear sense of his own limitations and of the conditions under which he could create, anyone acquainted with his prefaces and letters will acknowledge. But his own genius absorbed him; and he read for recreation, for escape, for historical backgrounds needed in his own tales, for the chance acquisition of motifs which might stimulate his own imagination—in short, for his own purposes."⁵

Reading to stimulate the imagination was a chief end for both writers. "Keep thy imagination sane," Hawthorne admonished Sophia, for "that is one of the truest conditions of communion with Heaven."⁶ Lewis credited his reading of George MacDonald's *Phantastes*, which he bought and read in 1916 at age eighteen, being "waist-deep in Romanticism," for altering his imagination: "What it actually did to me was to convert,

---

3. Warren, "Hawthorne's Reading," *The New England Quarterly*, December, 1935, 480. Note also Marion L. Kesselring's "Hawthorne's Reading," *Bulletin of the New York Public Library*, March, 1949, 133.

4. See Lewis's essays on Chaucer, Shakespeare, Bunyan, Addison, and Shelley in *Selected Literary Essays*.

5. Warren, "Hawthorne's Reading," 480.

6. Hawthorne, Letter of 18 October 1841, *Selected Letters of Nathaniel Hawthorne*, 96.

even to baptize . . . my imagination."⁷ Critics have referred to Hawthorne's "freedom of imagination" and his "refined imagination," both perhaps another way of describing Lewis's "baptized imagination." Baptism, the Christian rite symbolizing death, burial, and resurrection or mortification and renewal, speaks also of initiation and identification. All of these seem to apply to Lewis's acknowledged indebtedness to MacDonald, along with a kind of "*good* Death," as he put it, to his "waist-deep" Romanticism. For Hawthorne, as for Lewis (also Coleridge, Wallace Stevens et al.), the imagination is more powerful than reality: "After all, the utmost force of man can do positively very little towards making grand things, or beautiful things; the imagination can do so much more, merely on shutting one's eyes, that the actual effect seems meagre . . ."⁸ Similarly, while watching boys sail their miniature boats on Frog Pond near Boston, Hawthorne noted: ". . . there is something that kindles the imagination more than the reality would. If we see a real, great ship, the mind grasps and possesses, within its real clutch, all that there is of it; while here, the miniature ship is the representative of an ideal one, and so gives us a more imaginative pleasure."⁹ Lewis would undoubtedly understand and approve not only these comments but also Hawthorne's statement in the Custom House Introduction to *The Scarlet Letter*: "The floor of our familiar room has become a neutral territory, somewhere between the real world and fairy-land, where the Actual and the Imaginary may meet, and each imbue itself with the nature of the other."¹⁰ Both writers, knowing the great power of the imagination, also knew the importance of balance between the real and the ideal.

Both writers knew the value of fairy-land and fairy tales, for as Lewis said, "Sometimes fairy stories may say best what's to be said,"¹¹ Hawthorne wrote five children's books— *Grandfather's Chair, Famous Old People, Liberty Tree, A Wonder-Book for Girls and Boys*, and *Tanglewood Tales*. Lewis wrote seven children's books—*The Narnia Chronicles* (*The Lion, the Witch and the Wardrobe, Prince Caspian, The Voyage of the 'Dawn Treader', The Silver Chair, The Horse and His Boy, The Magician's Nephew,* and *The Last Battle*). In addition, he wrote *Boxen: The*

---

7. Lewis, Preface, *George MacDonald: 305 Readings*, xxxiii.
8. Hawthorne, *English Notebooks*, 74–75.
9. Hawthorne, *The American Notebooks*, 233–34.
10. Hawthorne, "The Custom House," *The Scarlet Letter*, 35.
11. Lewis, "Sometimes Fairy Stories May Say Best What's to be Said," *Of Other World: Essays and Stories*, 35.

Imaginary World of the Young and *Letters to Children*. He said, ". . . it certainly is my opinion that a book worth reading only in childhood is not worth reading even then."[12] Similarly, Hawthorne remarked to Washington Irving, "I sent you 'The Wonder Book,' because, being meant for children, it seemed to reach a higher point, in its own way, than anything that I had written for grown people."[13]

Traumatic events in the lives of both writers had significant effects on their futures. When Hawthorne was about nine he was injured while playing in the schoolyard, being hit on the foot by a ball, had to be carried home, and was incapacitated for about fifteen months. During this crucial time when young people enjoy physical activity, Hawthorne lived a restricted life, using crutches and limping, lying down a lot, reading and daydreaming to pass the time. Such restrictions probably led even further to his habits of introspection and seclusion. Anne Tyler has said, "I know a poet who says that in order to be a writer, you have to have had rheumatic fever, but I believe that any kind of setting-apart situation will do as well."[14] In addition to his foot injury setting him apart, Hawthorne's inveterate shyness and the derisive laughter from his classmates when he recited or gave speeches resulted in further isolation.

Lewis's "setting-apart" situations were his self-acknowledged physical ineptitude and the trauma of attending English boarding schools. "What drove me to write was the extreme manual clumsiness from which I have always suffered," he said. "I attribute it to a physical defect which my brother and I both inherit from our father: we have only one joint in the thumb. The upper joint (that farthest from the nail) is visible, but it is a mere sham; we cannot bend it . . . Nature laid on me from birth an utter incapacity to make anything . . . With a tool or a bat or a gun, a sleeve-link or a corkscrew, I have always been unteachable. It was this that forced me to write." In addition, he was subjected to oppressive bullying at English boarding schools, of which he said, "Life at a vile boarding-school is in this way a good preparation for the Christian life, that it teaches one to live by hope."[15]

---

12. Lewis, "Sometimes Fairy Stories May Say Best What's to be Said," *Of Other Worlds: Essays & Stories*, 38.

13. Hawthorne, Letter of 16 July 1852, *Selected Letters of Nathaniel Hawthorne*, 164–65.

14. Anne Tyler, "Still Just Writing," *The Writer on Her Work: Contemporary Women Writers Reflect on Their Art and Situation*, Edited by Janet Sternburg, 11.

15. Lewis, *Surprised by Joy*, 12, 36.

Part I: Personal Backgrounds and Worldviews

Another traumatic event experienced by both writers was the death of their mothers, Hawthorne's in 1849, Lewis's in 1908. (Hawthorne's father died of yellow fever in Surinam, leaving his family impoverished, when Nathaniel was just four; Lewis felt alienated from his father and spoke disparagingly of him for his invectives which filled him with "boundless terror and dismay."[16]) Hawthorne recounts his visit to his dying mother's bedside: ". . . I was moved to kneel down close by my mother and take her hand . . . I found the tears slowly gathering in my eyes. I tried to keep them down; but it would not be—I kept filling up, till, for a few moments, I shook with sobs. For a long time, I knelt there, holding her hand; and surely it is the darkest hour I ever lived."[17]

Lewis, just nine years old at the time, having prayed earnestly for his mother to be healed and hoping for a miracle, which was not to come. He tells of "a night when I was ill and crying both with headache and toothache and distressed because my mother did not come to me. That was because she was ill too," dying of cancer. Unlike Hawthorne, in his forties when his mother died and able to see her and hold her hand, the young Lewis "was taken into the bedroom where my mother lay dead; as they said, 'to see her,' in reality, as I at once knew, 't see it.'" "Grief," he said "was overwhelmed with terror." His childish faith is deeply shaken, as he concludes: "With my mother's death all settled happiness, all that was tranquil and reliable, disappeared from my life . . . It was sea and islands now; the great continent had sunk like Atlantis."[18] Conversely, Hawthorne, though grief-stricken, found assurance in the hope of Heaven: "Oh what a mockery, if what I saw were all, —let the interval between extreme youth and dying age be filled up with what happiness it might! But God would not have made the close so dark and wretched, if there were nothing beyond; for then it would have been a fiend that created us, and measured out our existence, and not God. It would be something beyond wrong—it would be insult—to be thrust out of life into annihilation in this miserable way. So, out of the very bitterness of death, I gather the sweet assurance of a better state of being."[19] Interestingly, Lewis's faith was shaken at the death of his mother, Flora, whereas Hawthorne's faith, especially in the reality of immortality and Heaven, was enhanced by the death of his mother, Elizabeth.

16. Ibid., 39.
17. Hawthorne, *The American Notebooks*, 429.
18. Lewis, *Surprised by Joy*, 21.
19. Hawthorne, *The American Notebooks*, 429.

Both men were immeasurably influenced by two other women, respectively, who became their wives. For Hawthorne it was Sophia Peabody, whom he credited with rescuing him from his reclusive "lonely chamber" period in Salem:

> Here sits thy husband in his old accustomed chamber, where he used to sit in years gone by, before his soul became acquainted with thine . . . By and bye[sic], the world found me out in my lonely chamber, and called me forth—not, indeed with a loud roar of acclamation, but rather with a still, small voice, and forth I went, but found nothing in the world that I thought preferable to my old solitude, till at length a certain Dove was revealed to me . . . Living in solitude till the fullness of time was come, I still kept the dew of my youth and the freshness of my heart, and had these to offer to my Dove . . . Thou only hast taught me that I have a heart—thou only hast thrown a light deep downward, and upward, into my soul.[20]

Further, Hawthorne credited Sophia with making him conscious of God's love and assurance of Heaven: "Oh, dearest blessedest Dove, I never felt sure of going to Heaven, till I knew that you loved me; but now I am conscious of God's love in your own . . . Even amid the Joys of Heaven, we shall love to look back to our earthly bliss, and treasure it forever in the sum of our infinitely accumulating happiness."[21] Because his heart was "touched"—by God, by Sophia, by God through Sophia, he asserts—he has begun to be a "being of reality" and "inheritor of eternity." His repeated use of Biblical language is pertinent—for example, "still, small voice," a phrase used to describe the prophet Elijah's encounter with Yahweh (I Kings 19:11–12) and "till the fullness of time was come," used to describe the coming of Jesus to redeem humankind (Galatians 4:4—"But when the fullness of time was come, God sent forth his Son, made of a woman, made under the law"). Clearly, Hawthorne thought of his "heavenly Dove," as he called her, as epitomizing the Holy Trinity!

Nathaniel and Sophia were not married until 1842, when Nat was thirty-eight, his life more than half over. Jack Lewis and Joy Gresham nee Davidman were married in 1956, when Jack was fifty-eight, first a registry office affair for the purpose of giving Joy English nationality, and later by an ecclesiastical ceremony performed at Joy's bedside as she was dying of

---

20. Hawthorne, Letter of 4 October 1840, *Selected Letters of Nathaniel Hawthorne*, 79–80.

21. Ibid., Letter of 23 September 1839, 63.

Part I: Personal Backgrounds and Worldviews

cancer. Joy lived to enjoy three years and four months of marriage to Jack. Like Hawthorne, who revered Sophia for her spiritual influence on him, Lewis recognized a similar influence of Joy, recalling the words of Coventry Patmore's *The Rod, the Root and the Flower*—that Woman "'is both Heaven and the way . . . Heaven becomes very intelligible and attractive when it is discerned to be—Woman.' She is a reflection of the divine and has the power to make evident to man truths that he would miss without knowledge of her body."[22] Joy apparently inspired at least four of Jack's books—*Till We Have Faces*, which she extensively influenced and may have co-written, *The Four Loves*, *Reflections on the Psalms*, and *A Grief Observed*, the intimate, personal book that Lewis wrote after her death. In this moving book, Lewis wrote this poignant tribute to Joy: "A good wife contains so many persons in herself. What was H. not to me? She was my daughter and my mother, my pupil and my teacher, my subject and my sovereign; and always, holding all these in solution, my trusty comrade, friend, shipmate, fellow-soldier."[23] Hawthorne might have written the same tribute for Sophia, perhaps only adding "heavenly Dove." In each case, the relationship is a kind of mystical experience. Lewis writes, "We are 'taken out of ourselves' by the loved one while she is here. Then comes the tragic figure of the dance in which we must learn to be still taken out of ourselves though the bodily presence is withdrawn, to love the very Her, and not fall back to loving our past, or our memory, or our sorrow, or our relief from sorrow, or our own love."[24] Undoubtedly, Lewis and Hawthorne each loved his "very Her."

Considerably more mundane, in the full sense of the adjective's etymology (Latin *mundus*, "world," "secular, worldly, quotidian, everyday"), but no less trenchant, was another relationship and activity shared by both authors: male camaraderie enjoyed on walking tours, which both men relished. It is easy to imagine the two of them walking and communing together on a wide range of subjects. If the relationships with their mothers, respectively, constituted *storge* and even *agape* and their relationships with their wives, respectively, constituted *philia*, *eros*, and even *agape*, their relationships with walking companions constituted *philia* and perhaps even *agape*. Lewis was apparently recalling walking tours when he wrote of friendship in *The Four Loves*: "Those are the golden sessions; when four

22. Sayer, *Jack: C. S. Lewis and His Times*, 232.

23. Lewis, *A Grief Observed*, 55–56. "H" stands for Helen, which was Joy's first name, though never used.

24. Ibid., 59.

or five of us after a hard day's walking have come to our inn; when our slippers are on, our feet spread out towards the blaze and our drinks at our elbows; when the whole world, and something beyond the world, opens itself to our minds as we talk; and no one has any claim on or any responsibility for another but all are freemen and equals as if we had first met an hour ago, while at the same time an Affection mellowed by the years enfolds us. Life—natural life—has no better gift to give. Who could have deserved it?"[25] This vivid description seems to suggest that the camaraderie, or perhaps "fellowship" is the more appropriate term, is not simply or totally "mundane" after all, for, he mentions that, "something beyond the world," that is, something otherworldly, opens itself to their minds. Lewis wrote the following on the dust jacket of the original American edition of *Perelandra*: "My happiest hours are spent with three or four old friends in old clothes tramping together and putting up in small pubs." Lewis's walking tours reportedly began with Cecil Harwood, a lifelong friend whom Lewis dubbed "Lord of the Walks," and Owen Barfield, a fellow-Inkling and classmate at Oxford, with whom Lewis took an annual Easter walking tour. Lewis introduced his brother Warnie to walking tours and reportedly took no fewer than eight tours between 1931 and 1939. Lewis delighted in spending vacation days each year on walking tours through villages and countryside. According to George Sayer, "Jack's view of nature was essentially mystical . . . [His] enjoyment of such scenes was as great as that of the most romantic of the romantic poets."[26]

It should come as no surprise that Hawthorne loved walking tours also, especially in view of the fact that the English Romantic poets, Wordsworth in particular, loved walking tours. It is reported that Wordsworth walked 175,000 to 180,000 English miles, at age twenty-one setting off on a two-thousand mile journey on foot, spending holidays in 1790 on an extensive walking tour of Europe—including the Alps, areas of France, Switzerland, and Italy—and in 1828 touring the Rhineland with Coleridge. (When Hawthorne visited the Lake District with his family he tells of visiting Dove Cottage in Grasmere and Wordsworth's grave in Saint Oswald's church.) Like the Romantic poets, Hawthorne and Lewis apparently made walking tours less a mode of traveling than a mode of being, walking as a major stimulant, walking as a form of thinking, walking as part of the writing process. Hawthorne's most frequent walking

25. Lewis, *The Four Loves*, 77.
26. Sayer, *Jack: C. S. Lewis and His Times*, 148.

companion was Horatio Bridge, fellow-classmate at Bowdoin College and lifetime friend and supporter, whom Hawthorne would later call "the best friend I ever had or shall have (of the male sex)."[27] They took extended walking tours, or "excursions" as he sometimes called them, of Maine in 1837 and western Massachusetts in 1838. Other walking companions were Ellery Channing, Bronson Alcott, Emerson, Thoreau, even Margaret Fuller, and his sister Elizabeth (Ebe). In his Notebooks he enthusiastically described such excursions: "We cast aside all irksome forms and straight-laced habitudes, and delivered ourselves up to the free air, to live like the Indians or any less conventional race, during one bright semicircle of the sun."[28]

Both writers also enjoyed the male conviviality of various clubs of which they were a part. The best known was the Inklings (the name perhaps suggesting those who dabble in ink), an informal group of friends who met twice a week, on Tuesday mornings at the Eagle and Child Pub (Bird and Baby) and on Thursday evenings in Lewis's rooms in Magdalen College—"theoretically," Lewis said, "to talk about literature, but in fact nearly always to talk about something better. What I owe to them all is incalculable . . . Is any pleasure on earth as great as a circle of Christian friends by a good fire?"[29] This "confraternity," as Lewis once called it, met from 1939 until about 1962. Those attending included Tolkien, Warnie, Charles Williams, Hugo Dyson, Humphrey Havard, Owen Barfield, Nevill Coghill, John Wain, and others.[30] Lewis may have had the Inklings in mind when he wrote about the value of friendship: "In each of my friends there is something that only some other friend can fully bring out. By myself I am not large enough to call the whole man into activity; I want other lights than my own to show all his facets . . . Of course the scarcity of kindred souls—not to mention practical considerations about the size of the rooms and the audibility of voices—set limits to the enlargement of the circle; but within those limits we possess each friend not less but more as the number of those with whom we share him increases. In this, Friendship exhibits a glorious 'nearness by resemblance' to Heaven

---

27 Wineapple, *Hawthorne: A Life*, 51.

28. Hawthorne, *The American Notebooks*, 355.

29. Lewis, Letter of 21 December 1941, *The Collected Letters of C. S. Lewis*, II, 501.

30. For a complete discussion of the Inklings, see Humphrey Carpenter's *The Inklings: C. S. Lewis, J. R. R. Tolkien, Charles Williams and Their Friends* (1978). Carpenter lists eighteen who attended the meetings, not a comprehensive list.

itself . . ."³¹ Just as Lewis relished "something beyond the world" in his walking tours, so he relished a glorious "nearness by resemblance" to Heaven in meetings of the Inklings.

Less widely known is the similar clubbiness of Hawthorne, who while a student at Bowdoin was a charter member of the secret Pot-8-O Club (the name reflective of the abundance of potatoes grown in Maine), which met weekly at Ward's Tavern for imbibing (cider?), eating (roasted potatoes?), and poetasting (at least fourteen lines). Another college club was the Androscoggin Loo Club, featuring weekends in the woods with food and drink. A third was the Navy Club, formed at the end of the term by fourteen class members who had no part in the commencement exercises, meeting weekly at Ward's Tavern for a meal and attendant conviviality. Hawthorne's closest equivalent to Lewis's Inklings was the Boston Saturday Club, founded in 1855 for literary discussions, with dinner meetings the last Saturday of each month at the Parker House in Boston. Regular participants included literary, social, and political figures, such as James Russell Lowell, Oliver Wendell Holmes, Henry Wadsworth Longfellow, Ralph Waldo Emerson, John Greenleaf Whittier, and others. In a letter to Henry A. Bright, Hawthorne wrote: "I meet Longfellow and all the other prominent literary people at the monthly dinner of the Saturday Club, of which I found myself a member on my return [from England in 1860]. It is an excellent institution, with the privilege of first-rate society, and no duties but to eat one's dinner."³² Unlike Lewis, who was reportedly the cynosure of the Inklings group, Hawthorne was reportedly reclusive even at the Saturday Club. Yet his friend Horatio Bridge offered this description: ". . . though taciturn, he was invariably cheerful with his chosen friends, and there was much more of fun and frolic in his disposition than his published writings indicate." William Allingham, an Irish poet, gave these impressions of Hawthorne at the Saturday Club: "The shy man, through his veil of fanciful sketch and tale, shows me more of his mind and heart than any pen-dipper of them all. What a pensive, sympathetic humanity makes itself felt everywhere. He is no pessimist, save as regards man's efforts to alter the natural condition of

---

31. Lewis, *The Four Loves*, 61–62.

32. Hawthorne, Letter of 17 December 1860, *Selected Letters of Nathaniel Hawthorne*, 232. It should be noted that utopian Brook Farm was originally called "Hedge's Club" or "Hedge Club." Hawthorne spent less than a year at Brook Farm. He was put in charge of shoveling a hill of manure referred to as "the Gold Mine." He was never part of the Transcendental Club, established in 1840.

human life, and the natural effect of human actions. His fixed faith is that man is a spirit with his real life flowing from and to a finer world than that of the senses."[33] For both Hawthorne and Lewis the regular meetings of these informal clubs, characterized by spirited discussion, readings, encouragement, and light-hearted whimsy washed down with spirits, served to foster and enhance *philia*, which Lewis described as "the most spiritual of loves . . . even, if you like, angelic."[34]

The two writers also shared a mutual dislike of each other's compatriots, John Bull and Uncle Jonathan respectively. As noted above, Lewis, in expressing his great admiration for the works of Hawthorne, bemoaned the fact that "such a genius should be a beastly American!" Similarly, in a letter to his brother, Lewis asked, "What else do you expect from a set of squatters and damned money grubbing Puritans like the Yanks? You remember Wilde's wheeze, 'When good Americans die they go to Paris'—'But where do bad Americans go when they die?'—'Oh, they go to America.'"[35] During and immediately after the war, however, Lewis altered his view of (Uncle) "Sammy," expressing appreciation for "the extraordinary goodness of our American friends" and remarked that "every *third* meal we eat is 'on America.'"[36]

"For my part," Hawthorne wrote in a letter to Longfellow, "I have no love for England nor Englishmen . . . ,"[37] and in *Our Old Home* he wrote: "An American is not very apt to love the English people, as a whole, on whatever length of acquaintance . . . They are beset by a curious and inevitable infelicity, which compels them, as it were, to keep up what they seem to consider a wholesome bitterness of feeling between themselves and all other nationalities, especially that of America."[38] Again he wrote: "Though the individual Englishman is sometimes preternaturally disagreeable, an observer standing aloof has a sense of natural kindness towards them in the lump."[39] Interestingly, this attitude is diametrically opposite to that which he attributes to the English: "If an Englishman

---

33. Edward Waldo Emerson, *The Early Years of the Saturday Club, 1855–1870*, 209, 215–16.

34. Lewis, *The Four Loves*, 87.

35. Lewis, Letter of 8 January 1917, *The Collected Letters of C. S. Lewis*, I, 266.

36. Ibid., Letters of 3 June 1948 and 7 March 1949, II, 856, 923.

37. Hawthorne, Letter of 30 August 1854, *Selected Letters of Nathaniel Hawthorne*, 186.

38. Hawthorne, *Our Old Home*, 86.

39. Ibid., *Our Old Home*, 328.

were individually acquainted with all our twenty-five millions of Americans—and liked every man of them, and believed that each man of those millions was a Christian, honest, upright, and kind, —he would doubt, despise, and hate them in the aggregate, however he might love and honor the individuals."[40]

Their mutual dislike of Englishmen and Americans, respectively, carried over to their attitudes toward England itself. Lewis remarked, "I have no patriotic feeling for anything in England except Oxford, for which I would live and die."[41] Lewis arrived at University College, Oxford, in 1917, where, except for what A. N. Wilson calls "periods of exile," he was to spend the rest of his life—in this "unspoilt Gothic paradise."[42] In *Surprised by Joy* he expressed his first taste of Oxford, a comical experience when he sallied out of the railway station on the wrong side, heading mistakenly toward the sprawling suburb of Botley. Though he was all agog for "dreaming spires" and "last enchantments," he got to open country and only then turned around and there "behind me, far away, never more beautiful since, was the fabled cluster of spires and towers."[43] In letters to Arthur Greeves he wrote: "The place is on the whole absolutely ripping. If only you saw the quad, on these moonlit nights with the long shadows lying half across the level, perfect grass and the tangle of spires & towers rising beyond in the dark!" Later he rhapsodizes about an Oxford morning: "It was a perfectly lovely morning with a deep blue sky, all the towers and pinnacles gleaming in the sun & bells ringing everywhere."[44]

Sixty years earlier, Hawthorne visited Oxford and rhapsodized even more eloquently:

> ... I find Oxford exceedingly picturesque, and rich in beauty and grandeur, and in antique stateliness . . . gray, weather-stained, and picturesquely time-worn fronts of famous colleges and halls of learning, everywhere about the streets, with arched

---

40. Hawthorne, *The English Notebooks*, 41. Perhaps Hawthorne is echoing Jonathan Swift's famous assertion: "I have ever hated all nations professions and communities and all my love is towards individuals . . . but principally I hate and detest that animal called man, although I heartily love John, Peter, and so forth" (September 19, 1725, letter to Alexander Pope, *The Correspondence of Jonathan Swift*, III, 103).

41. Quoted in Griffin, *Clive Staples Lewis: A Dramatic Life*, 7.

42. Wilson, *C. S. Lewis: A Biography*, 48–49.

43. Lewis, *Surprised by Joy*, 184.

44. Lewis, Letters of 6 May 1917 and 13 May 1917, *They Stand Together: The Letters of C. S. Lewis to Arthur Greeves*, 181, 183.

> entrances, passing through which, we found grassy quadrangles within, with perhaps a cloistered walk around, old gray towers and turrets, ivy grown; quaint bits of sculpture . . . The world surely has not another place like Oxford; it is a despair to see such a place, and ever have to leave it; for it would take a lifetime, and more than one, to comprehend and enjoy it satisfactorily.[45]

Initially, though, he described Oxford as "an ugly old town, of crooked and irregular streets; gabled houses, mostly plastered of a buff or yellow hue . . . and as for the buildings of the university, they seem to be scattered at random without any reference among one another."[46] Later, in his chapter "Near Oxford" in *Our Old Home*, he provides one of the most vivid descriptions of Oxford, as he prepares to leave:

> And now I take leave of Oxford without even an attempt to describe it,—there being no literary faculty, attainable or conceivable by me, which can avail to put it adequately, or even tolerably, upon paper. It must remain its own sole expression, and those whose sad fortune it may be never to behold it have no better resource than to dream about gray, weather-stained, ivy-grown edifices, wrought with quaint Gothic ornament, and standing around grassy quadrangles,—where cloistered walks have echoed to the quiet footsteps of twenty generations,—lawns and gardens of luxurious repose, shadowed with canopies of foliage, and lit up with sunny glimpses through archways of great boughs,—spires, towers, and turrets, each with its history and legend,—dimly magnificent chapels, with painted windows of rare beauty and brilliantly diversified hues, creating an atmosphere or richest gloom,—vast college halls, high-windowed, oaken-panelled, and hung round with portraits of the men, in every age, whom the university has nurtured to be illustrious,—long vistas of alcoved libraries, where the wisdom and learned folly of all time is shelved . . . make all these things vivid in your dream, and you will never know nor believe how inadequate is the result to represent even the merest outside of Oxford . . .[47]

Again, he summarizes: ". . . I find Oxford exceedingly picturesque, and rich in beauty and grandeur, and in antique stateliness," and, with great dramatic irony, describes the quadrangle of Lewis's "Maudlin College"

---

45. Hawthorne, *The English Notebooks*, 109, 118.

46. Ibid., 43.

47. Hawthorne, *Our Old* Home, 278–79.

(mistakenly spelling it in accordance with the pronunciation of Magdalen). Perhaps Lewis, had he read these lyric, rhapsodic descriptions of his beloved Oxford, might have responded: "Quite! Good show, old chap! Good show (beastly Yank though you are)!"

Part II

Mutual Themes

4

Myths Retold and Myths Made

WHETHER IN OXFORD OR Salem, Headington Quarry or Concord, these two writers, though at a chronological and geographical remove, wrote of numerous mutual themes. "Theme," sometimes used interchangeably with "motif," is a central, guiding idea or subject recurring implicitly or explicitly in a literary work, an abstract concept made concrete through representation in a character, image, or action, often providing a dominant impression and unifying thread in a work.[1]

Both writers placed great value on myth, a theme which functions significantly in the work of each. Treated here as a theme, motif, or topos, myth has, of course, been variously defined, ranging from "a way of thinking" to "a large, controlling image that gives philosophic meaning to the facts of ordinary life." Lewis, having referred often to myth, defines it as follows: "A *myth* is a description or a story introducing supernatural personages or things, determined not, or not only, by motives arising from events within the story, but by the supposedly immutable relations of the personages or things: possessing unity: and not, save accidentally,

---

1. A "motif," from the German *leitmotif*, meaning "a leading or guiding" concept or pattern, is a synonym but is sometimes applied more specifically to a recurring design in more than one work. A third term applied to common themes or topics in medieval literature is *topoi*, putatively originated by Ernst R. Curtius in *European Literature and the Latin Middle Ages* (1953, 1967). Lewis himself refers to Dr. Curtius and his work, as well as to themes in medieval literature, in *The Discarded Image: An Introduction to Medieval and Renaissance Literature* (82, 200, 202). Donald E. Glover is one of the few critics to explicitly specify and discuss a wide-ranging selection of themes in Lewis's work (at least twenty-eight) in *C.S. Lewis: The Art of Enchantment*. As Melville wrote in *Moby Dick*, "To produce a mighty book, you must choose a mighty theme" (452).

Part II: Mutual Themes

connected with any given place or time."² Lewis discussed myth further in his essay "On Myth" in *An Experiment in Criticism*: It is "a particular kind of story which has a value in itself—a value independent of its embodiment in any literary work." Then he specifies six characteristics: 1) it is extra-literary (here he mentions Hawthorne, along with five other writers); 2) the pleasure of myth depends hardly at all upon such narrative elements as suspense or surprise; 3) we feel very little sympathy and no empathy for the characters; 4) being "fantastic," myth deals with "impossibles and preternaturals"; 5) the mythopoeic experience may be sad or joyful but is always grave, never comic; and finally 6) "the experience is not only grave but awe-inspiring. We feel it to be numinous. It is as if something of great moment had been communicated to us."³ Further, Lewis described "a good myth" as "a story out of which ever varying meanings will grow for different readers and in different ages."⁴ The hallmark of "a true myth," he said, is that "you have seen nothing like it before you read the book, but after that you see things like it everywhere."⁵

In 1851 Hawthorne published *A Wonder-Book for Girls and Boys*, another of what he called his "baby books," this one a retelling and modernizing of six Greek myths which he had loved as a child (Perseus and the Gorgon's Head; Midas and the Golden Touch; Pandora and the Box; Hercules and the Three Golden Apples in the Garden of the Hesperides; Baucis and Philemon and the Miraculous Pitcher; and Bellerophon,

---

2. Lewis, "The 'Great War' Letters, Series I, Letter 4, *The Collected Letters of C. S. Lewis*, III, 1619.

3. Lewis, "On Myth," *An Experiment in Criticism*, 43–44. *Numinous*, a term coined by Rudolph Otto in *The Idea of the Holy* (1917) (from *numen*, "a deity, an indwelling, guiding spirit") denotes the aspect of deity, a sense of awesome otherness that transcends or defies comprehension in purely rational terms. Lewis included Otto's book as one of the ten books that most influenced his thinking. He summarizes his concept of the numinous in the Introduction to *The Problem of Pain*, where he characterizes it as an uncanny dread, "a direct experience of the really supernatural, to which the name Revelation might properly be given," distinguishing it from fear based on knowledge of danger and from the morally good. He cites an example from Kenneth Grahame's *The Wind in the Willows*, where Rat and Mole approach the god Pan, part man, part goat: "'Rat, ' [Mole] found breath to whisper, shaking, 'Are you afraid?' 'Afraid?' murmured the Rat, his eyes shining with unutterable love. 'Afraid! Of *Him*? O, never, never! And yet—and yet—O Mole, I am afraid!'" (Grahame, 136). Had it been current in his time, Hawthorne would undoubtedly have shared Lewis's appreciation of the term and its referent, for much of the numinous appears in the work of both writers.

4. Lewis, Letter of 22 September 1956, *The Collected Letters of C. S. Lewis*, III, 789.

5. Ibid., Letter of 10 February 1958, 919.

Pegasus, and the Chimaera). Almost immediately he began work on a sequel titled *Tanglewood Tales for Girls and Boys*, published in 1853, consisting of six more myths retold (Theseus and the Minotaur; Hercules, the Giant Antaeus, and the Pygmies; Cadmus and the Dragon's Teeth; Ulysses and Circe's Palace; Ceres, Pluto, Proserpina, and the Pomegranate Seeds; Jason, Medea, and the Golden Fleece). Hawthorne questioned whether "these old legends, so brimming over with everything that is most abhorrent to our Christianized moral sense, —some of them so hideous, others so melancholy and miserable . . . was . . . the stuff that children's playthings should be made of? How were they to be purified? How was the blessed sunshine to be thrown into them?" he wondered.[6] He concluded that his retelling of the myths caused them to be "done up in excellent style, purified from all moral stains, re-created as good as new, or better, and fully equal, in their own way, to Mother Goose. I never did anything else so well as these old baby stories," he vaunted.[7] His retelling of the tales did not demythologize but re-mythologized them, altering but not vitiating them of their fascination and strength.

Interestingly, Lewis gave Roger Lancelyn Green advice on his classic "retellings" of traditional myths and legends, including *Heroes of Greece and Troy* (1960), resembling Hawthorne's similar retellings. Walter Hooper's observation that Lewis considered Green's retelling of tales to be "unparalleled" is borne out clearly in a letter to Green: "Thanks very much for the *Old Greek Fairy Tales*. I was not quite in my *marchen* mood—you know how one's literary weather changes—at the moment, but I believe you have done the job very well."[8] Lewis's own equivalent mythic tales for children are the seven Chronicles of Narnia, which can be profitably examined vis-à-vis Hawthorne's twelve mythic tales, both authors being myth-users and myth-makers. Lewis remarked that he had "tried to do what I can for children—in a mythical and fantastic form—by my seven 'Narnian' fairy tales."[9]

6. Hawthorne, "The Wayside: Introductory," *Tanglewood Tales for Girls and Boys*, 240.

7. Hawthorne, "Introductory Note," *A Wonder-Book for Girls and Boys*, xii.

8. Lewis, Letter of 29 August 1958, *The Collected Letters of C. S. Lewis*, III, 967. *Marchen* is a German term for fairy tale or folktale, such as the stories of Jakob and Wilhelm Grimm (*Volksmarchen*) or the tales of E.T.A. Hoffmann and others (*Kunstmarchen*).

9. Ibid., Letter of 16 January 1959, 1011. Responding to a question about books of Christian instruction, Lewis said that many "seem to me namby-pamby and 'sissie' and calculated to nauseate any child worth his salt."

Part II: Mutual Themes

There are at least seven common, constituent elements of myth, most of which are manifest in both Hawthorne and Lewis: the hero/heroine; a task, purpose or quest; a formidable adversary, often a lethal monster; exploits performed and battles fought; magical accoutrements and weapons; various helpers; and the final victory, a triumph, with boons bestowed and the heroic victor apotheosized.

Traditionally, a hero is a person of supernatural or superhuman power, physical and moral strength, prowess, fortitude, and virtue, widely admired, even idealized and idolized for noble deeds. Perhaps unfortunately, the term has become widely used simply to denote the leading character in a work, the protagonist. Lewis had little explicitly to say about the hero (other than to observe that to use a poet not as a poet but as a saint or hero, may be seen as using the poet for an alien purpose[10]). Lewis apparently never refers to the two seminal works on the hero—Lord Raglan's *The Hero* (1936) or Joseph Campbell's *The Hero with a Thousand Faces* (1949). Raglan traced great heroes of folklore, tale, epic, and scripture ranging from ancient civilizations of Asia Minor and Greece to Norse legends (which would have been of particular interest to Lewis) to English tales, all putatively derived from religious rites and ritual dramas that supposedly fulfilled a basic human need to believe in something beyond this mortal life. He specifies twenty-two patterned motifs characterizing the hero.[11] Campbell discusses the mythological adventure of the hero, formulaic rites of passage, what he calls "the nuclear unit of the monomyth"—separation, initiation, return: "A hero ventures forth from the world of common day into a region of supernatural wonder: fabulous forces are there encountered and a decisive victory is won: the hero comes back from this mysterious adventure with the power to bestow boons on his fellow man."[12]

If Hawthorne's retold tales present the hero with at least seven faces, Lewis's mythic Narnia tales present the hero with a single face—the noble Aslan (Turkish for "lion"), wild and neither a safe nor *tame* lion but good, both "good and terrible at the same time"—and sub-hero helpers, such as the Pevensie children—Peter, Susan, Lucy, Edmund—Jill Pole, even Eustace Scrubb, [13] and certainly the courageous, noble mouse Reepi-

---

10. Lewis, *The Personal Heresy*, 98–99.
11. Raglan, *The Hero*, 174–75.
12. Campbell, *The Hero with a Thousand Faces*, 30.

13. The obnoxious, self-absorbed Eustace Scrubb, cousin of the Pevensie children, is anything but heroic until after his dramatic transformation by Aslan, his

cheep. In Hawthorne's *Wonder-Book* and *Tanglewood Tales* the heroes are illustrious and their monster adversaries are formidable. The first, Perseus, one of the best-known heroes of Greek myth, has been called a model for the very career of a hero (Homer called him "the most renowned of all men"). With the help of magical flying slippers, mystical wallet, and helmet of invisibility provided by helpful nymphs, Perseus kills the dragon-monster Gorgon named Medusa, who had the power to transform into stone any poor mortal who fixed his eyes upon her face. Her counterpart in Lewis is the White Witch in *The Lion, the Witch, and the Wardrobe* (also known as Jadis in *The Magician's Nephew*, progenitor of a long line of witches, including the Green Witch in *The Silver Chair*). The White Witch, who turns faun Tumnus and other creatures into stone, later unpetrified by Aslan, is also called Lilith, descended from the giants on one side and, on the other, one of the Jinn (Islamic term for various species of demons and spirits)—"bad all through," as Mrs. Beaver tells the Pevensie children.[14] Only Aslan can dispatch the Witch, though her death is questioned in *Prince Caspian*, when dwarf Nikabrik seeks to call her up for power through black sorcery.

Hercules, with "heroic limbs and figure," is no Lewisian Lion but is clad in a shaggy lion's skin and has "chased a very swift stag . . . [and] caught it by the antlers, and carried it home alive."[15] Similarly, the Pevensie siblings hunt the White Stag, "who would give you wishes if you caught him,"[16] but unlike Hercules, they do not succeed in catching the stag, who instead leads them into the thicket, where they discover the lamp-post and wardrobe door.

The "numskull of a Giant" Antaeus, whom Hercules encounters and strangles by lifting him off Mother Earth, resembles the not-very-clever Giant Rumblebuffin, a "good giant" who assists in the battle against the White Witch. "In some folk-tales we meet giants who are not dangerous," Lewis said. "But they still affect us in much the same way. A *good* giant is legitimate: but he would be twenty tons of living, earth-shaking oxymoron."[17]

"undragoning" in *The Voyage of the "Dawn Treader."* His namesake in Hawthorne's retold myths is the exemplary, honorific Eustace Bright, raconteur, brilliant student at Williams College. The name "Eustace" means "fruitful" (derived from the Greek). Ultimately, the two diametrically opposite figures prove to be eminently "fruitful."

14. Lewis, *The Lion, the Witch, and the Wardrobe*, 88.
15. Hawthorne, *A Wonder-Book*, 127.
16. Lewis, *The Lion, the Witch, and the Wardrobe*, 202.
17. Lewis, "On Stories," *Of Other Worlds: Essays and Stories*, 9.

Part II: Mutual Themes

Bellerophon, one of the seven heroic destroyers of monsters, slays the Chimera, "the ugliest and most poisonous creature, and the strangest and unaccountablest, and the hardest to fight with, and the most difficult to run away from, that ever came out of the earth's inside. It had a tail like a boa constrictor; its body was like I do not care what; and it had three separate heads, one of which was a lion's, the second a goat's, and the third an abominably great snake's." Hawthorne's account is both ironic and comic, belying Lewis's conclusion, cited above, that myth may be sad or joyful but always grave and never comic. Note further the ironic, comic tone in Hawthorne's narrative describing the Chimera: "O, the mischief, and mischief, and mischief that this naughty creature did! With its flaming breath it could set a forest on fire, or burn up a field of grain, or, for that matter, a village, with all its fences and houses. It laid waste the whole country round about, and used to eat up people and animals alive, and cook them afterwards in the burning oven of its stomach." Then as if it were not enough that this "unaccountablest" of monsters is merely "naughty" and mischievous in devastating the entire countryside, "eating up" people and animals alive, then cooking them in the burning oven of its stomach, the description concludes with these admonitory words: "Mercy on us, little children, I hope neither you nor I will ever happen to meet a Chimaera!"[18] Lewis's description of the "old sad creature" which Eustace Scrubb encounters but does not recognize, "because he had read none of the right books," is remarkably similar: "The thing that came out of the cave was something he had never even imagined—a long lead-coloured snout, dull red eyes, no feathers or fur, a long lithe body that trailed on the ground, legs whose elbows went up higher than its back like a spider's, cruel claws, bat's wings that made a rasping noise on the stones, yards of tail."[19] Lewis's description of "the two lines of smoke [that] were coming from its two nostrils . . . like the smoke of a fire that will not last much longer" is similar to Hawthorne's description of "a hot blast of fire [that] came flaming out of each of [the Chimera's] three mouths." Such descriptions verge on the mock-heroic, downplaying or deflating the elevated descriptions of formidable creatures, in effect altering the

---

18. Hawthorne, *A Wonder-Book*, 202–03

19. Lewis, *The Voyage of the "Dawn Treader"*, 69. Of course, it should be remembered that this old and dying dragon is the form of Octesian, one of the lost Narnian lords. The pervasive irony and humor in Hawthorne's retold myths and in Lewis's Narnia tales merit a study all its own.

referent of *awful* from "inspiring impressive awe" to the current sense of "unpleasant or dreadful."

From the blood of Medusa springs Pegasus, the fabulous winged horse, favorite of the nine Muses and symbol of poetic inspiration, given to Bellerophon to assist in the slaying of the Chimera, after which he flew to heaven and was made a constellation. Pegasus, or at least a winged horse, appears in Lewis's *The Great Divorce*, when an angelic Burning One painfully removes the red lizard of lust from the shoulder of a Ghost. Flung broken-backed on the turf, the hideous, writhing reptile grows and changes into a great silvery stallion with mane and tail of gold. "It was smooth and shining, rippled with swells of flesh and muscle, whinnying and stamping with its hoofs. At each stamp the land shook and the trees dindled," whereupon "in joyous haste the young man leaped upon the horse's back" and rode off "like a shooting star" into the heavens. What Bellerophon was unable to achieve, Lewis's "new-made man," rescued from the red lizard of lust, seems to achieve with triumph.[20] Lewis uses an action parable, with mythical figures, to dramatize how grace brings repentance and transforms the ugliness of sin into the transcendent beauty of artistic expression.

Subsequently and sequentially, Theseus, the chief Attic hero, slays the Minotaur, that "bull-headed villain"; Cadmus, with the assistance of Athena, overcomes a dragon, "the scaly wretch," and sows its teeth on the plain; King Ulysses, bold and prudent, overcomes the one-eyed Cyclops, numerous monsters of the sea and land, and the evil enchantress Circe; and Jason leads the heroic Argonauts in quest of the Golden Fleece guarded by an execrable dragon and to dethrone the wicked king Pelias from the throne, which is rightfully his, as Lewis's Prince Caspian reclaims the throne from the usurping tyrant Miraz.

There is abundant magic afoot in these mythic tales of both authors. In a notebook entry, Hawthorne wrote of an image and idea he considered using in a future tale: "An old volume in a large library, —every one to be afraid to unclasp and open it, because it was said to be a book of magic."[21] It was Lewis who wrote about the magic book in *The Voyage of the "Dawn Treader."* Lucy finds herself in a large library lined with floor-to-ceiling books and a Magic Book of spells lying on a reading desk in the middle of the room. Lucy is at first unable to open the book but when she unfastens the two leaden clasps, it opens easily. After seeing a picture of herself, one

---

20. Lewis, *The Great Divorce*, 106–12.
21. Hawthorne, *The American Notebooks*, 14.

Part II: Mutual Themes

of Aslan the Lion, and one of two friends she spies on, Lucy begins reading a story that refreshes her spirit but soon discovers that she cannot turn pages back to read again—only the right-hand pages could be turned, not the left-hand ones. When she discovers the spell to make hidden things visible, Aslan appears to rebuke her for using magic to spy on her friends and assures her that he will relate the refreshing story for years and years.

The magic of myth shows up in numerous other instances and figures in the Chronicles. There are evil figures which the White Witch calls up—the Ghouls, the Boggles, the Ogres, the Minotaurs, the Cruels, the Hags, the Specters, the people of the Toadstools, the Incubuses, the Wraiths, the Horrors, the Efreets, the Sprites, the Orknies, the Wooses, the Ettins.[22] But there are also the figures of good, such as the Nymphs who lived in the wells, the Dryads who lived in the trees, the Visible Naiads, the Maenads, the Satyrs, the Dwarfs, the Giants, the Centaurs, the Talking Beasts, the Fauns.[23] The evil figures know myopically only of the Deep Magic, whereas the good figures know of the Deeper Magic from before the dawn of time.

Positioned in strategic places in *Prince Caspian*, there are five distinctive mythic dances—*oreibasia*—which convey a sense of the awe-inspiring, the numinous, which Lewis said characterizes myth. The first occurs just after the creatures in hiding have been revealed to Caspian, and Trufflehunter states that the Dryads and Naiads have sunk into a deep sleep, perhaps never to stir again. Just before he drops off to sleep, Caspian hears a wild but dreamy musical sound—drums and flutes—from the depth of the woods, then sees dozens of fauns dancing in the moonlight, whereupon he and Trufflehunter join in the dance. The next morning he thinks it was all a dream—until he finds the grass covered with little cloven hoofprints.

The second mythic dance occurs just before Lucy sees Aslan in the woods. In this case it is the trees dancing a lilt, "a complicated country dance" (for, Lucy thinks, "when trees dance, it must be a very, very country dance indeed").[24] The third dance is the Bacchanalian romp with the trees, Bacchus and his entourage, occurring just after Aslan's stentorian roar and just before the climactic battle in Aslan's How. It is led by Bacchus himself, the Roman god of wine and revelry, son of Zeus, identified

---

22. Lewis, *The Lion, the Witch, and the Wardrobe*, 149, 165.
23. Lewis, *Prince Caspian*, 47.
24. Ibid., 134.

Myths Retold and Myths Made

with the Greek Dionysus.²⁵ In his classic study *Dionysus: Myth and Cult*, Walter F. Otto notes that Dionysus was "the god of ecstasy and terror, of a wildness and of the most blessed deliverance . . . Dionysus, himself, who raises life into the heights of ecstasy, is the suffering god. The raptures which he brings rise from the innermost stirrings of that which lives."²⁶ Like Aslan himself, who is not a tame lion, not "safe" but good, Dionysus is fully a god: "most terrible and yet most gentle."²⁷ Lewis describes Bacchus as "a youth, dressed only in a fawn-skin, with vine-leaves wreathed in his curly hair. His face would have been almost too pretty for a boy's if it had not looked so extremely wild." He is accompanied by "a lot of girls . . . as wild as he,"²⁸ Maenads or Bacchantes, female votaries of Bacchus / Dionysus who traditionally took part in the wild drinking and dancing to the loud, rhythmic music of drums and high-pitched flutes. In addition, there appeared an old, enormously fat, jolly, intoxicated man on a donkey, dispensing "refreshments" and falling off his donkey crowned with vine leaves, only to be hoisted back on again. (Hawthorne would surely have relished the humor.) This is Silenus, foster-father, nurse, teacher, and follower of Bacchus, perhaps the son of Pan (Greek god of flocks and shepherds, forests and wild life, and fertility). This wild entourage shout "Euan, euan, eu-oi-oi-oi-oi," the traditional Bacchic cry, expressing the ecstatic joy of worshippers exulting in their god. Significantly, it is Lucy who recognizes who they are, remembering that Tumnus the Faun identified them long ago. Susan may speak for Hawthorne, who was concerned about the Christianizing of the pagan myths, when she says: "I wouldn't have felt very safe with Bacchus and all his wild girls if we'd not met them with Aslan," to which Lucy wisely responds, "I should think not."²⁹

---

25. Many of the ancients wrote stories about Bacchus, including Apollodorus, Herodotus, Homer, Ovid, Seneca, Virgil, and Euripides. Lewis apparently knew of Euripides's *Bacchae* even before he saw it performed in Greek at the Arts Theatre in Cambridge in February of 1956, an experience he called "simply overwhelming" (*The Collected Letters of C. S. Lewis*, III, 711).

26. Otto, *Dionysus: Myth and Cult*, 65, 180.

27. Euripides, *Bacchae*, 53.

28. Lewis, *Prince Caspian*, 152. Cf. Caravaggio's enigmatic self-portrait *Sick Bacchus*, which Francine Prose has called "the evil twin of *Boy with a Basket of Fruit*, which features another young man with bare shoulders, dark curls, and bunches of grapes" (*Caravaggio, Painter of Miracles*, 31).

29. Ibid., 154.

Part II: Mutual Themes

The fourth dance occurs at the denouement of *Prince Caspian*, when the battle against the Telmarines has been engaged. Aslan exclaims, "We will make holiday," and, as with the romp after his "resurrection" in *The Lion, the Witch, and the Wardrobe*, with the Pevernsie girls on his back, he leads the whole party of "Bacchus and his Maenads leaping, rushing, and turning somersaults, the beasts frisking around them, and Silenus and his donkey bringing up the rear."[30] It is important to realize that Aslan is fully in control, and, with Bacchus and the Maenads in his service, he commands Bacchus to deliver the river-god from his chains. In the town of Beruna, Aslan and "the wild people" liberate a school classroom having a dull history lesson, turning out Miss Prizzle and freeing little Gwendolyn, who readily believes. They free another schoolroom where "a tired-looking girl was teaching arithmetic to a number of boys who looked very like pigs."[31] They free farm animals along the way—sad old donkeys, chained dogs, harnessed horses—and a boy who was being beaten, the abuser's stick bursting into flower. Finally, they rescue a weeping boy's ill aunt (who turns out to be Caspian's old nurse), with Bacchus dipping a pitcher in the cottage well and handing her "not water but the richest wine, red as red-currant jelly, smooth as oil, strong as beef, warming as tea, cool as dew."[32] Lewis here dramatizes what he had expressed in *Miracles*: God incarnate in Jesus "is constantly doing all the things that nature-gods do: He is Bacchus, Venus, Ceres all rolled into one." Further, in discussing miracles of fertility, he notes: "The earliest of these was the conversion of water into wine at the wedding in Cana. This miracle proclaims that the God of all wine is present. The vine is one of the blessings sent by Yahweh: He is the reality behind the false god Bacchus."[33] Hawthorne, intent on "purifying" the pagan myths, "throwing blessed sunshine" into them so they would conform to "our Christianized moral sense," would likely have concurred with this assertion.

One final mythic dance is positioned at the very end of *Prince Caspian*, the evening before Aslan makes a doorway in the air. With a roaring woodland bonfire on a midsummer night, "Bacchus and Silenus and the Maenads began a dance, far wilder than the dance of the trees; not merely a dance for fun and beauty (though it was that too) but a magic dance

---

30. Ibid., 191–92
31. Ibid., 196.
32. Ibid., 198.
33. Lewis, *Miracles: A Preliminary Study*, 119, 141.

of plenty . . ."[34] The magic dance produces a feast of the most exquisite, delicious viands—meats and cakes and fruit and wines.

Lewis skillfully uses pagan myth to communicate an awe-inspiring, numinous experience "of great moment" in the Christian life. The chorus in Euripides's *Bacchae* makes it clear that Bacchus is the "god of joy" who "delights in feasts" such as the one just noted, and David Franklin astutely concludes in his commentary on the play that "the dominant emotion for the participants was joy."[35] Similarly, when the "tired-looking girl" in the classroom looks out the window and sees "the divine revelers singing up the street . . . , a stab of joy went through her heart."[36] A point "of great moment" would seem to be that victory in the novel and in the Christian life is accomplished through joy rather than through the violence of battle, though that sometimes plays a role as well. As the prophet Nehemiah reminded his people in a time of great adversity, "Do not be grieved, for the joy of the Lord is your strength."[37]

Yet another joyful mythic dance occurs near the end of *The Silver Chair*, when Jill Pole, Eustace Scrubb, and Puddleglum the marshwiggle escape from the horrors of Underland, domain of the Green Witch. This is "the Great Snow Dance," performed by "trim little fauns and dryads with leaf-crowned hair floating behind them, . . . done every year in Narnia on the first moonlit night when there is snow on the ground . . . , a kind of game as well as a dance, because every now and then some dancer will be the least little bit wrong and get a snowball in the face, and then everyone laughs."[38] This is also a magic dance of plenty for the god of joy delights in feasts, in this case a late supper of "real meaty, spicey [sic] [sausages], fat and piping hot and burst and just the tiniest bit burnt. And great mugs of frothy chocolate, and roast potatoes and roast chestnuts, and baked apples with raisins, stuck in where the cores had been, and then ices just to freshen you up after all the hot things," followed the next morning with a breakfast of scrambled eggs and toast.[39] The point is that joy brings strength and victory and freedom and celebratory dancing and delightful satisfaction of festive eating and drinking.

34. Lewis, *Prince Caspian*, 205.
35. Euripides, *Bacchae*, 23, 8.
36. Lewis, *Prince Caspian*, 196.
37. Nehemiah 8:10.
38. Lewis, *The Silver Chair*, 192–93.
39. Ibid., 203, 205.

Part II: Mutual Themes

An even greater mythic dance precedes these—the vision of the "Great Dance" lasting a whole year, at the conclusion of *Perelandra*:

> Set your eyes on one movement and it will lead you through all patterns and it will seem to you the master movement. But the seeming will be true . . . There seems no plan because it is all plan: there seems no center because it is all center . . . It seemed to be woven out of the intertwining undulation of many cords or bands of light, leaping over and under one another and mutually embraced in arabesques and flower-like subtleties . . . even then, at the very zenith of complexity, complexity was eaten up and faded, as a thin white cloud fades into the hard blue burning of the sky, and a simplicity beyond all comprehension, ancient and young as spring, illimitable, pellucid, drew him with cords of infinite desire into its own stillness.[40]

Dance is "one of the most ancient forms of magic," the incarnation of eternal energy, symbolizing cosmic matrimony or the union of heaven and earth, union of space and time.[41] This great cosmic dance symbolizes unity in the midst of diversity, harmony in the midst of difference, concord in the midst of variance, stability in the midst of vicissitude, stillness in the midst of turning worlds. The reader of Lewis's space-time trilogy gets the sensation, as Ransom did, not of following an adventure but of enacting or reliving a myth. He "saw reality and thought it was a dream." When he recognizes the garden of the Hesperides, meets the original of the Cyclops, a giant in a cave and a shepherd, the question is inevitable: "Were all the things which appeared as mythology on earth scattered through other worlds as realities?"[42] An affirmative answer is implied.

Even in the third novel of the trilogy, *That Hideous Strength*, which Lewis called "a modern fairy tale for grown-ups" and "a 'tall story' about devilry,"[43] Lewis both uses and makes myth. To oppose the sinister, totalitarian N.I.C.E., National Association of Co-ordinated Experiments, Dr. Ransom, revealed as the great Pendragon of Logres, reappears, along with Merlin, magician from the time of King Arthur. In a climactic chapter titled "The Descent of the Gods," celestial spirits dance: "It seemed to each that the room was filled with kings and queens, that the wildness of their dance expressed heroic energy and its quieter movements had

40. Lewis, *Perelandra*, 218.
41. Cirlot, *A Dictionary of Symbols*, 76.
42. Lewis, *Perelandra*, 47, 45.
43. Lewis, *That Hideous Strength*, Inscription and Preface, 7.

seized the very spirit behind all noble ceremonies." And dance they did! "It was some round dance, no modern shuffling: It involved beating the floor, clapping of hands, leaping high."[44] Even the mortals are "caught up into the *Gloria*"!

Lewis wrote *Till We Have Faces: A Myth Retold* in 1956, reinterpreting the classical myth of Cupid and Psyche from the *Metamorphoses* or *The Golden Ass* of Lucius Apuleius. The book is dedicated to Joy Davidman, who apparently had a greater role in its writing than is recognized. In a letter written the following year he said, "I think it much my best book but not many people agree,"[45] and again in two subsequent letters he said, "I think it far and away my best book, but it has, with the critics and the public, been my one great failure: an absolute 'flop'. No one seems to have the slightest idea what I'm getting at in it."[46] In the Apuleius account, Venus, jealous of Psyche's beauty, orders her son Cupid to make her fall in love with the ugliest of men, but Cupid falls in love with her himself and whisks her off to a fabulous palace where he can make nightly visits unseen by anyone, but forbidding Psyche to look upon his face. Her two sisters, motivated by envy, persuade Psyche that her lover might be a hideous serpent who will consume her, so when she holds a lamp over him, she trembles with love, spilling hot oil on him. Roused, he angrily rebukes her and vanishes, whereupon Psyche, desolate and disconsolate, wanders in search of Cupid. Venus assigns what are considered impossible tasks, but with aid she accomplishes them. Cupid returns, forgives Psyche, secures permission from Jupiter to marry her, sees her immortalized, and arranges their reconciliation with Venus: happy ever after.[47]

---

44. Lewis, *That Hideous Strength*, 326. Dancing was a significant aspect of Jewish life in Bible times, with eleven different Hebrew terms used to describe the act in the Old Testament and two Greek terms in the New Testament.

Pagans used a form of dance to honor their gods (I Kings 18:26). The Psalmist urges the people to praise God with dance (Psalm 149:3; 150:4). David rejoices that "weeping may last for the night but a shout of joy comes in the morning ... for [God] has turned for me my mourning into dancing" (Psalm 30:5, 11). The prophet Jeremiah speaks of Yahweh's "lovingkindness" (*hesed*, "faithfulness"), Who assures His people that they will "take up your tambourines and go forth to the dances of the merrymakers" (Jeremiah 31:3, 4).

45. Lewis, Letter of 7 August 1957, *The Collected Letters of C. S. Lewis*, III, 873.

46. Ibid., Letter of 28 April 1960, Letter of 26 August 1960, 1148, 1181.

47. Lewis apparently followed the Robert Graves translation, published in 1950. Erich Neumann's *Amor and Psyche: The Psychic Development of the Feminine*, an illuminating commentary on Apuleius's tale discussing the psychological characteristics of the feminine, appeared in German in 1952, with the English version appearing in

Part II: Mutual Themes

Lewis said the idea of rewriting this classic myth, with the palace invisible, had been in his mind since he was an undergraduate, noting that he had been at work on Orual (Psyche's unattractive sister and narrator) for thirty-five years. He said that "Apuleius got it all wrong. The elder sister (I reduce her to one) couldn't *see* Psyche's palace when she visited her. She saw only rock & heather. When P. said she was giving her noble wine, the poor sister saw & tasted only spring water. Hence her dreadful problem: 'is P. mad or am I blind?' As you see, tho' I didn't start from that, it is the story of every nice, affectionate agnostic whose dearest one suddenly 'gets religion', or even every lukewarm Christian whose dearest gets a Vocation. Never, I think, treated sympathetically by a Christian writer before. I do it all thro' the mouth of the elder sister."[48] As Orual remonstrates with the Fox near the end of the novel, he says to her, "For mortals, as you said, will become more and more jealous. And mother and wife and child and friend will all be in league to keep a soul from being united with the Divine Nature."[49] What a profound application of the myth to Christian experience this is!

Whereas Hawthorne attempted to render pagan myths palatable to Christian sensitivity, Lewis Christianized pagan myths and used them to dramatize Christian truths. For example, he said, "Psyche is an instance of the *anima naturaliter Christiana* ["soul by nature Christian"] making the best of the Pagan religion she is brought up in and thus being guided (but always 'under the cloud', always in terms of her own imagination or that of her people) towards the true God. She is in some ways like Christ not because she is a symbol of him but because every good man or woman is like Christ. What else could they be like?"[50]

1956, the same year as Lewis's novel.

48. Lewis, Letter of 2 April 1955, *The Collected Letters of C. S. Lewis*, III, 590. Cf. the striking scene of blindness in the stable at the end of *The Last Battle*, when the dwarfs see only a pitch-black, smelly little hole of a stable instead of sky, trees, and flowers. Instead of the aromatic beauty of wild violets they perceive filthy stable litter, and instead of the glorious feast they think they are eating hay, an old turnip, and a raw cabbage leaf; instead of golden goblets of rich red wine, they think they are drinking dirty water from a trough (*The Last Battle*, 144–47).

49. Lewis, *Till We Have Faces*, 304.

50. Lewis, Letter of 10 February 1957, *The Collected Letters of C. S. Lewis*, III, 830. For a more complete discussion of Lewis's *Till We Have Faces* and its recurring image of veils, masks, and faces vis-à-vis Hawthorne's short story "The Minister's Black Veil" and *The Blithedale Romance*, see chapter 10, "The Black Veil and the White."

In 1959 Lewis began work on yet another retelling of a classic myth, that of Menelaus, king of Sparta, younger brother of Agamemnon, and husband of Helen. When Helen was abducted by Paris, prince of Troy, Menelaus and Agamemnon fought together in the Trojan War to reclaim her. According to Euripides, the gods fashioned an imitation Helen, an "Eidolon," an image without real existence, an ideal apparition. In his "Notes to *After Ten Years*," Roger Lancelyn Green states that Lewis's story "was to turn on the conflict between dream and reality" but says he did not know, nor did Lewis, what exactly would have happened if he had gone on with the story.[51] The theme of conflict between dream and reality was one of great interest to Hawthorne as well, one that recurs in his work.

For those who may consider Lewis's use of myth in general to be inappropriate and the wild Bacchanalian romps and dances in particular to be incongruous in works with Christian underpinnings, it is important to understand further his view of myth. In 1931, the year of his conversion, Lewis wrote to Arthur Greeves expressing his fascination with "the idea of the dying and reviving god" and went on to say that "the story of Christ is simply a true myth: a myth working on us in the same way as the others, but with this tremendous difference that *it really happened*: and one must be content to accept it in the same way, remembering that it is God's myth where the others are men's myths . . . "[52] Early captivated by Northern mythology (Norse and Celtic), Lewis went much further than Hawthorne in expanding on the meaning and significance of myth, his fullest statement coming in his 1944 essay "Myth Became Fact," in which he argues that Christianity, specifically the Incarnation, is a "true myth," myth become fact: "Now as myth transcends thought, Incarnation transcends myth. The heart of Christianity is a myth which is also a fact. The old myth of the Dying God, *without ceasing to be myth*, comes down from the heaven of legend and imagination to the earth of history. It *happens*—at a particular date, in a particular place, followed by definable historical consequences. We pass from a Balder or an Osiris, dying nobody knows where, to a historical Person crucified (it is all in order) *under Pontius Pilate*. Becoming fact it does not cease to be myth: that is the miracle."[53]

---

51. "Notes on *After Ten Years*," in Lewis, *Of Other Worlds: Essays and Stories*, 146–48.

52. Lewis, *They Stand Together: The Letters of C. S. Lewis to Arthur Greeves*, 427.

53. Lewis, "Myth Became Fact," *God in the Dock: Essays on Theology and Ethics*, 66–67. Balder in Norse myth is god of light, wisdom, and righteousness; he was killed by his brother but is prophesied to return again at the final destruction of the world. Osiris is the ancient Egyptian god of fertility, lord of the underworld, and judge of the

Part II: Mutual Themes

For his part, Hawthorne included a chapter titled "Myths" midway through his novel *The Marble Faun*, one of Lewis's favorite works. He demonstrates that in a fallen world no longer are the old Arcadian myths true. The mythological Arcadia was a secluded, pastoral, sparsely populated, Eden-like area in the middle of the Peloponnesus, inhabited by shepherds and hunters, an area adopted by poets as a symbol of peaceful, rustic existence. Donatello the Faun leads his friend Kenyon to such an enchanted nook, a certain little dell, where water from a fountain once splashed into an urn in the arms of a marble nymph, but now the urn has a great crack from top to bottom and "the lady of the fountain" can only watch the basin fill itself through a channel she cannot control. The young Count narrates a myth of his progenitor, a young knight who loved and was loved by the water nymph, who refreshed him and gladdened his spirit whenever he came to the fountain. But one day when he called the nymph she did not come nor ever came again, and the water shrank away from his hands—because the guilty man had polluted the pure water by trying to wash away a blood stain! The Count tells how he was familiar with woodland creatures, habitually calling the furry and feathered people, but when he does so this time only a brown venomous lizard of the tarantula species responds. Trembling, Donatello cries, "They shun me! All Nature shrinks from me, and shudders at me! I live in the midst of a curse, that hems me round with a circle of fire! No innocent thing can come near me!" The Count can only retire to his tower, and Kenyon depart to read an antique edition of Dante. Nature has no cure for human ills. The loss of innocence is the price paid for experience.

Hawthorne was influenced by the Faun of the Greek sculptor Praxiteles, on display in the Vatican Museum in Rome. He wrote in his notebook, "It seems to me that a story, with all sorts of fun and pathos in it, might be contrived on the idea of the faun's species having become intermingled with the human race . . . The moral instincts and intellectual characteristics of the faun might be most picturesquely brought out without detriment to the human interest of the story."[54] He saw the faun as "a natural and delightful link betwixt human and brute life, with something of a divine character intermingled."[55] Donatello is originally a prelapsarian

---

dead. As with Balder, Osiris's jealous brother slew him, but Isis revived him to reign another day.

54. Cited in Meltzer, *Nathaniel Hawthorne: A Biography*, 124–25.

55. Cited in Turner, *Nathaniel Hawthorne: A Biography*, 336.

creature, a sylvan figure, an innocent noble savage until he rescues Miriam from her strange, sinister antagonist by casting him over the precipitous Tarpeian Rock. Sin and death enter the world, spoiling the Arcadian ideal.

Henry James argued against Hawthorne's use of myth in the novel: ". . . I think it a pity that the author should not have made [the faun] more definitely modern, without reverting so much to his mythological properties and antecedents, which are very gracefully touched upon, but which belong to the region of picturesque conceits, much more than to that of real psychology." James seems to violate his own rule about the necessity of granting a writer his *donnee*, his starting-point, his set of "givens," so as not to be guilty of "tampering with his flute and then criticizing his music."[56]

Hyatt H. Waggoner says, "However beautiful the old Arcadian myths are, however sad it is that we have lost our innocence, they are not true any longer in a fallen world. (In Hawthorne's terminology, the old pagan legends are 'myths,' the Biblical story in Genesis a symbolic truth, perhaps not literally true historically but true as a type of the human condition. He never refers to the Genesis story as a 'myth.') Donatello, now that he has known sin, cannot re-enter Arcadia."[57] Or, in Christian terms, there is no return to Eden. Hawthorne saw the old pagan myths being rendered false by the Fall while the Biblical stories remained true, whereas Lewis saw the old pagan myths imaging Christianity's "true myths," which became fact.

---

56. James, "The Art of Fiction," *The Future of the Novel: Essays on the Art of Fiction*, 17–18.

57. Waggoner, *Hawthorne: A Critical Study*, 215–16.

5

Scientists and Scientism

JUST AS HAWTHORNE AND Lewis valued myth in its many ramifications they devalued and even derogated what Lewis called "scientism" (the –ism suffix customarily renders the noun pejorative), which he defined as "a certain outlook on the world which is casually connected with the popularization of the sciences, though it is much less common among real scientists than among their readers. It is, in a word, the belief that the supreme moral end is the perpetuation of our own species, and that this is to be pursued even if, in the process of being fitted for survival, our species has to be stripped of all those things for which we value it—of pity, of happiness, and of freedom."[1] Clyde S. Kilby has defined "scientism" as "the popular unthinking assumption that there is no truth other than truth revealed by the scientific method,"[2] and Colin Duriez defines it as "the idolatry of science, where it becomes the sole authority, the model, and arbiter of truth . . ."[3]

Lewis has been accused of being anti-science, of maligning science and scientists, of attacking science and libeling scientists, but such is not the case. To be sure, he spoke of the "pseudo-scientific" as being "the worst rubbish," of the traditional faith "making too many concessions to the modern scientific outlook," of the danger of science "setting up to be a philosophy," of science being "run as a kind of religion," of "scientocracy" offering to free us of (rational) fears.[4]

 1. Lewis, "A Reply to Professor Haldane," *Of Other Worlds: Essays and Stories*, 76–77.
 2. Kilby, *The Christian World of C. S. Lewis*, 175.
 3. Duriez, *The C. S. Lewis Encyclopedia*, 183.
 4. Lewis, Letter of 26 July 1950, *Collected Letters of C. S. Lewis*, III, 45; Letter of 30 April 1941, II, 482; Letter of 26 March 1940, II, 372; Letter of 31 September 1957, III, 886–87; Letter of 8 December 1959, III, 1104.

In his essay "Is Theology Poetry?" Lewis makes clear the nature of his opposition:

> Long before I believed Theology to be true I had already decided that the popular scientific picture at any rate was false. One absolutely central inconsistency ruins it . . . The whole picture professes to depend on inferences from observed facts. Unless inference is valid, the whole picture disappears. Unless we can be sure that reality in the remotest nebula or the remotest part obeys the thought-laws of the human scientist here and now in his laboratory—in other words, unless Reason is an absolute—all is in ruins. Yet those who ask me to believe this world picture also ask me to believe that Reason is simply the unforeseen and unintended by-product of mindless matter at one stage of its endless and aimless becoming. Here is flat contradiction. They ask me at the same moment to accept a conclusion and to discredit the only testimony on which that conclusion can be based. The difficulty is to me a fatal one; and the fact that when you put it to many scientists, far from having an answer, they seem not even to understand what the difficulty is, assures me that I have not found a mare's nest but detected a radical disease in their whole mode of thought from the beginning."[5]

He concludes that when one understands this situation he is compelled to regard the scientific cosmology as being, in principle, a myth! Further, in a letter to Professor Douglas Bush, Lewis stated that "Magic and 'science' are twins *et pour cause*, for the magician and the scientist both stand together, and in contrast to the Christian . . . in so far as both make Power their aim, believe Power to be attainable by a technique, and in the practice of that technique are ready to defy ordinary morality."[6] It should be noted that in remarking upon this "strong family likeness" between magic and "science" he places the latter in quotes, suggesting pseudo-science, faux-science, or quasi-science.

Dr. Ransom, a character in *That Hideous Strength* and the other novels of the space trilogy, perhaps speaks for Lewis: "The physical sciences, good and innocent in themselves, had already, even in Ransom's own time, begun to be warped, had been subtly manoeuvred in a certain direction. Despair of objective truth had been increasingly insinuated into

---

5. Lewis, "Is Theology Poetry?" *Screwtape Proposes a Toast and Other Pieces*, 54–55.

6. Lewis, Letter of 28 March 1941, *The Collected Letters of C. S. Lewis*, II, 475. Douglas Bush, born in Canada, was a Milton scholar who taught at Harvard, and, like Lewis, was writing a volume for the Oxford History of English Literature.

Part II: Mutual Themes

the scientists; indifference to it, and a concentration upon mere power, had been the result."[7]

Parallels can be noted in the fiction of Hawthorne. In her study of Flannery O'Connor vis-à-vis Hawthorne, Wendy Piper argues that Hawthorne presents "an ongoing critique of modern scientism," undermines the rationalism of the modern era, and "collapses the dichotomy between subject and object upon which modern scientific objective is founded."[8] "In the name of reform, perfection, and power," she says further, Hawthorne's "scientists / idealists attempt to transcend history, flesh, and fleshly limitation, in order to come to know, and hence assume control over, the object of their investigation."[9] For Hawthorne, it is the subjectivism which results from the imbalance of head and heart that distinguishes modern scientific, dichotomous thinking and characterizes his depiction of scientists. Randall Stewart has well said, "Hawthorne more than once warns of the dangers of an exclusively scientific attitude toward life. Such an attitude, he thought, was apt to result in the dehumanizing of the experimenter and the sacrifice of the victims . . . Hawthorne . . . did not share the unqualified enthusiasm of his century for the onward march of science, for it could not have been unintentional with him that his blackest villains . . . are men of scientific training."[10]

At least six men of "science" in Hawthorne's fiction illustrate the obsession, the *idée fixe*, the monomania for control, the cold rationalism, the imbalance of head and heart, the sacrifice of human love for knowledge and power. Edward Wagenknecht has well said that "nothing he ever wrote more reflects Hawthorne's mistrust of science than 'The Birthmark.'"[11] Hawthorne states in the opening sentence that Aylmer is an eminent "man of science" and that he possessed a "degree of faith in man's ultimate control over Nature. He had devoted himself . . . too unreservedly to scientific studies ever to be weaned from them by any second passion," even the love of his beautiful young wife, Georgiana. He sacrifices her life by attempting, with an elixir vitae, to remove a tiny crimson birthmark from her cheek,

---

7. Lewis, *That Hideous Strength: A Modern Fairy-Tale for Grown-Ups*, 203.

8. Piper, *Misfits and Marble Fauns, Religion and Romance in Hawthorne and O'Connor*, 41, 11, 3.

9. Ibid., 38.

10. Stewart, *Nathaniel Hawthorne: A Biography*, 248–49.

11. Wagenknecht, *Nathaniel Hawthorne: The Man, His Tales and Romances*, 41. Cf. Melville's Captain Ahab casting his quadrant to the deck with a curse: ". . . with thy impotence thou insultest the sun! Science! Curse thee, thou vain toy" (*Moby Dick*, 493).

"for he was confident in his science, and felt that he could draw a magic circle round her within which no evil might intrude." He arrogantly imagined himself to have "acquired from the investigation of Nature a power above Nature, and from physics a sway over the spiritual world."[12]

Aylmer's obsession with the diminutive bloody hand on his wife's check is no trivial matter to be solved by a simple Helena Rubinstein treatment, for it is described as the "sole token of human imperfection,"[13] symbol of original sin. Though he is motivated by an egregious hubris, though he is presumptuous in thinking he can improve on" Nature's fairest work," though he usurps the prerogatives of Providence in attempting through science to produce a "magic circle" into which no evil can intrude, Aylmer's idealism may strike the reader as ambivalent, suggesting at once a seemingly admirable intent but also a presumptuous, insensitive abuse and sacrifice of the one who loves him. Several Notebook entries containing ideas that apparently led to the story seem to reinforce this ambivalence: "A person to be in the possession of something as perfect as mortal man has a right to demand; he tries to make it better, and ruins it entirely"; "a person to spend all his life and splendid talents in trying to achieve something naturally impossible, —as to make a conquest over Nature"; "a person to be the death of his beloved in trying to raise her to more than mortal perfection; yet this should be a comfort to him for having aimed so highly and holily."[14] The three entries suggest that Hawthorne carefully pondered different perspectives for the story: the first emphasizes that Aylmer violates the "right" to possess absolute perfection and ironically in attempting to improve on Nature—ruins it; the second emphasizes the irony of the degree of effort expended to achieve the impossible—achieve perfection by conquering Nature; the third emphasizes that even though Aylmer causes the death of his beloved in attempting to make her perfect he should be consoled by his high, holy aim. With typical irony, Hawthorne has Georgiana, in her dying

12. Hawthorne, "The Birthmark," *The Complete Short Stories of Nathaniel Hawthorne*, 227, 231, 233.

13. Ibid., 237. Aylmer's view of the birthmark and his monomaniacal attempt to remove it resembles Captain Ahab's search for the white whale, which to him represented the "incarnation of all those malicious agencies. . . the intangible malignity. . . all the subtle demonisms of life and thought, all evil. . . all the general rage and hate felt by his whole race from Adam down" (Melville, *Moby Dick*, 183). Ahab's "fatal pride" (511) is also that of Aylmer. Melville refers to "the ineffaceable, sad birth-mark in the brow of man [which] is but the stamp of sorrow in the signers" (461). Hawthorne's story preceded Melville's novel by eight years (1843 and 1851, respectively).

14. Hawthorne, *The American Notebooks*, 165, 184.

moment, pronounce a blessing on Aylmer for his good intention: "You have aimed loftily; you have done nobly." However one may assess Aylmer's motivation and action, it is unmistakable that the story dramatizes the devastating ruin wrought by scientific idealism carried to the extreme.

A scientist / villain similar to Aylmer is Dr. Giacomo Rappaccini, a botanist and physiologist in "Dr. Rappaccini's Daughter." In fact, Roy R. Male sees Rappaccini as "a hardened, power-mad Aylmer."[15] As Wendy Piper has noted, "The tragic potential for misuse of the modern scientific attitude is the subject of 'Rappaccini's Daughter.'"[16] Similarly, Hubert H. Hoeltje concludes that "Doctor Rappaccini, who sacrifices his own daughter to science, is the very counterpart of Goethe's Mephistopheles—the embodiment of intellect divorced from love or moral purpose—with consequences devastating and unspeakably shocking."[17] It is said that Rappaccini "cares infinitely more for science than for mankind. His patients are interesting to him only as subjects for some new experiment. He would sacrifice human life, his own among the rest, or whatever else was dearest to him, for the sake of adding so much as a grain of mustard seed to the great heap of his accumulated knowledge." Accordingly, being "as true a man of science as ever distilled his own heart in an alembic," he "was not restrained by natural affection from offering up his child in this horrible manner as the victim of his insane zeal for science," though he argues that he did it to render his daughter Beatrice "as terrible as [she was] beautiful," not leaving her in "the condition of a weak woman, exposed to all evil and capable of none."[18] Accordingly, he imbued her with poisons from her birth onward until her nature had itself become the deadliest poison in existence. The kernel idea for the story appears in a Notebook citation, attributed to Sir T. Browne: "A story there passeth of an Indian king that sent unto Alexander a fair woman, fed with aconite and other poisons, with this intent complexionally to destroy him."[19] The difference, of course, is that Rappaccini intends the poison infusion not as a means of destroying its recipient but as a means of rendering her inviolable and the infusion of Giovanni to secure a companion for her,

15. Male, *Hawthorne's Tragic Vision*, 59.

16. Piper, *Misfits and Marble Fauns: Religion and Romance in Hawthorne and O'Connor*, 30.

17. Hoeltje, *Inward Sky: The Mind and Heart of Nathaniel Hawthorne*, 234.

18. Hawthorne, "Dr. Rappaccini's Daughter," *The Complete Short Stories of Nathaniel Hawthorne*, 260–61, 271, 275.

19. Hawthorne, *The American Notebooks*, 184.

though he is apparently motivated partly in seeking to outdo his professional rival, Professor Pietro Baglioni. When Giovanni administers an antidote produced by Professor Baglioni, Beatrice, like Georgiana, dies as another man of science, Baglioni, looks on from an upstairs window with a shout of triumph mixed with horror. Beatrice is the victim, mistreated and violated by three men of science who are villains in varying degrees.

Yet another of Hawthorne's aberrant scientists is Dr. Cacaphodel, a researcher in chemistry and alchemy, in "The Great Carbuncle." His name is perhaps a compounded derivative from *caca*, a slang expression meaning "excrement," and *asphodel*, a plant of the lily family, the classic flower of death. It is said that Dr. Cacaphodel "had wilted and dried himself into a mummy by continually stooping over charcoal furnaces, and inhaling unwholesome fumes during his researches," having "drained his body of all its richest blood, and wasted it, with other inestimable ingredients, in an unsuccessful experiment," being "so estranged from natural sympathies, by the absorbing spell of the pursuit, as to acknowledge no satisfaction at the sight of human faces . . ."[20] His scientific experiments have already estranged, deranged, and dehumanized him. He is one of seven searchers for the Great Carbuncle, a mysterious, deep-red garnet[21] the quest of which one considers but little better than trafficking with the Evil One. Each construes the carbuncle in his own way and, as with the crew members of Melville's *Pequod* viewing the gold doubloon nailed by Ahab to the mast-head, it functions "like a magician's glass, to each and every man in turn but mirrors back his own mysterious self."[22] The eminent chemist / alchemist, who vents his disdain for those who do not regard "the interests of science," believes his possession of the Great Carbuncle will crown his "scientific reputation" so he returns to his laboratory with "a prodigious piece of granite, which he ground to powder, dissolved in acids, melted in the crucible, and burned with the blow-pipe, and published the result of his experiments in one of the heaviest folios of the day." What could be a more ironic, more satirical, more scathing statement about scientism than the narrator's conclusion that for Dr. *Merde*-Death "the gem itself could not have answered

---

20. Hawthorne, "The Great Carbuncle," *The Complete Short Stories of Nathaniel Hawthorne*, 81.

21. Is there cogent irony in Hawthorne's use of "carbuncle," not only a deep-red gem but also a bacterial infection in painful, pus-filled boils.

22. Melville, *Moby Dick*, 428.

Part II: Mutual Themes

better than the granite"?[23] Dr. Cacaphodel's "scholarly" paper may be included in one of the "gigantic folios and black-letter quartos" or one of the "little parchment-covered duodecimos" which line the shelves of Dr. Heidegger's study, along with a bronze bust of Hippocrates, Greek physician and "Father" of modern medicine. Half a century before, the doctor's fiancée, afflicted with "some slight disorder," had swallowed one of her lover's prescriptions—and, like Georgiana and Beatrice, —died on their wedding evening.[24] On the present occasion, the doctor has assembled four elderly persons for another of his scientific experiments—to restore them to the bloom of youthfulness with water he has supposedly secured from the Fountain of Youth. Apparently Hawthorne pondered variations for such a story, as suggested by a Notebook entry: "A man, arriving at the extreme point of old age, grows young again, at the same pace at which he has grown old; returning upon his path, throughout the whole of life, and then taking the reverse view of matters. Methinks it would give rise to some odd concatenations."[25]

In this story the distinction between science and magic is blurred, for the doctor takes a ponderous black leather-bound folio, releases the silver clasps on this reputed "book of magic" (as Lucy Pevensie does in Lewis's *The Voyage of the "Dawn Treader"*) and removes a fifty-five-year-old rose, which blooms again when he applies the water. The four persons each quaff the magic water, are restored to the happy prime of youth, cavort as they did when young, then age again when the vessel containing the Water of Youth is overturned and broken. The four persons resolve to make a pilgrimage to find the Fountain of Youth; only the doctor seems to have learned the lesson that even if one has a "second chance," the opportunity to relive one's life, it is unlikely that there will be any repentance, any change, only a re-enactment of original foibles and folly—essentially the same truth conveyed in Lewis's *The Great Divorce*.

Hawthorne's most egregious scientist / villain would seem to be Roger Chillingworth, reputedly "a person of great skill in physic" as an

---

23. Hawthorne, "The Great Carbuncle," *The Complete Short Stories of Nathaniel Hawthorne*, 89. Cf. Lewis's Episcopal Ghost in *The Great Divorce* who rejects repentance and Heaven to return so he can present a paper at a Theological Society—in Hell.

24. Hawthorne, "Dr. Heidegger's Experiment," *The Complete Short Stories of Nathaniel Hawthorne*, 114.

25. Hawthorne, *The American Notebooks*, 285. The Notebook entry seems more exactly to anticipate F. Scott Fitzgerald's "The Curious Case of Benjamin Button," which was apparently inspired by a remark of Mark Twain to the effect that it was a pity that the best part of life came at the beginning and the worst part at the end.

"eminent Doctor of Physic from a German university," "a modern man of science... provided with a distilling apparatus, and the means of compounding drugs and chemicals, which the practiced alchemist knew well how to turn to purpose," "a man of thought, —the bookworm of great libraries" who "sought truth in books... [and] gold in alchemy," one familiar "with the ponderous and imposing machinery of antique physic," a "scholar" and "man of skill" "extensively acquainted with the medical science of the day," of "the medical and chirurgical profession."[26] There is some perverse name-dropping when he claims knowledge of innovative medical secrets learned not only from Indians in the wilderness but also lessons as old as Paracelsus, speaks knowingly of Kenelm Digby, and reportedly was associated with Doctor Simon Forman[27]—nefarious alchemists and occultists all.

Chillingworth differs from Aylmer, Rappaccini, Cacophodel, and Heidegger in that his motivation is totally malicious, with no honorific intent: he obsessively seeks to avenge the unfaithfulness of his wife Hester by diabolically seeking out her partner in adultery and destroying him, both body and soul. As Darrel Abel has said, "The physician was enabled to effectuate his malice by his adeptness in a science which Hawthorne looked upon as dangerous if applied outside its proper sphere."[28] But what, one might ask, would Hawthorne conceive to be the "proper sphere" for pseudo-scientific occultism, alchemy, necromancy, black magic? Rather, he seems to show that such "scientism" *has* no proper sphere and that its practice leads in its extremity to outright diabolism, as it does for Chillingworth. With a deliberate act of his will, "*he chose* to withdraw his name from the roll of mankind," cutting himself off from

---

26. Hawthorne, *The Scarlet Letter*, 100, 111, 116, 69, 70, 109–10, 71, 103, 111, 109.

27. Ibid., 68, 111, 117. Paracelsus was born Phillipus Auroleus Theophrastus Bombastus von Hohenheim (1493–1541), German-Swiss physician, alchemist, botanist, occultist. He is credited with the introduction of opium, mercury, and principles of magnetism into the study of medicine, and is considered the most original medical thinker and pioneer of the 16th century. Kenelm Digby (1603–1665) was an English courtier, diplomat (in conflict with the Puritans), and scientific experimenter (originating the so-called Powder of Sympathy, a kind of salve used to treat injuries), astrologer, and alchemist. Simon Forman (1552–1611) was a notorious Elizabethan astrologer, occultist, and herbalist who was implicated in the plot to kill Sir Thomas Overbury. Ben Jonson and others characterized Forman as either a fool or an evil magician in league with the devil—"Devil Forman."

28. Abel, *The Moral Picturesque: Studies in Hawthorne's Fiction*, 212.

the community of mankind, effecting "a new purpose, dark."[29] He became "a striking evidence of man's faculty of transforming himself into a devil, if he will only, for a reasonable space of time, undertake a devil's office," becoming "the arch-fiend standing there with a smile and scowl to claim his own."[30] When he thrusts aside Dimmesdale's vestment and apparently glimpses the minister's own scarlet letter, anyone seeing the physician's ecstasy would have "no need to ask how Satan comports himself when a precious human soul is lost to heaven, and won into his kingdom."[31] For further evidence one need only check with Lewis's Screwtape.

Coldly (living up to his name), apathetically, heartlessly, Chillingworth "has violated, in cold blood, the sanctity of a human heart,"[32] an act as diabolical as Ethan Brand's psychological experiment on Esther, by which he "wasted, absorbed, and perhaps annihilated her soul, in the process."[33] The imagery of fire, devil, and hell is similar in the novel and in the story: "Sometimes a light glimmered out of the physician's eyes, burning blue and ominous, like the reflection of a furnace, or, let us say, like one of those gleams of ghastly fire that darted from Bunyan's awful doorway in the hill-side, and quivered on the pilgrim's face."[34] Chillingworth's decline illustrates Lewis's point about spoiled goodness: "Goodness is, so to speak, itself: badness is only spoiled goodness. And there must be something good first before it can be spoiled . . . evil is a parasite, not an original thing. The powers which enable evil to carry on are powers given it by goodness. All the things which enable a bad man to be effectively bad are in themselves good things—resolution, cleverness, good looks, existence itself."[35] In his dialogue with Hester, Chillingworth reminds her, "All my life had been made up of earnest, studious, thoughtful, quiet years, bestowed faithfully for the increase of my own knowledge . . . and faithfully, too, for

29. Hawthorne, *The Scarlet Letter*, 109. Emphasis added.

30. Ibid., 155, 143.

31. Ibid., 127. Hawthorne seems to imply the contrast to "the joy in heaven over one sinner who repents" (Luke 15:7).

32. Ibid., 179.

33. Hawthorne, "Ethan Brand," *The Complete Short Stories of Nathaniel Hawthorne*, 480. Though his violating experiment resembles those of Chillingworth, Aylmer, and Rappaccini, Brand is not a scientist so his case will be discussed below in another context. Other Hawthorne scientists and physicians in minor works include Hippocrates Jenkins, a villainous fraud in "The Haunted Quack," and Septimius Felton, in the unfinished novel of that name, who seeks the Elixir of Life that will bring earthly immortality.

34. Hawthorne, *The Scarlet Letter*, 119.

35. Lewis, *Mere Christianity*, 44–45.

Scientists and Scientism

the advancement of human welfare. No life had been more peaceful and innocent than mine; few lives so rich with benefits conferred. Dost thou remember me? Was I not, though you might deem me cold, nevertheless a man thoughtful for others, craving little for himself,—kind, true, just, and of constant, if not warm affections? Was I not all this?" he asks Hester, to which she replies: "All this, and more."[36] Clearly, he represents goodness spoiled, a good man perverted, though even then his execrable flaw is detectable—he has no "warm affections"; his heart is cold.

After Dimmesdale's death, Chillingworth's vengeful energy seems to desert him and he "positively withered up, shriveled away, and almost vanished from mortal sight, like an uprooted weed that lies wilting in the sun." When "there was no more Devil's work on earth for him to do, it only remained for the unhumanized mortal to betake himself whither his Master would find him tasks enough, and pay him his wages duly."[37] The physician dies within a year and leaves a substantial bequest for illegitimate Pearl, the elf-child, the alleged demon offspring, who becomes the wealthiest heiress of her day. Hawthorne states, "we would fain be merciful" to Chillingworth, surmising whether "hatred and love be not the same thing at bottom," each supposing "a high degree of intimacy and heart-knowledge," each rendering "one individual dependent for the food of his affections and spiritual life upon another," each leaving "the passionate lover, or the no less passionate hater, forlorn and desolate by the withdrawal of his subject. Philosophically considered, therefore, the two passions seem essentially the same, except that one happens to be seen in a celestial radiance, and the other in a dusky and lurid glow. In the spiritual world, the old physician and the minister—mutual victims as they have been—may, unawares, have found their earthly stock of hatred and antipathy transmuted into golden love."[38] What is one to conclude about the ultimate disposition of this pseudo-scientific villain? Hawthorne's Puritan / Calvinist background would dictate, "The soul who sins will die" (Ezekiel 18:4), but if one finishes the same chapter, the final verse states, "'I have no pleasure in the death of anyone who dies,' declares the Lord God. 'Therefore repent and live.'" Jesus himself

---

36. Hawthorne, *The Scarlet Letter*, 158.

37. Ibid., 236. Hawthorne seems to have in mind here the Apostle Paul's assertion that "the wages of sin is death, but the free gift of God is eternal life in Christ Jesus our Lord" (Romans 6:23), but who, one might ask, is the Master who exacts and pays the wages—the Devil or God?

38. Ibid., 236.

warned, "Unless you repent, you will all likewise perish" (Luke 13:5), but he also declared, "The one who comes to me I will certainly not cast out" (John 6:37). Is Hawthorne suggesting that no one, not even such a monster of scientism, is beyond the pale of grace, that Chillingworth himself, perhaps influenced by the repentant confession of the minister whom he victimized, repented during his final year and demonstrated his change of heart in his graciousness toward Pearl? Or is Hawthorne simply reverting to Romantic sentiment, which says that "love wins," as suggested by his earlier comment concerning Hester: "It is to the credit of human nature, that, except where its selfishness is brought into play, it loves more readily than it hates. Hatred, by a gradual and quiet process, will even be transformed to love, unless the change be impeded by a continually new irritation of the original feeling of hostility"?[39] Could this unresolved conundrum be one of the reasons Lewis considered this novel to be inferior to *The House of the Seven Gables* and *The Marble Faun*,[40] inscribing in one of his copies of *The Scarlet Letter*, "I had forgotten the curious badness of the writing in many places"?[41]

The epitome of scientism in Lewis is illustrated by the physicist and materialist Edward Rolles Weston, who appears in *Out of the Silent Planet* and again in *Perelandra*. He is first introduced to Dr. Elwin Ransom, a philologist at Cambridge University, apparently modeled in part on J. R. R. Tolkien and Owen Barfield, by Dick Devine, Weston's co-conspirator to kidnap a human sacrifice for rulers of Malacandra (Mars): "*The* Weston . . . The great physicist. Has Einstein on toast and drinks a pint of Schrodinger's blood for breakfast."[42] Weston is a scientific idealist seeking to use whatever means necessary, even the destruction of humans and of human values, usurping the prerogatives of the Almighty himself, to assure not just the survival but also the immortality of humanity. He arrogantly tells Ransom, "As far as we know, we are doing what has never been done in the history of man, perhaps never in the history of the uni-

---

39. Ibid., 147. Cf. the irony in Lewis's *The Great Divorce* when the Big Ghost meets Len, one of the solid people who on earth had murdered their mutual friend Jack but is now in "heaven," along with Jack, because they both repented and asked for "the Bleeding Charity," which the Big Ghost refuses to do, instead insisting on his "rights" (28).

40. Lewis, Letter of 28? October 1917, I, 340.

41. In the Marion E. Wade Center, Wheaton College.

42. Lewis, *Out of the Silent Planet*, 13. Edwin Schrodinger (1887–1961) was a distinguished Austrian physicist and theoretical biologist, pioneer of quantum mechanics, known for important contributions to physics, especially the Schrodinger wave equation. He shared the Nobel Prize for Physics in 1933.

verse. We have learned how to jump off the speck of matter on which our species began: infinity, and therefore perhaps eternity, is being put into the hands of the human race. You cannot be so small-minded as to think that the rights or the life of an individual or of a million individuals are of the slightest importance in comparison with this." Like Hawthorne's devotees of scientism, Weston is unscrupulous, obsessive, monomaniacal. Unable or unwilling to learn the Malacandrian language, he attempts to express in broken English his secular humanistic beliefs: "Me care for man—care for our race—what man begets . . . man's loyalty to humanity. . . Make man live all the time,"[43] though he, as a "Bent" one, is willing to sacrifice any one, every one, all who oppose him. Even his associate Devine "was quite ready to laugh at Weston's solemn scientific idealism [for] he didn't give a damn . . . for the future of the species . . ."[44] At times Lewis' characterization verges on stereotype, as when Weston says, "I do not call classics and history and such trash education . . ."[45] He gets at least some of his just due when all of the Malacandrian *hrossa, pfifltriggi, sorns,* and even *eldila* erupt in derisive laughter at him when he tries to palliate them by dangling before them "a brightly coloured necklace of beads, the undoubted work of Mr. Woolworth." Perhaps the most damning assertion about Weston and his danger to humanity is the narrator's statement that "the stars in their courses were fighting against Weston."[46]

Lewis commented on the danger posed by Weston's unscrupulous scientism: ". . . The danger of 'Westonism' I mean to be real. What set me about writing the book was the realisation [sic] that . . . thousands of people, in one form or another depend on some hope of perpetuating and improving the human species for the whole meaning of the universe—that a 'scientific' hope of defeating death is a real rival to Christianity." In another letter, interestingly to science fiction author Arthur C. Clarke, Lewis said, "I don't of course think that at the moment many scientists are budding Westons: but I do think (hang it all, I *live* among scientists!) that a point of view not unlike Weston's is on the way . . . I agree Technology is *per se* neutral: but a

---

43. Lewis, *Out of the Silent Planet*, 138–39.
44. Ibid., 30.
45. Ibid., 27.
46. Ibid., 128. Lewis is citing Judges 5:20—"the stars in their courses fought against Sisera," the formidable Canaanite general, who was killed by Heber's wife Jael, who hammered a tent spike into his head as he slept (Judges 4:21).

Part II: Mutual Themes

race devoted to the increase of its own power by technology with complete indifference to ethics *does* seem to me a cancer in the universe."[47]

Lewis's expression of concern about the proliferation of Weston's point of view, particularly the increase of power by scientific technology resulting in indifference to ethics, was made in 1943, the year both *The Abolition of Man*[48] and *Perelandra*, the second volume of his space trilogy, appeared. In the former Lewis defends the objectivity of virtues and values, epitomized by the Tao, and deplores the atrophy of chests, which balance the cerebral and visceral aspects, thus ultimately resulting in "the abolition of man." "We make men without chests," he says, "and expect of them virtue and enterprise . . . We remove the organ and demand the function . . . We laugh at honour and are shocked to find traitors in our midst. We castrate and bid the geldings be fruitful."[49]

Like Hawthorne, Lewis suggests the close relationship between magic and science:

> The serious magical endeavour and the serious scientific endeavour are twins: one was sickly and died, the other strong and throve. But they were twins. They were born of the same impulse . . . There is something which unites magic and applied science while separating both from the 'wisdom' of earlier ages. For the wise men of old the cardinal problem had been how to conform the soul to reality, and the solution had been knowledge, self-discipline, and virtue. For magic and applied science alike the problem is how to subdue reality to the wishes of men: the solution is a technique; and both, in the practice of this technique, are ready to do things hitherto regarded as disgusting and impious . . .

---

47. Letter of 9 August 1939. Letter of 7 December 1943, II, 262, 594. Sir Arthur Charles Clarke (1917—), chairman of the British Interplanetary Society, is perhaps best known as the author of *2001: A Space Odyssey* (1968) and numerous other science fiction books. In 1943 he was offended by Lewis's *Perelandra*, particularly the passage in chapter 6, page 81, beginning "He was a man obsessed" and ending with "to these minds a welcome corollary." See *From Narnia to A Space Odyssey: The War of Ideas Between Arthur C. Clarke and C. S. Lewis* (2003), consisting of the letters, as well as stories and essays by Lewis and Clarke.

48. In a letter of 20 February 1955, written to an American lady, Lewis said, "I'm so pleased about the *Abolition of Man*, for it is almost my favourite among my books but in general has been almost totally ignored by the public" (*Letters to an American Lady*, 37).

49. Lewis, *The Abolition of Man*, 35.

Later he summarizes the problem and suggests a solution: "It might be going too far to say that the modern scientific movement was tainted from its birth: but I think it would be true to say that it was born in an unhealthy neighbourhood and at an inauspicious hour. Its triumphs may have been too rapid and purchased at too high a price: reconsideration, and something like repentance, may be required."[50]

Reconsideration and repentance—they constitute the solution to aberrant scientism, Lewis says. Accordingly, in what is perhaps the denouement of *Perelandra*, after Weston has been possessed by "the Force," becoming the dehumanized Un-Man, Ransom pleads with him, "Say a child's prayer if you can't say a man's. Repent your sins."[51] But, of course, Weston does not, perhaps cannot, repent and, like Ethan Brand, is cast into a fire-pit, "a terrible place where clouds of steam went up for ever and ever."[52]

Such was the end of the one who hubristically claimed, "I've become conscious that I'm a man set apart. Why do I do physics? Why did I discover the Weston rays? Why did I go to Malacandra? It—the Force—has pushed me on all the time. I am being guided. I know now that I am the greatest scientist the world has yet produced."[53] Ransom senses that he is in the presence of a monomaniac, with Weston "like an actor who cannot think of anything but his celebrity, or a love who can think of nothing but his mistress, tense, tedious, and unescapable, the scientist pursued his fixed idea."[54] His *idée fixe*, set to initiate a new era of misery for the universe,

> is the idea that humanity, having now sufficiently corrupted the planet where it arose, must at all costs contrive to seed itself over a larger area: that the vast astronomical distances which are God's quarantine regulations, must somehow be overcome. This for a start. But beyond this lies the sweet poison of the false infinite—the wild dream that planet after planet, system after system, in the end galaxy after galaxy, can be forced to sustain, everywhere and for ever, the sort of life which is contained in the loins of our own species—a dream begotten by the hatred of death upon the fear of true immortality, fondled in secret by thousands of ignorant men and hundreds who are not ignorant.

50. Ibid., 87–88–89.
51. Lewis, *Perelandra*, 171.
52. Ibid., 182–83.
53. Ibid., 93.
54. Ibid., 89.

Part II: Mutual Themes

> The destruction or enslavement of other species in the universe, if such there are, is to these minds a welcome corollary."[55]

Ransom soon learns that he has been brought to unfallen, pristine Perelandra (Venus) to refute the evil, diabolical arguments that Weston presents to the Green Lady Queen Tinidril and King Tor, her husband, who are tempted, like Adam and Eve, to disobey the command of Maleldil not to live on the Fixed Land. The Floating Islands, twenty-three of them, as opposed to the Fixed Land, seem to represent living by faith and submitting to the Divine will. Hour after hour, day after day Weston argues biological philosophy, emergent evolution, purposive dynamism, Life Force spiritualism, the vortex of self-realization, an "all is one" monism, planetary imperialism, and more. He tempts the Lady with "independence," with "being a full woman," with being "older" and wiser, with tasting new fruits, with finding Death and branching out, with rebellious feminism, with braving a terrible risk for her child, lover, and people, with being a risk-bearer out of love for the King, with the feminist argument about men laboring to keep women down to mere childbearing and ignoring the high destiny for which they were created, with the idea that the Fall in Thulcandra (Earth) was fortunate, with vanity by means of a cheap pocket mirror and gown of feathers and leaves. Ransom does his best to counter each of the temptations, though he feels an assault on his faith and often succumbs to an appalling weariness and malaise. Maleldil gives him longed-for rest, but then he is compelled to fight Weston physically until he smashes the grotesque head with a stone and hurls his dehumanized body into the abyss.

Hawthorne's Chillingworth becomes Lewis's Weston; they are cut from the same cloth or, more accurately, from the same asbestos fibers. As Chillingworth becomes an "unhumanized mortal" with once a human heart, who has "become a fiend," having transformed himself into a Devil, Weston becomes a "dehumanized mortal," the Un-man, the Thing, having called the Force into him completely.[56] A significant difference, however, is that Weston's malicious, unmitigated hatred has no chance of being "transmuted into golden love," as Chillingworth's stock of hatred and antipathy are said possibly to be.

55. Ibid., 81–82. This is part of the passage that Arthur C. Clarke found so objectionable.

56. For a full discussion of Weston's diabolism and demon possession, Lewis's description of which is one of the most vivid in all of fiction, along with discussion of evil, the Evil One, and *Felix Culpa*, see chapter 9.

In *That Hideous Strength*, the final volume of the space trilogy, Lewis gives a final turn of the screw to scientism's "outer rim of devilry," as the N.I.C.E., the National Institute of Co-ordinated Experiments, a sinister, totalitarian organization of scientists, attempts to use technology for gaining social, psychological, and political control. Though Weston is gone, Westonism has proliferated, now no longer limited to a few individuals but spreading to a technocracy of scientific materialism seeking to remake the human race, eradicating outdated values like freedom, dignity, and beauty. "If Science is really given a free hand it can now take over the human race and re-condition it," one official says, "make man a really efficient animal."[57] "The Kingdom is going to arrive: in this world: in this country. The powers of science are an instrument."[58] Leader Filostrato says, "It is the beginning of all power . . . The giant time is conquered. And the giant space—he was already conquered too . . . It is the beginning of Man Immortal and Man Ubiquitous . . . Man on the throne of the universe . . . Man's power over Nature means the power of some men over other men with Nature as the instrument. There is no such thing as Man—it is a word. There are only men. No! It is not Man who will be omnipotent, it is some one man, some immortal man. Alcasan, our Head is the first sketch of it."[59] Alcasan is literally only a head, a scientific experiment of a new species— Chosen Heads who never die, the supposed "next step in evolution, the emergence of Bodiless Men." In his diary, Lewis wrote of writing "a horror play . . . to turn on the idea of a scientist who discovers a means of keeping the brain and motor nerves alive in a corpse by means of injections. The victim is kept in cold storage but occasionally allowed a turn round the house, wearing a mask: the scientist tells people he is a poor fellow whose face was badly smashed in the war. He is always sitting over fires and complaining of being cold and always being chased away by the scientist for obvious reasons."[60] Surely Hawthorne would have relished the idea!

"The Hideous Strength" confronts Ransom the Director and Pendragon of Logres, Jane and Mark Studdock, newly returned Merlin, and others as it did in the days when Nimrod built the Tower of Babel. Victory over the N.I.C.E. is won when the gods descend, initiating an exultant

---

57. Lewis, *That Hideous Strength*, 41.
58. Ibid., 79.
59. Ibid., 178.
60. Lewis, *All My Road Before Me: The Diary of C. S. Lewis*, 238.

dance of heroic energy, and Merlin pronounces the curse of Babel on their enemies so they cannot understand each other's gibberish. All is joy and gladness as Mark and Jane are happily reunited, and Ransom returns to Perelandra to be healed of the wound on his heel, where the mad scientist Weston had bitten him. Lewis and Hawthorne would seem to agree that healing of the bite of Westonism is possible only through reconsideration and repentance.

6

The "Great Power of Blackness": Sin—Original, Besetting, Unpardonable

IT MAY HAVE BEEN, at least in part, the dark villainy depicted by Hawthorne that resonated with Lewis as it did with Herman Melville, who acknowledged in his essay "Hawthorne and His Mosses" that it was that blackness which so fixed and fascinated him.

> Whether Hawthorne has simply availed himself of this mystical blackness as a means to the wondrous effects he makes it to produce in his lights and shades; or whether there really lurks in him, perhaps unknown to himself, a touch of Puritanic gloom—this, I cannot altogether tell. Certain it is that this great power of blackness in him derives its force from its appeals to that Calvinistic sense of Innate Depravity and Original Sin, from whose visitation, in some shape or other, no deeply thinking mind is always and wholly free. For, in certain moods, no man [certainly not his American cousin] can weigh this world, without throwing in something, somehow like Original Sin, to strike the uneven balance.[1]

A similar power of blackness recurs in Lewis's work as well, and one can trace the spectrum of evil in both authors, from the villainy of scientistic monomania to the nadir of evil in the archfiend himself.

The theme of "Innate Depravity and Original Sin" recurs in the work of both writers. Though Hawthorne never alludes explicitly to Original Sin, that is, inherited sin, the effect which the sin of Adam has

---

1. Melville, "Hawthorne and His Mosses," *Herman Melville*. Edited by R. W. B. Lewis, 42–43.

as a precondition of all human life[2], there is ample evidence that he held this belief. In an 1836 entry in his Notebook, he wrote: "There is evil in every human heart, which may remain latent, perhaps, through the whole of life; but circumstances may rouse it to activity . . . The appetite might be observed first in a child, and then traced upwards, manifesting itself in crimes suited to every stage of life."[3] Evil, Hawthorne suggests, is both innate, present from birth, and latent, hidden, present but invisible. Original Sin, as Randall Stewart has noted, "refers not so much to covert acts as to the whole nature of man, his limitations, his fallibility, his self-involvement, the 'wrongness' of his attitudes, the absence of contrition and humility, the presence of pride."[4] Interestingly, the British philosopher T. E. Hulme wrote, "We may define Romantics, then, as all who do not believe in the Fall of Man," those who do not "believe in Original Sin."[5] Applying this criterion, neither Hawthorne nor Lewis could be considered a "Romantic."

Miriam, in Hawthorne's *The Marble Faun*, says to Kenyon, "The story of the Fall of Man! . . . that very *sin into which Adam precipitated himself and all his race. . .*"[6] As Hyatt H. Waggoner has well said, "Over and over again [Hawthorne] retold the story of the Fall, and now and then he managed to imagine its sequel, the redemption effected by the Second Adam. Loss of innocence compelled his imagination."[7] In a real sense, *The Marble Faun* is Hawthorne's story of the Fall of man, and garden / Eden imagery recurs in such works as "Rappaccini's Daughter," "The New Adam and Eve," *The House of the Seven Gables*, and *The Blithedale Romance*.

The passing down of evil and its proclivities from generation to generation is a common theme in the work of both writers. *The House of the Seven* Gables "can be read as a parable on the nature and effects of Original

---

2. See, for example, Romans 5:12—"Therefore, just as sin entered the world through one man, and death through sin, and in this way death came to all men, because all sinned" and Psalm 51:5—"Behold, I was brought forth in iniquity, and in sin my mother conceived me."

3. Hawthorne, *The American Notebooks*, 29–30.

4. Stewart, *American Literature and Christian Doctrine*, 36–37.

5. Hulme, *Speculations: Essays on Humanism and the Philosophy of Art*, 256.

6. Hawthorne, *The Marble Faun*, 434. Emphasis added. Cf. I Corinthians 15:21–22—"For since by a man came death, by a man also came the resurrection of the dead. For as in Adam all die, so also in Christ all shall be made alive."

7. Waggoner, *Hawthorne: A Critical Study*, 259.

Sin."[8] As Phoebe contemplates the striking resemblance between the living judge and the portrait of his ancestor, the narrator observes that "a deeper philosopher than Phoebe" might have noted something very terrible, for "it implied that *the weaknesses and defects, the bad passions, the mean tendencies, and the moral diseases which lead to crime are handed down from one generation to another*, by a far surer process of transmission than human law has been able to establish in respect to the riches and honors which it seeks to entail upon posterity."[9]

Similarly, as titular Young Goodman Brown makes his way into the forest on his nefarious purpose, the figure he sees sitting under an old tree bears "*a considerable resemblance to him[self] . . . [T]hey might have been taken for father and son.*"[10] This devil figure informs Brown that he was good friends with both his grandfather and father, having assisted the former when he lashed a Quaker woman in the streets of Salem and the latter when he set fire to an Indian village in King Philip's war. Brown's pious old catechism teacher, Goody Cloyse, utters what appears to be both an imprecation and an identification when she exclaims, "The devil!" upon seeing the dark figure, who replies, "Then Goody Cloyse knows her old friend?" She says further, "Yea, truly is it, and *in the very image of my old gossip Goodman Brown, the grandfather of the silly fellow that now is.*"[11] "Gossip" here is a blended form of *god* and *sib*, a godparent, one who has sponsored another at his / her baptism; in other words, young Brown's grandfather, acting as catechist, had sponsored Goody Cloyse, his catechumen, at her initiation, her confirmation into diabolism at a witches' sabbath. Subsequently, when young Brown approaches the evil "congregation," he feels "*a loathful brotherhood by the sympathy of all that was wicked in his heart. He could have well nigh sworn that the shape of his own father beckoned him to advance*, looking downward from a smoke wreath . . ."[12] Is Hawthorne, in fact, dramatizing the recurring statement in the Pentateuch that the Almighty is "visiting the iniquity of the fathers on the children, on the third and the fourth generations of those who hate [him]?"[13]

---

8. Ibid., 161.

9. Hawthorne, *The House of the Seven Gables*, 108. Emphasis added.

10. Hawthorne, "Young Goodman Brown," *The Complete Short Stories of Nathaniel Hawthorne*, 248. Emphasis added.

11. Ibid., 249–50. Emphasis added.

12. Ibid., 254. Emphasis added.

13. See Exodus 21:5, 34:7, Numbers 14:18, and Deuteronomy 5:9.

Part II: Mutual Themes

The devil figure's exhortations to the young initiate to hasten farther into the forest are so aptly expressed that "*his arguments seemed rather to spring up in the bosom of his auditor* than to be suggested by himself." Brown proceeds farther into "the heart of the dark wilderness . . . , *rushing onward with the instinct that guides moral man to evil.*"[14] Hawthorne is clearly suggesting that young Brown's compulsion to go deeper into the heart of darkness comes not from something learned externally but from impulses that spring up from within, from instinct, an inborn, natural tendency to act this way—innate depravity, inherited sin.

One of Hawthorne's most obvious symbols of original sin is the titular birth-mark, which the author calls variously "the visible mark of earthly imperfection," "the fatal flaw of humanity which Nature, in one shape or another, stamps ineffaceably on all her productions," "the symbol of [Georgiana's] liability to sin, sorrow, decay, and death," "the symbol of imperfection," "that sole token of human imperfection."[15] Another symbol of original sin is the seven-gabled house of the Pyncheons, bearing the ominous curse of Matthew Maule. The narrator early raises the question of "whether each inheritor of the property—conscious of wrong, and failing to rectify it—did not *commit anew the great guilt of his ancestor,* and *incur all its original responsibilitie*s," echoing the idea that Original Sin is "original" with each person. The implied answer to this "awful query" would seem to be a strong affirmative in this self-described "history of retribution for the sin of long ago."[16] Hawthorne seems intent on stressing that sin is at once original, inherited, and "original" with each person. For example, Roderick Elliston in "Egotism; or, The Bosom Serpent" tells of how it was reputed that a snake "once crept into the vitals of my great grandfather and dwelt there many years, tormenting the old gentleman beyond mortal endurance. In short it is a family peculiarity. But, to tell you the truth, I have no faith in this idea of the snake's being an heirloom. He is my own snake, and no man's else," then adds, "There is poisonous stuff in any man's heart sufficient to generate a brood of serpents."[17]

---

14. Hawthorne, "Young Goodman Brown," *The Complete Short Stories of Nathaniel Hawthorne*, 250, 252. Emphasis added.

15. Hawthorne, "The Birthmark," *The Complete Short Stories of Nathaniel Hawthorne*, 227, 228, 237.

16. Hawthorne, *The House of the Seven Gables*, 24, 42.

17. Hawthorne, "Egotism; or, The Bosom Serpent," *The Complete Short Stories of Nathaniel Hawthorne*, 346.

The "Great Power of Blackness": Sin—Original, Besetting, Unpardonable

Lewis, for his part, would doubtless have concurred with Hawthorne's descriptions. He defined sin as "the turning away of the will from God."[18] But perhaps his most vivid description of sin is this one: "The only way in which I can make real to myself what theology teaches about the heinousness of sin is to remember that every sin is the distortion of an energy breathed into us—an energy which, if not thus distorted, would have blossomed into one of those holy acts whereof 'God did it' and 'I did it' are both true descriptions. We poison the wine as He decants it into us; murder a melody He would plan with us as the instrument. We caricature the self-portrait He would paint. Hence all sin, whatever else it is, is sacrilege."[19] He is saying that sin is energy distorted (like the "bent ones" in the Space Trilogy), wine poisoned, melody murdered, a self-portrait caricatured—in short, *sacrilege*, literally, the temple robbed, the holy profaned, the sacred desecrated. Accordingly, the beauty and innocence of Narnia are perverted and degraded when Jadis, the wicked Queen of Charn, is awakened from enchanted sleep by Digory Kirke and taken inadvertently to the newly created Narnia: "though the world [was] not five hours old an evil [had] already entered it."[20] Digory's motivation has been honorific, for he sought a magic apple to cure his ill mother, which it does at the end: "the smell of the Apple of Youth was as if there was a window in the room that opened on Heaven." Lewis dramatizes his point "about a Dark Power in the universe—a mighty evil spirit who was held to be the Power behind death and disease, and sin." "Badness," he says further, "consists in pursuing [good things] by the wrong method, or in the wrong way, or too much . . . [W]ickedness, when you examine it, turns out to be the pursuit of some good in the wrong way."[21]

Even Weston in the first two novels of the interplanetary trilogy purports to seek a means of guaranteeing the survival of mankind, and the scientists of the so-called National Institute for Co-ordinated Experiments in the third novel allegedly seek to recondition the human race and make man "a really efficient animal," but in all cases the villainous agents with their questionable motivation and dissolute means corrupt their already dubious ends. In a letter Lewis questioned whether the evil in the trilogy would make the novels unsuitable for a family to read: ". . .

---

18. Lewis, Letter of 28 March 1949, *The Collected Letters of C. S. Lewis*, II, 929.
19. Lewis, *Letters to Malcolm: Chiefly on Prayer*, 69.
20. Lewis, *The Magician's Nephew*, 119.
21. Lewis, *Mere Christianity*, 44–45.

Part II: Mutual Themes

because in the last one there is so much evil, in a form not, I think, suitable for their age . . . I daresay the *Silent Planet* is alright: *Perelandra*, little less so: T.H.S [*That Hideous Strength*] most unsuitable."[22] Most assuredly, the evil and the ominous shadow which it casts is hideous—dreadful, revolting, ugly, appalling, horrible to witness.

Lewis seems less haunted by the Fall and loss of innocence than Hawthorne, but he devotes an entire chapter in *The Problem of Pain* to "human wickedness" and one to "the fall of man." He essentially reiterates the view of the church fathers that we sin "in Adam," whom God created perfectly good and completely happy, but he disobeyed God and became what we now see. "Our present condition," Lewis says, "is one of original sin, and not merely one of original misfortune . . . we are members of a spoiled species."[23] In *Perelandra* Lewis dramatizes the contrast between paradise lost in Thulcandra (Earth) and paradise saved in Perelandra (Venus).

Very likely Hawthorne would have concurred with Lewis's view of Total Depravity: "I disbelieve that doctrine, partly on the logical ground that if our depravity were total we should not know ourselves to be depraved, and partly because experience shows us much goodness in human nature."[24] Both writers believed in innate depravity and universal depravity, but not in total depravity, apparently not recognizing what some theologians call prevenient grace, that is, grace that precedes all human decision and endeavor, implying that God in His sovereignty takes the initiative on behalf of needy sinners, dead in trespasses and sins.[25]

Both writers see pride as the basic sin underlying all sins, the besetting sin whereby a person "tries to set up on its own, to exist for itself"; "it is the fall in every individual life, and in each day of each individual life, the basic sin behind all particular sins: at this very moment you and I are either committing it, or about to commit it, or repenting it," Lewis writes.[26] "The Fall," he writes in a letter, "is, in fact, Pride. The possibility of this wrong preference is inherent in the v. fact of having, or being, a

---

22. Lewis, Letter of 22 February 1954, *The Collected Letters of C. S. Lewis*, III, 432–33.

23. Lewis, *The Problem of Pain*, 85.

24. Ibid., 66–67.

25. Cf. Ephesians 2:1—"And you were dead in your trespasses and sins," and Romans 5:8, 10—"While we were still helpless, at the right time Christ died for the ungodly. . . . While we were enemies, we were reconciled to God through the death of His son . . ."

26. Lewis, *The Problem of Pain*, 75.

self at all."[27] "The Great Sin," according to Lewis, is Pride or Self-Conceit: "According to Christian teachers, the essential vice, the utmost evil, is Pride ... Pride leads to every other vice: it is the complete anti-God state of mind ... Pride is spiritual cancer: it eats up the very possibility of love, or contentment, or even common sense."[28]

Similarly, "pride, in Hawthorne's analysis, is the root evil, for pride is a voluntary separation [from human sympathy and connection] ... Hawthorne's stories emphasize the obstacles to free, reciprocal relationships. An obstacle may be pride, or egoism, or solitary ambition, or secret sin ... "[29] A poignant example is Roderick Elliston in "Egotism; or, The Bosom Serpent," who is serpent-possessed, reputedly having a snake in his bosom, which seemed "the symbol of a monstrous egotism to which everything was referred, and which he pampered, night and day, with a continual and exclusive sacrifice of devil worship." His egotism, his pride, leads to most of the other deadly or capital sins[30]--envy, avarice or covetousness, gluttony, lust, anger, sloth. According to Roderick's theory "every mortal bosom harbored either a brood of small serpents or one overgrown monster that had devoured all the rest."[31] In the end, the serpent / fiend is exorcised when Roderick for an instant is able to forget himself and think of the unselfish love and hope of his faithful wife, Rosina. Lewis's words seem an apt commentary and accompanying caveat on Roderick's change: "To love and admire anything outside yourself is to take one step away from utter spiritual ruin; though we shall not be well so long as we love and admire anything more than we love and admire God."[32] Roderick wails, "Forgive! Forgive!" and then sits up "like a man renewed, restored to his right mind, and rescued from the fiend which had so miserably overcome him ...," like the Gerasene demoniac.[33] Like

27. Lewis, Letter of 20 July 1943, *The Collected Letters of C. S. Lewis*, II, 585.

28. Lewis, *Mere Christianity*, 121–22, 125.

29. Stewart, *Nathaniel Hawthorne: A Biography*, 255, 261.

30. For a fuller discussion of the Seven Deadly Sins in Lewis's work, see Gerard Reed's *C. S. Lewis Explores Vice and Virtue* (2001). Cf. *The Seven Deadly Sins*, Edited by Ian Fleming (1962), *Deadly Sins* (William Morrow, 1993), and Solomon Schimmel's *The Seven Deadly Sins: Jewish, Christian, and Classical Reflections on Human Psychology* (1997).

31. Hawthorne, "Egotism; or, The Bosom Serpent," *The Complete Short Stories of Nathaniel Hawthorne*, 342, 344.

32. Lewis, *Mere Christianity*, 127.

33. Hawthorne, "Egotism; or, The Bosom Serpent," *The Complete Short Stories*, 347. Cf. Mark 5:15—"And they came to Jesus and observed the man who had been

Part II: Mutual Themes

Roderick, Hollingsworth, in *The Blithedale Romance*, has a "dark, self-delusive egotism"; his "godlike benevolence has been debased into all-devouring egotism."[34]

In the work of both writers a multiplicity of figures display overweening *hubris* in varying ways, forms, and degrees, though most are anything but heroic—Ethan Brand, Chillingworth, Aylmer, Rappaccini, Roderick Elliston, Owen Warland, Jaffrey Pyncheon, Hollingsworth, Mr. Smooth-it-away, and others in Hawthorne, Screwtape, Weston, Jadis, Mr. Enlightenment, Lord Feverstone with the rest of N.I.C.E., and others in Lewis.

Lewis suggested that the deeper a sin the less the sinner / victim suspects its existence: ". . . the more a man was in the Devil's power, the less he would be aware of it, on the principle that a man is still fairly sober as long as he knows he's drunk."[35] A key example would be Eustace Scrubb, who sleeps on the dragon's tail while filled with greedy, dragonish thoughts, being unaware that he had *become* a dragon and needed to be un-dragoned,[36] as he subsequently was by Aslan. Lewis said further that there are two errors concerning sin: we can minimize our sins, "whitewashing" them, or we can exaggerate them, "blackening" them. Rather than doing either, he says, we should "call them by their ordinary names and try to see them as you wd. see the same faults in somebody else—no special blackening or whitewashing."[37] Further, in a letter to Walter Hooper, Lewis said we should "distrust states of mind which turn our attention upon ourselves. Even at our sins we should look no longer than is necessary to know and to repent them . . . "[38]

The danger of having an excessive, unhealthy interest in sin is perhaps best dramatized by Hawthorne's Ethan Brand, who travels throughout the world for eighteen years in search of the Master Sin, the Unpardonable Sin, only to discover that it has grown in his own breast. This example counters Lewis's view that the less a victim is aware of a sin's existence, the deeper it is, for Brand is obsessively aware of the sin, which could be no deeper in his heart. When the lime-burner asks Brand what that sin is, he replies: "The sin of an intellect that triumphed over the sense of brotherhood with

demon-possessed sitting down, clothed and in his right mind . . ."

34. Hawthorne, *The Blithedale Romance*, 96, 89.

35. Lewis, "Answers to Questions on Christianity," *God in the Dock: Essays on Theology and Ethics*, 56–57.

36. Lewis, *The Voyage of the "Dawn Treader,"* 75, 89–92.

37. Lewis, Letter of 13 October 1961, *The Collected Letters of C. S. Lewis*, III, 1285.

38. Ibid., Letter of 30 November 1954, 535.

man and reverence for God, and sacrificed everything to its own mighty claims! The only sin that deserves a recompense of immortal agony!"[39] Hawthorne sketched the basis of the story "Ethan Brand," originally titled "The Unpardonable Sin,"[40] in his Notebook: "The search of an investigator for the Unpardonable Sin;—he at last finds it in his own heart and practice . . . The Unpardonable Sin might consist in a want of love and reverence for the Human Soul; in consequence of which, the investigator pried into its dark depths, not with a hope or purpose of making it better, but from a cold philosophical curiosity;—content that it should be wicked in whatever kind of degree, and only desiring to study it out. Would not this, in other words, be the separation of the intellect from the heart?"[41]

For Hawthorne, the sin too heinous and egregious to be forgiven is characterized by at least six elements: 1) it is a cold and calculating intellectual sin; 2) it demonstrates a lack of love and reverence for the human soul; 3) it shows an imbalance, even a separation, between the head and the heart; 4) it involves violation, an obsessive prying and analyzing of another; 5) it involves estrangement from the community of humankind; 6) it involves a hardening of the heart and the impossibility of repentance, as symbolized at the end of the story with the lime-burner's query, "Was the fellow's heart made of marble?"

Though related, Hawthorne's view of this sin does not seem to conform to that of the three synoptic gospels. Matthew's gospel quotes Jesus as saying, "Therefore I say to you, any sin and blasphemy shall be forgiven men, but blasphemy against the Spirit shall not be forgiven. And whoever shall speak a word against the Son of Man, it shall be forgiven him, but whoever shall speak against the Holy Spirit, it shall not be forgiven him, either in this age or in the age to come."[42] There is some controversy among theologians about the nature of this sin, but a common view is that "the sin consists in the conscious, malicious, and willful rejection and slandering, against evidence and conviction, of the testimony of the Holy Spirit respecting the grace of God in Christ, attributing it out of hatred and enmity to

---

39. Hawthorne, "Ethan Brand," *The Complete Short Stories of Nathaniel Hawthorne*, 478.

40. Mellow, *Nathaniel Hawthorne in His Times*, 283. (See also Brenda Wineapple, *Hawthorne: A Life*, 199.) It seems curious that James Playsted Wood chose to title his biography of Hawthorne *The Unpardonable Sin: A Life of Nathaniel Hawthorne*.

41. Hawthorne, *The American Notebooks*, Edited by Claude M. Simpson, 251.

42. Matthew 12:31–32. Cf. Mark 3:29–30 and Luke 12:10. See also Hebrews 6:4–6 and 10:26–29.

the prince of darkness . . . In committing that sin man willfully, maliciously, and intentionally attributes what is clearly recognized as the work of God to the influence and operation of Satan."[43] It was said that Brand "had conversed with Satan himself in the lurid blaze of this very kiln," having been accustomed "to evoke a fiend from the hot furnace of the lime-kiln, night after night, in order to confer with him about the Unpardonable Sin . . ."[44]

Other theologians have added helpful clarification:

> The sin against the Holy Spirit is not to be regarded simply as an isolated act, but also as the eternal symptom of a heart so radically and finally set against God that no power which God can consistently use will ever save it. This sin, therefore, can be only the culmination of a long course of self-hardening and self-depraving. He who has committed it must be either profoundly indifferent to his own condition, or actively and bitterly hostile to God . . . The sin against the Holy Spirit cannot be forgiven, simply because the soul that has committed it has ceased to be receptive of divine influences, even when those influences are exerted in the utmost strength which God has seen fit to employ in his spiritual administration.[45]

Another theologian writes, "According to the Scripture . . . the chief sins of men consist in their wrong judgments, in thinking and believing evil to be good and good to be evil. This in its highest form, as our Lord teaches us, is the unpardonable sin or blasphemy against the Holy Ghost. It was because the Pharisees thought that Christ was evil, that His works were the works of Satan, that He declared that they could never be forgiven."[46] Still another major theologian has written: "The degree to which the soul has hardened itself and become unreceptive to multiplied offers of the grace of God here determines the degree of guilt. Final obduracy is the sin against the Holy Spirit and is unpardonable, because the soul through it has ceased to be receptive of divine influence."[47] The common views seem to be: blasphemy against the Holy Spirit by attributing His work to Satan, calling good evil and evil good, continued self-hardening and self-depraving, leading to unfeeling indifference and hostility toward

43. Berkhof, *Systematic Theology*, 253.

44. Hawthorne, "Ethan Brand," *The Complete Short Stories of Nathaniel Hawthorne*, 477.

45. Strong, *Systematic Theology: A Compendium*, 650–51.

46. Hodge, *Systematic Theology*, 306–07.

47. Thiessen, *Introductory Lectures in Systematic Theology*, 270.

The "Great Power of Blackness": Sin—Original, Besetting, Unpardonable

God. Brand and Weston become so hardened and depraved that they are beyond the reach of repentance; as Brand says, "Freely, were it to do again, would I incur the guilt."[48]

Agnes McNeill Donohue concludes that "the unpardonable sin of Ethan Brand corresponds most accurately with the biblical and Calvinistic unforgivable sin, and goes beyond Hawthorne's early description of how he could dramatize the commission of the unpardonable sin," for "Hawthorne's apostate blasphemes against the Holy Spirit by violating the soul of another human being and studying it out of cold curiosity. This violation is blasphemous because the investigator has cooly [sic] and defiantly assumed the role of the deity."[49] Though Brand demonstrates some of the biblical characteristics of this sin, this view seems dubious for several reasons. First, there is no evidence that Brand was an "apostate," one who has "fallen away" from faith in God, though indeed he remembers how he had been "a simple and loving man . . . with what tenderness, with what love and sympathy for mankind, and what pity for human guilt and woe . . . ; with what reverence he had then looked into the heart of man . . ."[50] He had led "a solitary and meditative life" before he adopted his monomaniacal *idée fixe* and lost his hold on "the magnetic chain of humanity," but there is no evidence whatsoever that he ever had genuine faith in God. Brand's compatriot Goodman Brown might seem a more likely candidate for "apostate," for Brown, just three months married to Faith, willfully leaves her behind, goes into the forest for an apparently previously arranged rendezvous with the devil at a witches' Sabbath, "loses" his Faith (though he is still married to her), and no hopeful verse was carved on his tombstone, "for his dying hour was gloom."[51] Second, the gospels nowhere indicate that either violation of a human soul per se or usurping the role of deity constitutes blasphemy against the Holy Spirit.

If the Unpardonable Sin is, in fact, a cold, calculating sin of the intellect that violates the sanctity of the human heart, Ethan Brand, his marble heart at the end turned into snowy lime, is an egregious example, along

---

48. Hawthorne, "Ethan Brand," *The Complete Short Stories of Nathaniel Hawthorne*, 478.

49. Donohue, *Hawthorne: Calvin's Ironic Stepchild*, 214–15.

50. Hawthorne, "Ethan Brand," *The Complete Short Stories of Nathaniel Hawthorne*, 482.

51. Hawthorne, "Young Goodman Brown," *The Complete Short Stories of Nathaniel Hawthorne*, 256.

Part II: Mutual Themes

with Roger Chillingworth[52] and Lewis's Edward Weston. Just as Chillingworth was dehumanized and transformed into a very fiend, so Brand "became a fiend. He began to be so from the moment that his moral nature had ceased to keep the pace of improvement with his intellect."[53] Similarly, Lewis's Weston became dehumanized, "the thing," "the managed corpse, the bogey, the Un-man." He became fiend-possessed, the Enemy having "entered that body at Weston's own invitation, and without such invitation could enter no other. Ransom remembered that the unclean spirits, in the Bible, had a horror of being cast out into the 'deep.'" Interestingly and significantly, both Hawthorne and Lewis refer to and echo the biblical story of the Gerasene demoniac, as recorded in Mark 5:1–20 and Luke 8:26–39.

Like Hawthorne, Lewis also pondered and wrote of the Unpardonable Sin, offering wise counsel to a worried correspondent. He reminded him that John Bunyan thought he had at one time committed the unforgivable sin, [54] then added: "It has always puzzled me very much that Our Lord should have told us there is an unforgivable sin and yet not told us what it is. If it is a particular sin which could be done at a particular time, the warning does not seem to be any use—like being told that there is a poisonous vegetable but not told which it is. But it may mean persistence in ordinary sin, a final refusal to repent or even to *try* to reform . . . I have no doubt that the fear you mention is simply a temptation of the devil, an

---

52. Chillingworth, like Brand, who subjected the girl Esther to a psychological experiment and perhaps destroyed her soul in the process, is said to have violated, in cold blood, the sanctity of a human heart. Yet, surprisingly, Hawthorne, in the Conclusion of the novel, says he "would fain be merciful" to Chillingworth and his companions, and he adds: "In the spiritual world, the old physician and the minister—mutual victims as they have been—may, unawares, have found their earthly stock of hatred and antipathy transmuted into golden love." Is this the impingement of a facile Romanticism or a notion of Inclusivism or Universalism, perhaps resembling what some readers sense in Lewis, possibly as an influence of his mentor George MacDonald?

53. Hawthorne, "Ethan Brand," *The Complete Short Stories of Nathaniel Hawthorne*, 482–83.

54. See Bunyan's *Grace Abounding to the Chief of Sinners*, wherein Bunyan repeatedly refers to the misery he endured from thinking he had committed the unpardonable sin. For example: "What, thought I, is there but one sin that is unpardonable? But one sin that layeth the soul without the reach of God's mercy, and must I be guilty of that? Must it needs be that? Is there but one sin among so many millions of sins for which there is no forgiveness, and must I commit this? Oh, unhappy sin! Oh, unhappy man!" (John Bunyan, *The Pilgrim's Progress* and *Grace Abounding*, 39).

effort to keep us away from God by despair."⁵⁵ As noted above, Weston is Lewis's clearest example of an unpardonable sinner, along with members of the N.I.C.E. in *That Hideous Strength*. Also most of the ghosts in *The Great Divorce* could be said to have committed the Unpardonable Sin, in the sense that their sins remain unpardoned because they persist obdurately in refusing to repent, including the man with bowler hat, the Intelligent Man (Ikey), the Big Man / Big Ghost, the liberal Episcopal Ghost, the "hard-bitten" Ghost, the vain woman, the grumbling, whining woman who *becomes* a grumble, the coquettish corpse, the several who love to describe the seamy side of Hell, the artist, the nagging, materialistic wife of Robert, the Ghost Pam, the Ghost / tragedian Frank. A notable exception is the man overwhelmed by the red lizard of lust on his shoulder, the repulsive reptile being removed by a Burning One (angel) when the man repents and submits, the lizard then being transformed into a flying stallion, symbolizing how divine grace brings forgiveness, pardon, and transformation.Lewis confirmed this in a letter: "The metamorphosis of the lizard into the stallion was meant to symbolize perfect sublimation, after painful struggle and agonizing surrender, not by ordinary psychological law but by supernatural Grace."⁵⁶

Hawthorne spoke little of grace, and perhaps for this reason he at times seemed to take a more jaundiced view of transformation, reconciliation, spiritual and moral reparation. "Be the stern and sad truth spoken," the narrator of *The Scarlet Letter* says, "that the breach which guilt has once made into the human soul is never, in this mortal state, repaired. It may be watched and guarded . . . but there is still the ruined wall, and, near it, the stealthy tread of the foe that would will over again his unforgotten triumph."⁵⁷ Similarly, the narrator of *The House of the Seven Gables* says, "It is a truth (and it would be a very sad one but for the higher hopes which it suggests) that no great mistake, whether acted or endured, in our mortal sphere, is ever really set right."⁵⁸ A breached, ruined wall, a great mistake which puts things awry—these are just several of the dire results, the devastating consequences, of sin, though perhaps Hawthorne's parenthesis, with its reference to "the higher hopes," could be said to offer the transforming effect of divine grace to which Lewis alludes.

---

55. Lewis, Letter of 11 May 1962, *The Collected Letters of C. S. Lewis*, III, 1340–41.
56. Ibid., Letter of 13 February 1958, 920.
57. Hawthorne, *The Scarlet Letter*, 184.
58. Hawthorne, *The House of the Seven Gables*, 272.

Part II: Mutual Themes

Other effects of sin appear in the work of both writers. "What is Guilt?" the narrator of Hawthorne's "Fancy's Show Box," asks and then answers: "A stain upon the soul." A dark, polluting stain though it is, the narrator later concludes: ". . . There is reason to believe that one truly penitential tear would have washed away each hateful picture, and left the canvas white as snow . . . Penitence must kneel, and Mercy come from the footstool of the throne, or that golden gate will never open!"[59]

Edward Wagenknecht has concluded that "like *The Scarlet Letter*, 'Young Goodman Brown' is not a story about a sin but about the consequences of a sin."[60] A consequence of sin in these two works is the loss of faith: ". . . such loss of faith is ever one of the saddest results of sin," the narrator of *The Scarlet Letter* says.[61] Accordingly, Goodman Brown, thinking he has seen the pink ribbons of his wife Faith fluttering from the sky in the ominous forest, cries out, "But where is Faith?" and "My Faith is gone!"[62] Here, of course, it is the loss of faith both in the Almighty and in his fellow humans, for he has apparently accepted the statements of the devil: "Depending upon one another's hearts, ye had still hoped that virtue were not all a dream. Now are ye undeceived. Evil is the nature of mankind. Evil must be your only happiness."[63] Resembling Brown in his demoralization is Father Hooper, who looks out from behind his Black Veil, symbol of secret sin, and sees "lo! on every visage a Black Veil!"[64]

Still another consequence of sin is estrangement from the community of humankind, especially noted with Hester Prynne, who is ostracized, cursed with a mark "more intolerable to a woman's heart than that which branded the brow of Cain." She, and later her illegitimate child Pearl, is banished as a pariah, forced to inhabit another sphere, to occupy "a circle of seclusion from human society," a "magic circle of ignominy, where the cunning cruelty of her sentence seemed to have fixed her forever . . . ," "a sort of magic circle [that] had formed itself about her, into which . . . none ventured, or felt disposed, to intrude. It was a forcible type

---

59. Hawthorne, "Fancy's Show Box," *The Complete Short Stories of Nathaniel Hawthorne*, 109, 112, 113.

60. Wagenknecht, *Nathaniel Hawthorne: The Man, His Tales and Romances*, 63.

61. Hawthorne, *The Scarlet Letter*, 81.

62. Hawthorne, "Young Goodman Brown," *The Collected Short Stories of Nathaniel Hawthorne*, 253, 252.

63. Ibid., 254.

64. Hawthorne, "The Minister's Black Veil," *The Collected Short Stories of Nathaniel Hawthorne*, 39.

of the moral solitude in which the scarlet letter enveloped its fated wearer, partly by her own reserve, and partly by the instinctive, though no longer so unkindly, withdrawal of her fellow-creatures."[65]

There are, of course, other consequences of sin in the work of these two writers, besides these five—a breach in the soul, a stain of guilt, things set awry, loss of faith, estrangement—such as seeds of evil planted and fructifying, spread of the poison of malignity, death—both physical and spiritual—violation of others, and, some would argue, educative effects of sin.[66]

As part of their mutual reaction to sin and its consequences, both Hawthorne and Lewis demonstrated a great deal of attentiveness to confession, acknowlegment of sin by a penitent sinner (the Greek verb is *homologeo*, "to speak the same thing, to assent, to agree with, to admit oneself guilty"). Hawthorne was so obsessed with confession that while visiting the Cathedral in Siena he reportedly sat meditating and noting the time penitents spent in the confessional. His note of his visit to St. Peter's served as preparation for his description of Hilda's confession in *The Marble Faun*: "In one of the transepts I found a range of confessionals, where the penitent might tell his sins in the tongue of his own country . . . If I had a murder on my conscience or any other great sin, I think I should have been inclined to kneel down there, and pour it into the safe secrecy of the confessional. What an institution that is! *Man needs it so, that it seems as if God must have ordained it.*"[67]

One of the masterful scenes in *The Marble Faun* is the visit of Hilda, self-proclaimed "daughter of the Puritans," to a confessional in St. Peter's. "Within her heart, was a great need. Close at hand, within the veil of the confessional, was the relief. She flung herself down in the penitent's place; and, tremulously, passionately, with sobs, tears, and the turbulent overflow of emotion too long repressed, she poured out the dark story which had infused its poison into her innocent life . . . When the hysteric gasp, the strife between words and sobs, had subsided, what a torture had passed away from her soul! It was all gone; her bosom was as pure now as in her childhood." She finds "access to the Divine Grace for every

---

65. Hawthorne, *The Scarlet Letter*, 77–78, 87, 225, 213.

66. The supposed educative effects of sin or *Felix culpa*, "the fortunate fall," are discussed in relation to Hawthorne's *The Marble Faun* and Lewis's *Perelandra* in Chapter 9.

67. Hawthorne, *The French and Italian Notebooks*, 59–60.

Part II: Mutual Themes

Christian soul,"[68] receiving blessing, relief, and peace after she divulges to the priest her knowledge of the murder.

Hawthorne's other great confession scene, this one from a Puritan perspective, occurs at the end of *The Scarlet Letter*, where Dimmesdale acknowledges his adulterous guilt not in a private confession to a priest but openly before God, his horror-stricken parishioners, and little Pearl, whose kiss breaks "a spell," and the diabolical, vengeful Chillingworth, over whom he triumphs. God "is merciful," Dimmesdale asserts; "he hath proved his mercy, most of all, in my afflictions. By giving me this burning torture to bear upon my breast! By sending yonder dark and terrible old man, to keep the torture always at red-heat. By bringing me hither, to die this death of triumphant ignominy before the people! Had either of these agonies been wanting, I had been lost forever! Praised be His name!"[69] There seems to be no reason to question the genuineness of Dimmesdale's penitence and confession, as some critics have done. Chillingworth is unquestionably the unrepentant sinner. Dimmesdale is the late-repentant sinner. For seven years he performed acts of penance (from the Latin *poena*, "penalty"—external disciplinary measures), such as plying his "bloody scourge" on his shoulders, fasting, keeping vigils, all of which made a "mockery of penitence," a synonym of "repentance" (Greek term *metanoeo*, "to change one's mind" and "to feel remorse"). He makes "a vain show of expiation" and "vain repentance." When Hester asks if his good works have not "sealed and witnessed" in penitence, he replies, "It is cold and dead, and can do nothing for me! Of penance, I have had enough! Of penitence, there has been none!" But when he confesses his "deep life-matter—which, if [it was] full of sin, was full of anguish and repentance likewise," for he "put in his plea of guilty at the bar of Eternal Justice."[70] Hester is the yet-to-be-repentant sinner. Like Dimmesdale, she bears a "long and dreary penance," freely and voluntarily, with her acts of charity as a Sister of Mercy. The narrator asks, "Had seven long years, under the torture of the scarlet letter, inflicted so much of misery, and wrought out no repentance?" The question is answered at the end of the book: "Here had been her sin; here, her sorrow; and here was yet to be her penitence."[71]

68. Hawthorne, *The Marble Faun*, 357–58, 356.
69. Hawthorne, *The Scarlet Letter*, 233.
70. Ibid., 133, 135, 136, 176, 231.
71. Ibid., 77, 149, 207, 238.

Lewis was also highly interested in confession, beginning in 1940 the practice of weekly confession to a priest. In a letter to Sister Penelope he wrote: "I am going to make my first confession next week . . . I wasn't brought up to that kind of thing . . . The *decision* to do so was one of the hardest I have ever made . . ."[72] In a subsequent letter he noted that "the confessor is the representative of Our Lord and declares His forgiveness . . ."[73] Again he wrote: "We do not doubt that there can be forgiveness without it [confession]. But . . . many people do not *feel* forgiven, i.e. do not effectively 'believe in the forgiveness of sins' without it . . . There is the gain in self-knowledge: most of [us] have never really faced the facts about ourselves until we uttered them aloud in plain words, calling a spade a spade. I certainly feel I have profited enormously by the practice."[74] Later still, he wrote about the value of confession in making the theoretical belief in forgiveness a distinct reality: "I had been a Christian for many years before I *really* believed in the forgiveness of sins, or more strictly, before my theoretical belief became a reality to me. I fancy this may not be so uncommon."[75]

Interestingly, Hawthorne seems to have recognized the benefits of confession as a part of or result of penitence, dramatizing key scenes of each in his fiction, whereas Lewis seems to have recognized the value of confession personally, not as a sacrament but as a means of rendering forgiveness of sin a deeper reality, yet dramatizing the practice in his work in less overt terms. For example, he makes an obverse point when Weston refuses to heed Ransom's urging to "say a child's prayer if you can't say a man's. Repent your sins."[76] Similarly, most of the Ghosts in *The Great Divorce* refuse to repent and confess, with the exception of the one with the lizard of lust on his shoulder. He does not explicitly confess but, one may perhaps assume, does repent, acknowledging that he is a lost soul and desperately in need of rescue, necessitating his being willing to submit and grant permission to the Burning One to forcibly remove the reptile. Finally, he cries, "Go on, can't you? Get it over. Do what you like,' bellowed the Ghost; but ended, whimpering, 'God help me. God help me.'"[77]

---

72. Lewis, Letter of 24 October 1940, *The Collected Letters of C. S. Lewis*, II, 452.
73. Ibid., Letter of 6 April 1953, III, 1540.
74. Ibid., Letter of 4 June 1941, III, 320.
75. Ibid., Letter of 15 April 1958, III, 935.
76. Lewis, *Perelandra*, 171.
77. Lewis, *The Great Divorce*, 110.

Part II: Mutual Themes

Although it would certainly be invalid to speak of a "*virtual* repentance and confession," would it not be valid to speak of a "*tacit* repentance and confession," that is, one that is *veritable* and genuine but unspoken orally, silent? The obnoxious Eustace Scrubb has an experience similar to that of the Ghost with the lizard of lust when he submits to Aslan to be un-dragoned: "I was afraid of his claws, I can tell you, but I was pretty nearly desperate now. So I just lay flat down on my back to let him do it."[78] Here there is the acknowledgment of desperate need, belief that the Lion can help him cease being a dragon and having "dragonish" thoughts, trust that even though great pain is involved this is the sole remedy, and total submission to the transformation. Edmund Pevensie, who had betrayed Aslan and his siblings by consorting with the White Witch, is shown speaking with Aslan: ". . . there they saw Aslan and Edmund walking together in the dewy grass, apart from the rest of the court. There is no need to tell you," the narrator remarks, what was said in the conversation, but it was one "which Edmund never forgot." That it included repentance and confession may be assumed, especially when Edmund goes to each of his siblings, shakes hands with them, and says to each of them in turn, "I'm sorry."[79]

In *That Hideous Strength*, the titular phrase itself being synonymous with "the great power of blackness," two central figures, Mark and Jane Studdock, contrast the N.I.C.E. participants by their tacit repentance and assumed confessions. Jane had abandoned her Christian belief in early childhood, whereas Mark had never believed at all. In the course of the novel, however, each begins to change. Jane thinks, "There might be a life after death: a Heaven: a Hell. The thought glowed in her mind for a second like a spark that has fallen on shavings, and then a second later, like those shavings, her whole mind was in a blaze . . ."[80] She subsequently begins "descending the ladder of humility . . . then she thought of Maleldil. Then she thought of her obedience and the setting of each foot before the other became a kind of sacrificial ceremony,"[81] whereupon she thinks of her husband Mark and makes her way to the lodge where she hopes he is waiting to be reconciled with her. Mark himself comes to realize that "with all his life-long eagerness to reach an inner circle he had chosen

---

78. Lewis, *The Voyage of the "Dawn Treader,"* 90.
79. Lewis, *The Lion, the Witch, and the Wardrobe*, 152–53.
80. Lewis, *That Hideous Strength*, 234.
81. Ibid., 382.

The "Great Power of Blackness": Sin—Original, Besetting, Unpardonable

the *wrong* circle."[82] Having witnessed the results of the diabolical totalitarian machinations and the overwhelming "descent of the gods," Mark demonstrates his tacit repentance and confession as he waits to be reconciled with his wife Jane, the bedroom window open, his clothes piled carelessly on a chair, the sleeve of his shirt hanging down the outside wall.

Both writers recognized that penance, consisting of external acts of humiliation, can never effect true penitence, which is manifested by confession of sin before God and reparation for wrongs done to fellow humans, this reparation not constituting repentance but rather being the fruit thereof. True penitence or repentance and confession serve to bring forgiveness and to dissipate that "great power of blackness."

---

82. Ibid., 360.

Part III

Characterization

7

Perpetuators and Victims of the Power of Blackness

ALTHOUGH THERE IS NO explicit evidence that either Hawthorne or Lewis was acquainted with the numerous discussions of character and characters by various nineteenth century writers, the likelihood of their having some knowledge seems strong. For example, in 1844, during his "Old Manse Period," when Hawthorne became acquainted with various figures in the Transcendentalist circle, Emerson published both a poem and several essays on "Character," in which he asserted that "character is centrality, the impossibility of being displaced or overset" (echoing what he had said seven years earlier in "The American Scholar": "Character is higher than intellect"), and "no change of circumstances can repair a defect of character."[1] Whether or not either writer had encountered these statements, it seems likely that both would have concurred (except Hawthorne may have disagreed with the final clause).

Both Hawthorne and Lewis demonstrated a keen interest in, concern for, and attention to *character*, that is, the moral disposition, distinguishing attitudes, beliefs, and demeanor of a person, similar to what Aristotle called *ethos*. For example, in various Notebook entries, Hawthorne pondered the effects of external conditions on a person's character: "To well

---

1. Emerson, "Character" and "The American Scholar," *The Selected Writings* of Emerson, 370–71, 54. Forty years later, in 1884, Henry James wrote in "The Art of Fiction": "What is character but the determination of incident? What is incident but the illustration of character?" (*Henry James: The Future of the Novel*). And in 1883, Mark Twain published *Life on the Mississippi*, in which he said, "When I find a well-drawn character in fiction or biography, I generally take a warm personal interest in him, for the reason that I have known him before—met him on the river" (111).

Part III: Characterization

consider the characters of a family of persons in a certain condition, —in poverty, and endeavor to judge how an altered condition would affect the character of each."[2] Lewis, in an early letter to his father, distinguished between "being a character"—apparently a distinctive, unusual, or even eccentric person—and "having character," surmising that Abraham "had character" but could hardly be called "a character," whereas a friend, though lacking in character, was distinctly "a character." He concludes by wondering if "you need to be at least elderly to be a character," in which case, "each generation, seeing the characters all among its elders, would naturally conclude that the phenomenon was passing away or ... perhaps the secret of being a character in the very highest degree is to be dead, for then the anecdotes cluster and improve unchecked."[3] Each reader of Hawthorne and Lewis may construct his or her own list of figures who do or do not display moral "character" and those who are "characters," in the more esoteric sense in which Lewis is using the term.

In his Notebook, Hawthorne specifies sixty-five "hints for characters" or "character vignettes,[4] and Darrel Abel lists and discusses no fewer than eighty-eight Hawthorne characters.[5] Both Hawthorne and Lewis reveal and develop characters in similar ways—for example, suggesting meaning through naming (as with Hawthorne's *Faith* Brown and Lewis's Elwin *Ransom*, Hawthorne's Pearl and Lewis's Aslan, Hawthorne's Dr. Cacophodel and Lewis's Prunapismia, Hawthorne's "Mr. Smooth-it-away" and Lewis's "Mr. Halfways," Hawthorne's Chillingworth and Lewis's Screwtape and Wormwood et al.). Both writers also reveal characters by having the author or narrator describe a person's distinguishing features, as Hawthorne does with Tobias (whose name means "the Lord is my good") and Dorothy Pearson, the Puritan couple who befriend and adopt the Quaker boy, and as Lewis does with the Green Lady in *Pere-*

---

2. Hawthorne, *The American Note-Books*, 110. In another entry he wrote: "A change from a gay young girl to an old woman; the melancholy events, the effects of which have clustered around her character, and gradually imbued it with their influence, till she becomes a lover of sick chambers, taking pleasure in receiving dying breaths and in laying out the dead; also having her mind full of funeral reminiscences, and possessing more acquaintances beneath the burial turf than above it" (11).

3. Lewis, Letter of 25 February 1928, *The Collected Letters of C. S. Lewis*, I, 747.

4. Hawthorne, *The American Note-Books*, 571. See also *The American Notebooks*, Edited by Claude M. Simpson, which specifies fifty-three characters, 821.

5. Abel, *The Moral Picturesque: Studies in Hawthorne's Fiction*, 320–21. Cf. Marjorie J. Elder's discussion of character in *Nathaniel Hawthorne: Transcendental Symbolist*, 108–16.

landra. In addition, the two writers reveal their characters through their physical appearance, through their thoughts and interior monologue, through their speech, through their gestures and actions, through what other characters think and say about them.

In his writing a Romance rather than a Novel, Hawthorne claimed "a certain latitude," "a license with regard to every-day Probability," a freedom from "fidelity, not merely to the possible, but to the probable and ordinary,"[6] a claim certainly applicable to his depiction of characters. Similarly, Lewis, in discussing Science Fiction, remarks that "it is absurd to condemn [such works] because they do not often display any deep or sensitive characterization. They oughtn't to. It is a fault if they do . . . Every good writer knows that the more unusual the scenes and events of his story are, the slighter, the more ordinary, the more typical his persons should be . . . We must not confuse slight or typical characterization with impossible or unconvincing characterization."[7] Perhaps such confusion has produced the conclusion that "by conventional standards, the greatest weakness of Lewis's fiction is certainly his characterization"[8] Yet, is there not truth in Peter Kreeft's comment that Lewis "describes his villains better than his heroes, damnation better than salvation, strange men better than ordinary men, inhabitants of other planets better than those of earth, and even *eldils* better than human beings"? And is it not important to note that "in minimizing Lewis's characterizations, we must not forget his supreme success: few writers of fiction *or* apologetics, and far fewer writers of both, have portrayed as compellingly attractive a God as Lewis has dared to portray. No God farther from the God of undersexed seminarians could be imagined: regal, male, and glorious. Like Aslan, 'of course he isn't *safe*. But he's good.'"[9]

William Luther White has well said, "It is not so much that Lewis attempted novelistic character development and failed, as that he lacked the usual modern interest in character delineation. His interest in fiction concentrated elsewhere. He was more concerned to evoke a sense of the numinous than he was to delineate character. He was more concerned with Everyman than he was with any particular man."[10] Like Hawthorne,

---

6. Hawthorne, Preface, *The House of the Seven Gables*, vii. Preface, *The Blithedale Romance*, 2.

7. Lewis, "On Science Fiction," *On Stories and Other Essays on Literature*, 60–61.

8. Kreeft, *C. S. Lewis: A Critical Essay*, 38.

9. Ibid., 40.

10. White, *The Image of Man in C. S. Lewis*, 68.

Part III: Characterization

Lewis suggested that certain fictional works should be called by a name other than "novel," perhaps a special form of novel; Hawthorne called it a Romance. The point both were stressing is that the work should be judged by its own rules, not condemned for failing to accomplish something it never intended to, something inappropriate for its genre. So to misjudge and condemn is, to use the metaphor suggested by Henry James, to tamper with the author's flute and then criticize his music—by failing to grant, not necessarily to accept and concur with, his *donnee*, his set of "givens," his starting-point, including his subject, his underlying idea, the underpinnings of the genre.[11]

Characters in the work of Hawthorne and Lewis seem naturally to fall into four categories—those who perpetuate "the power of blackness," those who are victimized by it, those who counteract it, and those who convey ambivalence. It may have been, at least in part, the dark villainy depicted by Hawthorne that especially resonated with Lewis. The force of evil symbolized by witches and witchcraft plays a significant role in both writers. The Puritans considered witchcraft to be "the furthest Effort of our Original Sin . . . a siding with Hell against Heaven and Earth . . . , a renouncing of God and advancing of a filthy devil into the Throne of the Most High . . ."[12] For Lewis, perhaps the subject of witchcraft could be

11. James, "The Art of Fiction," *Henry James: The Future of the Novel*, 17–18.

12. Mather, "A Discourse on Witchcraft," *What Happened in Salem*, Edited by David Levin, 98–99. Charles Wentworth Upham's *Lectures on Witchcraft* (1831) and *Salem Witchcraft* (1867), the standard works in the field, perhaps perpetuated the warped image of Cotton Mather, who was depicted as the man who instigated the witchcraft trials to satisfy his own lust for fame. (Some say Upham was the model for Judge Pyncheon in *The House of the Seven Gables*; others say the model was John Hathorne.) See also *Cotton Mather on Witchcraft* (1991, first published in 1692), Montague Summers, *The History of Witchcraft* (1925), Pennethorne Hughes, *Witchcraft* (1952), Marion L. Starkey, *The Devil in Massachusetts: An Enquiry into the Salem Witch Trials* (1949), Paul Boyer & Stephen Nissenbaum, *Salem-Village Witchcraft: A Documentary Record of Local Conflict in Colonial New England* (1971), Chadwick Hansen, *Witchcraft at Salem* (1969), John Demos, *Entertaining Satan: Witchcraft and the Culture of Early New England* (1982), and, more recently, Frances Hill, *A Delusion of Satan: The Full Story of the Salem Witch Trials* (1995), Mary Beth Norton, *In the Devil's Snare: The Salem Witchcraft Crisis of 1692* (2002), and Diane Conwell and Jonathan Sutherland, *Witches of the World* (2007). Conclusions have varied—for example: "The popular view holds that there was no witchcraft practiced at Salem and thus that there was never any real menace to society; the danger was illusory from start to finish. It is comforting to think this, but as we have seen, it is quite wrong. There was witchcraft at Salem, and it worked. It did real harm to its victims and there was every reason to regard it as a criminal offense. The popular view also holds that all of those executed for witchcraft at Salem were innocent, and as we have seen, this is also false, although it is true that

said to have come full circle in the 1941 study *Witchcraft*, by his fellow-Inkling Charles Williams, who wrote that witchcraft "is one exhibition among many—and more flagrant than some—of a prolonged desire of the human heart; few studies of the past can present that heart more terribly—whether in its original and helpless corruption."[13]

Unlike Lewis, Hawthorne had a familial association with witchcraft: his great-great-grandfather John Hathorne (he added the "w" to the family name, some say out of embarrassment) was one of the infamous "witch judges," blamed by many for playing a major role in the witchcraft trials in 1692 Salem. The testimony of eight afflicted souls, based on "spectral evidence,"[14] brought about the hanging of nineteen victims and death by torture of another. Legend has it that one of the victims, before her execution on Gallows Hill, pronounced a curse on Judge Hathorne and his descendants. In his Custom House Preface to *The Scarlet Letter*, Hawthorne referred to the need for expiation of the sins of his fathers: "I know not whether these ancestors of mine bethought themselves to repent and ask pardon of Heaven for their cruelties; or whether they are now groaning under the heavy consequences of them, in another state of being. At all events, I, the present writer, as their representative, hereby take shame upon myself for their sakes, and pray that any curse incurred by them—as I have heard, and as the dreary and unprosperous condition of the race, for many a long year back, would argue to exist—may be now and henceforth removed."[15] As Mark Van Doren has put it, "Witchcraft

---

the majority of those who died were innocent. Finally the popular view ascribes the blame for the shedding of innocent blood to a corrupt leadership motivated by their own discreditable lust for power, and particulary [sic] to the clerical leadership ... This is perhaps the most grotesque distortion of all ... As for the clergy's part, they acted throughout as a restraint upon the proceedings and it was their misgivings which finally brought the trials to an end" (Hansen, *Witchcraft at Salem*, 226). Other scholars have come to different conclusions: "Ultimately, whatever the reasons for the behavior of afflicted and confessors alike, the governor, council, and judges of Massachusetts must shoulder a great deal of the blame for allowing the crisis to reach the heights that it did ... They attempted to shift the responsibility for their own inadequate defense of the frontier to the demons of the invisible world, and as a result they presided over the deaths of many innocent people" (Norton, *In the Devil's Snare*, 308).

13. Williams, *Witchcraft*, 10.

14. "Spectral evidence" refers to "evidence" concerning the supposed appearance of a specter or subjective apparition of the suspected person (hallucinations, dreams, mere fancies), rather than the actual bodily person, eventually becoming a legal issue of the trials.

15. Hawthorne, *The Scarlet Letter*, 9–10.

Part III: Characterization

for [Hawthorne] was not fiction, it was fact; he still experienced its mystery and its guilt ... Witchcraft for Hawthorne was a state of the soul ..."[16]

Gaggles of witches appear in the work of both writers. Witch tales form bookends of Hawthorne's short fiction—three appearing at the beginning (1830, 1835) and one at the end (1851). In Hawthorne's earliest tale, "The Hollow of the Three Hills," set "in those strange old times," a woman meets with an "aged crone," "a withered hag," "that evil woman," more a spirit medium like the so-called Witch of Endor that King Saul consulted (I Samuel 28:7–25). At an appointed hour and place, where "the Prince of Evil and his plighted subjects" were said to have held perverted baptismal rites, the withered crone pours forth a "prayer that was not meant to be acceptable in heaven,"[17] conjuring visions of the consequences of the unfaithful woman's sins—her parents dishonored and shamed, her daughter abandoned to die, and her husband driven mad by the woman's perfidy. The story ends with a vision of the woman's funeral service and the witch / crone chuckling over the "sweet hour's sport," the woman dead, apparently unrepentant, unforgiven.

The backdrop of another early tale, "Alice Doane's Appeal," is the Salem witch trials of 1692, those "old witch times." The two young ladies who accompany the narrator on a walk to Gallows Hill (also called Witch Hill) are oblivious of that "witchcraft delusion" and are unmoved by the narrator's grotesque and mysterious tale of Leonard Doane, with his "diseased imagination," of his beautiful sister Alice, and of Walter Brome, who taunted Leonard with assertion of his involvement with Alice. Overshadowing all three is "a wizard, a small, gray, withered man, with fiendish ingenuity in devising evil and superhuman power to execute it ... ," whose diabolical machinations "cunningly devised that Walter Brome should tempt his unknown sister to guilt and shame, and himself perish by the hand of his twin-brother [Leonard],"[18] thus effecting incest, jealousy, murder of his *doppelganger* brother, and a concluding array of graveyard fiends and ghosts. Alice's "appeal" is directed to the specter of Walter, urging him to absolve her from all purported sinful stain. The narrator concludes by calling for two monuments—one to commemorate the errors of the earlier age

---

16. Van Doren, *Nathaniel Hawthorne: A Critical Biography*, 70, 35.

17. Hawthorne, "The Hollow of the Three Hills," *The Complete Short Stories of Nathaniel Hawthorne*, 103, 104.

18. Hawthorne, "Alice Doane's Appeal," *The Complete Short Stories of Nathaniel Hawthorne*, 559, 562.

Perpetuators and Victims of the Power of Blackness

and another for the no less egregious errors of the "people of the present," who "have no heartfelt interest in the olden time."

Hawthorne's finest witch-tale and assuredly one of the best of all his stories, "Young Goodman Brown," appeared in the same year as "Alice Doane's Appeal" (1835). Set in Salem village and forest environs around the time of the witch trials, the story describes Brown's night journey into the forest on a prearranged rendezvous with a devil figure at a witches Sabbat or coven. He progresses, or more accurately regresses, from naivete, intending to go on his evil purpose for one night and thereafter "cling to [his wife Faith's] skirts and follow her to heaven," to cynicism, thinking he has seen righteous people of the village in the forest, his dying hour therefore being gloom, with "no hopeful verse" carved on his tombstone. The tale alludes to three historical figures accused of witchcraft in 1692. One is Goody Cloyse (Sarah Cloyce), "pious teacher of the catechism," who was accused of being seen at a meeting of witches but was never tried. Another is Martha Carrier, referred to by the narrator and several seventeenth century witches' narratives as "this rampant hag" and who, according to the narrator, "had received the devil's promise to be queen of hell"; she was condemned to death and hanged in August of 1692, but in this story she and Goody Cloyse lead "the slender form of a veiled female," implied to be Faith Brown, to the witches' canopy of fire. The third is Goody (Martha) Cory (or Corey, called "Gospel Witch" because of her zealous church activity), who is accused in the story by Goody Cloyse of stealing her broomstick and called "that unhanged witch." The real Martha Cory was condemned in September, 1692, in a trial at which Judge Hathorne presided in a reportedly brutal and intolerant manner—and hanged (though in 1703 her excommunication was revoked). More witchcraft lore is included in this tale than in any of Hawthorne's stories. When Brown finds a pink ribbon caught in a tree, thinking it belongs to his wife Faith and that she is in the forest too, he cries out in despair, "My Faith is gone! . . . There is no good on earth; and sin is but a name . . . Come witch, come wizard, come Indian powwow, come devil himself . . ." Did Brown fall asleep and merely dream of a witches meeting, or did he actually encounter "righteous" people of Salem, and his own wife, trafficking with evil? Hawthorne never answers the question, but ultimately no answer is necessary, for the result is the same: Brown, like the woman in "The Hollow of the Three Hills," dies at the conclusion—in gloom and hopelessness.

Hawthorne's last short story, "Feathertop: A Moralized Legend," appeared in 1851, a year after *The Scarlet Letter*, but the witch Mother

Part III: Characterization

Rigby, with her enchanted pipe, is no Mistress Hibbins, though she is described as "one of the most cunning and potent witches in New England."[19] Eighteen times called a "witch," nine times "the old witch," and twice "the good old woman," she is described as "a witch of singular power and dexterity" and admits to dancing at witch meetings in the forest. Though she says she "didn't mean to dabble in witchcraft today," she makes a scarecrow with pumpkin head, three-cornered hat, and bewitched pipe, which gives a semblance of life as long as he puffs it. The story is a fairy tale anticipating Frank Baum's Wizard of Oz, Walt Disney's fantasies, and T. S. Eliot's "hollow men," "stuffed men," "headpiece filled with straw."[20] Several years earlier a Notebook entry referred to a magician who fabricated a scarecrow with pumpkin head and dispatched him / it into the world as "the symbol of a large class" minus intellect, heart, and soul. Witch Rigby sends the simulacrum forth into high society to woo the pretty Polly Gookin; he remains undetected except by a small child and a cur dog, until he spies himself in a mirror as "the wretched, ragged, empty thing" he really is, his existence ending not with a bang but with barely a whimper. The tale satirizes the pretentious high society coxcombs and charlatans of the world who, unlike this hollow man, never see themselves for what they really are.

Mistress Hibbins, in *The Scarlet Letter*, is arguably the most pernicious witch in all of American literature, yet she is typically passed over summarily in much of the criticism, albeit well labeled by one critic as "the embodiment of ubiquitous evil."[21] The narrator describes her as "the bitter-tempered widow of the magistrate" and twice as the Governor's "bitter-tempered sister."[22] She appears in four strategic scenes and is referred to five other times. She first appears as Hester and little Pearl leave the Governor's house after a meeting to determine if the illegitimate child will be taken from her mother. The witch-lady thrusts her head from a chamber-window and attempts to entice Hester to meet with the so-called Black Man in the forest, but Hester refuses, saying she would readily have gone and signed his book as well if Pearl had been taken from her. Witch Hibbins again appears

19. Hawthorne, "Feathertop: A Moralized Legend," *The Complete Short Stories of Nathaniel Hawthorne*, 315.

20. Eliot, "The Hollow Men," *The Complete Poems and Plays*, 56.

21. Male, *Hawthorne's Tragic Vision*, 114.

22. Hawthorne, *The Scarlet Letter*, 47, 107, 137. According to Diane Conwell and Jonathan Sutherland, a Mrs. Hibbens, sister of Governor Bellingham, was charged with witchcraft and executed in 1656 (*Witches of the World*, 245).

at the chamber-window, gazing upward, when Dimmesdale shrieks aloud during his night vigil on the scaffold. She appears a third time when she confronts Dimmesdale on his way back from the forest after the minister encounters Hester and Pearl at the brook-side, thereby showing "his sympathy and fellowship with wicked mortals, and the world of perverted spirits."[23] The fourth time she appears is during the climactic Election Day procession; "arrayed in great magnificence," she whispers to Hester about Dimmesdale being one of the Black Man's own servants signed and sealed, then invites Pearl to ride with her some fine night to see her father, "the Prince of the Air."[24]

Significantly, the witch-lady encounters Hester (twice), Dimmesdale, and Pearl and is referred to by Dimmesdale (twice), by Pearl (twice), and by the narrator, who says that Hibbins "was to die upon the gallows" and again that "a few years later [she] was executed as a witch."[25] "The figure of the witch, as conceived by seventeenth-century New Englanders," historian John Demos has said, "was powerful, dangerous, an altogether formidable adversary. But there developed subsequently a different image that is with us still—the witch as hag."[26] In Hawthorne's fiction, examples of both images appear, the witch being a diversified symbol of pernicious evil.

In addition to its role in the four witch tales and *The Scarlet Letter*, witchcraft plays a significant but less explicit and extensive role in *The House of the Seven Gables*, in which Hawthorne again adapts an incident from the Salem witch trials. When Sarah Good, one of the accused women, appears at the gallows, the Reverend Nicholas Noyes reportedly called on her to confess, telling her she knows she is a witch, to which she replies: "You are a liar. I am no more a witch than you are a wizard, and if you take away my life God will give you blood to drink."[27] The narrator of the novel states that old Matthew Maule was executed for the crime of witchcraft, being "one of the martyrs to that terrible delusion," who pro-

---

23. Ibid., 201–3.

24. Ibid., 219–21. Cf. Pearl's comment to the shipmaster: "'Mistress Hibbens says my father is the Prince of the Air!'" (224). Hawthorne is echoing Ephesians 2:1–2— "And you were dead in your trespasses and sins, in which you formerly walked according to the course of this world, according to the prince of the power of the air, of the spirit that is now working in the sons of disobedience."

25. Ibid., 47, 107.

26. Demos, *Entertaining Satan: Witchcraft and the Culture of Early New England*, 391.

27. Quoted from Robert E. Calef's *More Wonders of the Invisible World* (1700) by Hansen, *Witchcraft at Salem*, 126.

Part III: Characterization

nounced a curse on Colonel Pyncheon from the scaffold: "God will give him blood to drink." The curse was not only remembered for generations but became a part of the Pyncheon legacy: "If one of the family did but gurgle in his throat, a bystander would be likely enough to whisper, between jest and earnest, 'He has Maule's blood to drink!'"[28]

Even in his penultimate novel *The Blithedale Romance* (1852), Hawthorne, seeking to epitomize malevolence in a character, refers to wizardry and witchery. For example, the narrator says of Westervelt: "Every human being, when given over to the Devil, is sure to have the wizard mark upon him, in one form or another. I fancied that this smile, with its peculiar revelation, was the Devil's signet on the Professor." Further, he says of two other characters: ". . . I saw in Hollingsworth all that an artist could desire for the grim portrait of a Puritan magistrate, holding inquest of life and death in a case of witchcraft;—in Zenobia, the sorceress herself, not aged, wrinkled, and decrepit, but fair enough to tempt Satan with a force reciprocal to his own . . ."[29]

Hawthorne's depiction of witchery differs from Lewis's in that it is based solidly in historical American culture, whereas Lewis's is based in mythology. Lewis, for his part, was rather ambivalent about the existence of witches, suggesting that belief in their reality is perhaps anachronistic. For example, in *Mere Christianity* he states that "the reason we do not execute witches is that we do not believe there are such things. If we did—if we really thought that there were people going about who had sold themselves to the devil and received supernatural powers from him in return and were using these powers to kill their neighbours or drive them mad or bring bad weather—surely we would all agree that if anyone deserved the death penalty, then these filthy quislings did?" Lewis is discussing the natural Law of Decent Behavior, using the example of executing witches to illustrate the need to distinguish between differences of morality and differences of belief about facts. He states that "it may be a great advance in knowledge not to believe in witches: there is no moral advance in not executing them when you do not think they are there, [just as] you would not call a man humane for ceasing to set mousetraps if he did so because he believed there were no mice in the house."[30] In a letter to Sister Penelope he addresses the issue for clarification: "On Witches. I

---

28. Hawthorne, *The House of the Seven Gables*, 13–14, 25.
29. Hawthorne, *The Blithedale Romance*, 154, 194.
30. Lewis, *Mere Christianity*, 14–15.

didn't really mean to deny them, tho' I see I have given that impression. I was interested in them at the moment only as an illustration. I think my considered view wd. be much the same as yours. But if a truth, it is not a truth I am at all anxious to spread."[31] Unlike Hawthorne, Lewis speaks hypothetically, tentatively, equivocally, concluding that if witches are genuinely extant, it is a truth he does not wish to disseminate.

Lewis's witches appear in four of the Narnia tales. The White Witch, also known as Lilith (Assyrian / Babylonian for "of the night"), in ancient Semitic folklore a female demon or vampire that lives in desolate places and attacks children; in medieval Jewish folklore the first wife of Adam or a night-witch who preys upon infants, having reputedly come, on one side, from the Jinn (a general term for various species of demons and spirits) and, on the other side, from giants. Consequently, the witches are totally, completely evil, for, as Mr. Beaver tells the Pevensie children, "there isn't a drop of real human blood" in the White Witch, and Mrs. Beaver adds: ". . . She's bad all through."[32]

In a letter Lewis said, "The Witch is of course Circe, Alcina, etc. because she is (and they are) the same Archtype [sic] we find in so many fairy tales. No good asking where any individual author got *that*. We are born knowing the Witch, aren't we?"[33] "We are born knowing the Witch"—what a significant and illuminating statement that is! The Witch character in both Lewis and Hawthorne can legitimately and beneficially be viewed as an archetype, that is, an image, a character, a thematic pattern, a universal symbol which is part of what Carl Jung called the "collective unconscious."[34] Northrop Frye has defined *archetype* as "a symbol, usually an image, which recurs often enough in literature to be recognizable as an element of one's literary experience as a whole."[35] Lewis was obviously fascinated with the theory of arche-

---

31. Lewis, Letter of 29 July 1942, *The Collected Letters of C. S. Lewis*, II, 526.

32. Lewis, *The Lion, the Witch, and the Wardrobe*, 88.

33. Lewis, Letter of 30 July 1954, *The Collected Letters of C. S. Lewis*, III, 497. Circe is the enchantress in Homer's *Odyssey* known for her cruelty in changing men into swine. Alcina is a witch in Lodovico Ariosto's *Orlando Furioso*, known for her enchanted garden and skill in turning her lovers into animals or stones.

34. See Jung, *Archetypes of the Collective Unconscious*, Translated by R. F. C. Hull (1959). See also Maud Bodkin, *Archetypal Patterns in Poetry: Psychological Studies of Imagination* (1934), to which Lewis also refers. Cf. also Richard P. Sugg, Editor, *Jungian Literary Criticism* (1992), which includes some discussion of archetypes in Herman Melville (but not in Hawthorne) and a brief essay on Lewis's *Till We Have Faces*.

35. Northrop Frye, *Anatomy of Criticism*, 365.

types, especially in relation to myth, which he saw as images recovered from the collective unconscious. "The most interesting thing about this theory," he said, "is the strength of the emotional reaction it awakes in nearly all those who hear it . . . The emotional power of Jung's essay is, as far as it goes, a proof that he is quite right in claiming that certain images, in whatever material they are embodied, have a strange power to excite the human mind."[36]

The witch / wizard as archetype epitomizes the embodiment of ubiquitous evil, being a sinister unhuman / superhuman figure who has trafficked with the Devil, from whom she / he has received and perpetuates "the Power of Blackness." The *modus operandi* of the witch is deception (appearing as a being of light and beauty, masking the ugliness of evil) to entice humans to choose evil and oppose good, occasional divination, devotion to the Evil One, and ultimate damnation. For example, the following parallel descriptions illustrate most of these elements, most notably diabolical power, deceit, seduction, false promises, deprivation, and opposition to good: "The spells of witches have the power of producing meats and viands that have the appearance of a sumptuous feast, which the Devil furnishes. But a Divine Providence seldom permits the meat to be good, but it has generally some bad taste or smell, —mostly wants salt, —and the feast is often without bread."[37] Does this not sound like Lewis imagining the White Witch's enticement of Edmund by offering him enchanted Turkish Delight, "every piece sweet and light to the very center," so delicious "that anyone who had once tasted it would want more and more of it, and would even, if they were allowed, go on eating it till they killed themselves"? Later, in the Beavers' house, Edmund "had eaten his share of the dinner, but he hadn't really enjoyed it because he was thinking all the time about Turkish Delight—and there's nothing that spoils the taste of good ordinary food half so much as the memory of bad magic food."[38] The two passages are parallel but with differing emphases: one suggests that Divine Providence often causes Devil's food, though enticing, to taste and smell bad, whereas the other suggests that memory of a witch's bad food, though enticing, often spoils the taste of good ordinary food.

---

36. Lewis, "Psycho-analysis and Literary Criticism," *Selected Literary Essays*, 297, 299.

37. Hawthorne, *The American Note-Books*, 504.

38. Lewis, *The Lion, the Witch, and the Wardrobe*, 38–39, 95.

All three witches in Lewis's tales are tall, exquisitely beautiful, arrogant, regal, stern, and cold. The White Witch impresses Edmund as "a great lady, taller than any woman [he] had ever seen. She also was covered in white fur up to her throat and held a long straight golden wand in her right hand and wore a golden crown on her head. Her face was white—not merely pale, but white like snow or paper or icing-sugar, except for her very red mouth. It was a beautiful face in other respects, but proud and cold and stern."[39] Similarly, her progenitor (or earlier form or "doubtless the same kind," "of the same crew"), witch Jadis, is seven feet tall, dazzlingly beautiful, possessing "a look of such fierceness and pride that it took your breath away," and she "looked stronger and prouder than ever, and even, in a way, triumphant: but her face was deadly white, white as salt."[40] The third witch, self-proclaimed Queen of Underland in *The Silver Chair*, is the most beautiful lady Drinian had ever seen; "she was tall and great, shining, and wrapped in a thin garment as green as poison," and her face turns "very white" with anger when she is confronted by a sane Prince Rilian.[41] Witch Lilith had pronounced on Narnia a curse of perpetual winter but never Christmas until Aslan brings spring and deeper magic from before the dawn of time to redeem Edmund; witch Jadis destroyed the world of Charn by means of the "Deplorable Word" and brought evil into Narnia, then fled to the north, and the Tree of Protection kept her from Narnia; the Green Witch enchanted and held Prince Rilian captive for a decade in the Underland until the spell is broken and she, in the form of a green serpent, is slain. Significantly, the faces of all three are pale, pallid, white, "not so much a color as the visible absence of color; and at the same time the concrete of all colors . . . , such a dumb blankness, full of meaning . . .—a colorless, all-color of atheism from which we all shrink," as Melville's Ishmael expresses it in "The Whiteness of the Whale," *Moby Dick*."[42]

39. Lewis, *The Lion, the Witch, and the Wardrobe*, 33–34.
40. Lewis, *The Magician's Nephew*, 62, 48, 160.
41. Lewis, *The Silver Chair*, 51, 149.
42. Melville, *Moby Dick*, 194–95. Lewis's copy of *Moby Dick* in the Marion E. Wade Center at Wheaton College is well marked and annotated, at least through Chapter LVII. In a letter to Arthur Greeves, Lewis remarked: "I began *Moby Dick* on the week end when term ended, and thought, despite its obvious defects of rhetoric & un-dramatic dialogue, that I liked it . . ." (Letter of 3 April 1930, *The Collected Letters of C. S. Lewis*, I, 889). Perhaps Lewis was indebted also to Coleridge's description of the Spectre-Woman and her Deathmate in *The Rime of the Ancient Mariner* (which he referenced in numerous letters)—"*Her* lips were red, *her* looks

Part III: Characterization

The narrator of *The Magician's Nephew* summarizes in a rather understated way the unscrupulous machinations of witches in his comment about Jadis taking no notice of Polly because she wanted to use Digory and when she "had" Uncle Andrew she took no notice of Digory: "I expect most witches are like that. They are not interested in things or people unless they can use them; they are terribly practical."[43] Jadis, who purportedly returns to Narnia to reign as self-proclaimed queen there for a century, is apparently killed in a battle with Peter and the forces of Aslan, though a Hag in *Prince Caspian* insists, "who ever heard of a witch that really died? You can always get them back"—this just before her own head rolls on the floor from Trumpkin's sword slash,"[44] thus precluding Nikabrik's attempt to call up the accursed spirit by black sorcery.

The spectrum of "the power of blackness" in both Hawthorne and Lewis ranges from the villainy of scientistic monomania to the sorcery of witchcraft to the nadir of evil in the archfiend himself, with whom the former are in league. Lewis's most sustained discussion of the archfiend is his chapter on Milton's Satan in *A Preface to Paradise Lost*, where he specifies that Milton's Satan thinks himself "impaired," suffering from a sense of "injured merit"; he is entangled in contradictions, wanting hierarchy and not wanting hierarchy; he is a liar, having become a Lie more than merely a Liar (rather like the grumbling ghost in *The Great Divorce* who *becomes* a grumble); he argues nonsensically that he is a self-existent being rather than a created being; he possesses "the horrible co-existence of a subtle and incessant intellectual activity with an incapacity to understand anything. This doom he has brought upon himself; in order to avoid seeing one thing he has, almost voluntarily, incapacitated himself from seeing at all."[45] Though muted, these characteristics can be found in Lewis's own Screwtape.

---

were free, / Her locks were yellow as gold: / Her skin was as white as leprosy, / The Night-mare Life-in-Death was she" (III, 190–93).

43. Lewis, *The Magician's Nephew*, 72.

44. Lewis, *Prince Caspian*, 165–66.

45. Lewis, *A Preface to Paradise Lost*, 99. Harold Bloom, referring to Lewis as the foremost among "churchwardenly commentators," says, "I cannot locate C. S. Lewis's temper-tantrum Satan. Something has gone wrong with the hero-villain, but no one as yet is able to tell us what . . . One step onward and we would have the angelical C. S. Lewis advising us that the proper way to read *Paradise Lost* is to start with a good morning's hatred of Satan. Milton, a great poet and member of his own party-of-one without knowing it, would certainly not have agreed with his dramatic exegetes. He does not like Satan, but he certainly molds an energetic hero-villain in the tradition of

Perhaps most arresting of all the points Lewis makes in his *Preface* is this one concerning our "autobiographical" involvement: "to admire Satan . . . is to give one's vote not only for a world of misery, but also a world of lies and propaganda, of wishful thinking, of incessant autobiography," with our choices tending to move us ever so slightly each day toward that world.[46] For his part, Hawthorne refers to Satan on his visit to the cathedral of Chester, England, where he examines a carving of "Satan under the guise of a lion, devouring a sinner bodily, and again in the figure of a dragon, with a man half way down his gullet, the legs hanging out." This "grim mirthfulness," reminiscent of images by Hieronymus Bosch and Pieter Breugel, disturbed Hawthorne, especially its appearance in "the holy interior of a Cathedral"—unless, he concludes, "it were intended to contain everything that belongs to the heart of man, both upward and downward."[47] The "downward" element in the human heart seems most obvious—pernicious evil resulting in the victimizing devouring of the person, digesting symbolizing mastery, assimilation, dissolution, a vanquishing which suggests the victor incorporating the potentialities of the victim.[48] The "upward" element is somewhat less obvious—perhaps the sanctified setting offering the possibility of rescue, redemption, victory, even the promise of rebirth and resurrection. The most striking point of the two passages, however, is the "incessant autobiography," what "belongs to the heart of man," the idea that the spirit of self is in fact the spirit of Satan. Lewis summarized it well in *Mere Christianity*: "The moment you have a self at all, there is a possibility of putting yourself first—wanting to be the centre—wanting to be God, in fact. *That was the sin of Satan: and that was the sin he taught the human race.*"[49]

Such "grim mirthfulness," as Hawthorne called it, or mirthful grimness, appears in Lewis's *Screwtape Proposes a Toast*, where Screwtape complains of the deplorable gastronomic insipidity of the meal—a

---

Elizabethan-Jacobean drama" (*The Anatomy of Influence: Literature as a Way of Life*, 2011), 92, 249.

46. Lewis, *Preface to Paradise Lost*, 102.

47. Hawthorne, *The English Notebooks*, 167. The New Testament depicts the devil as a roaring lion prowling about, seeking someone to devour (I Peter 5:8) and as a great dragon (Revelation 12:3-4, 9; 20:2).

48. See, for example, Cirlot, *A Dictionary of Symbols*, 80-81-82. Cf. Screwtape's final letter, in which he refers to Wormwood as "as dainty a morsel as ever I grew fat on" and signed off as "Your increasingly and ravenously affectionate uncle." Note the further devouring imagery in *Screwtape Proposes a Toast*, discussed below.

49. Lewis, *Mere Christianity*, 49. Emphasis added.

Part III: Characterization

tasteless Graft sauce, lukewarm Casserole of Adulterers, a Trade Unionist garnished with Claptrap, albeit topped off with "sound old vintage *Pharisee*," a wine expertly blended of "different types of Pharisee . . . harvested, trodden, and fermented together to produce its subtle flavour. Types that were most antagonistic to one another on earth . . . How they hated each other up there where the sun shone!" What he really longed for was "to get one's teeth again into a Farinata, a Henry VIII, or even a Hitler! There was real crackling there; something to crunch; a rage, an egotism, a cruelty only just less robust than our own. It put up a delicious resistance to being devoured. It warmed your innards when you'd got it down."[50]

Lewis warns that "there are two equal and opposite errors into which our race can fall about the devils: "One is to disbelieve in their existence. The other is to believe, and to feel an excessive and unhealthy interest in them."[51] Again, in "Answers to Questions on Christianity," he writes: "No reference to the Devil or devils is included in any Christian creeds, and it is quite possible to be a Christian without believing in them. I do believe such beings exist . . . The degree to which humans were conscious of their presence would presumably vary very much. I mean, the more a man was in the Devil's power, the less he would be aware of it . . ."[52]

It may seem anomalous that with all of its discussion of hell, especially with teacher George MacDonald, there are no Satan, no devil, no devils or fiends in Lewis's *The Great Divorce*. Perhaps the criterion of consciousness of their presence indicates their great power over the ghosts, who are, in fact, in the process of becoming more diabolical. Reference to Satan appears only in the epigraph from MacDonald: "There is no heaven

---

50. Lewis, *The Screwtape Letters with Screwtape Proposes a Toast*, 188–89, 208. The reference to Farinata, with its multiple significance, is especially appropriate in this context. Farinata degli Uberti (1212–1264) was a Florentine aristocrat who led Ghibeline forces in victory over the rival Guelphs. His body and his wife's were exhumed and burned as punishment for heretical beliefs. Dante comes upon Farinata in the sixth circle of the Inferno (Canto 10), reserved for heretics. He was reputedly fond of exquisite viands. Farina is a flour or meal made with cereal grains used in soups and puddings. Cf. the similar theme in *Perelandra*, where Ransom imagines bad men in Hell "melted down into their Master, as a lead soldier slips down and loses his shape in the ladle held over the gas ring. The question whether Satan, or one whom Satan has digested, is acting on any given occasion, has in the long run no clear significance" (173).

51. Lewis, Preface, *The Screwtape Letters*, ix.

52. Lewis, *God in the Dock: Essays on Theology and Ethics*, 56–57. It should be noted that the Westminster Confession of Faith does, in fact, refer to Satan in Chapter VI, Article 1: "Our first parents, being seduced by the subtilty and temptation of Satan, sinned, in eating the forbidden fruit."

Perpetuators and Victims of the Power of Blackness

with a little of hell in it—no plan to retain this or that of the devil in our hearts or our pockets. Out Satan must go, every hair and feather."

If the ghosts in *The Great Divorce* are oblivious of the unseen presence and power of devils, Hawthorne and Lewis most assuredly are not. Not only witches and wizards but also fiends, demons, devils, and the Archfiend himself seem to captivate the imagination of Hawthorne. Even the Hawthorne family cat was named Beelzebub (Hebrew *baal-zevuv*, literally "god of flies"—name for Satan).[53] Perhaps he was the inspiration for the grimalkin (a female cat or vicious old woman) which posted itself outside Judge Pyncheon's window in *The House of the Seven Gables*: "This grimalkin has a very ugly look. Is it a cat watching for a mouse, or the devil for a human soul? Would we could scare him from the window!" Subsequently, the entrance of Phoebe does scare him away: ". . . a strange grimalkin, which was prowling under the parlor window, took to his heels, clambered hastily over the fence, and vanished."[54]

Hawthorne seemed especially fascinated with the idea of demonic possession. In a Notebook entry, Hawthorne wrote of "a stove possessed by a Devil,"[55] and in another a steam engine is "possessed": "A steam engine in a factory to be supposed to possess a malignant spirit. It catches one man's arm, and pulls it off; seizes another by the coat-tails, and almost grapples him bodily;—catches a girl by the hair, and scalps her;—and finally draws in a man and crushes him to death."[56] Similarly, in one of his semi-autobiographical sketches, "The Devil in Manuscript," Hawthorne has the narrator relate his friend Oberon's frustration over repeated rejection of his manuscripts, until in utter despair he resolves to burn them, insisting that "there is a devil in this pile of blotted papers." Ignoring his friend's remonstrance, Oberon casts all his manuscripts into the hottest of the fire, which roars up the chimney, "like a demon with sable wings," causing a widespread conflagration in the wooden town, making Oberon "a triumphant author," for his "brain has set the town on fire!"[57]

---

53. The source may be Milton's *Paradise Lost* and / or the New Testament, which refers to this prince of demons in Matthew 10:25, 12:24, Mark 3:22, Luke 11:15. Screwtape addresses Beelzebub in *Screwtape Proposes a Toast*.

54. Hawthorne, *The House of the Seven Gables*, 245, 260.

55. Hawthorne, *The American Notebooks*, 235.

56. Ibid., 101.

57. Hawthorne, "The Devil in Manuscript," *The Complete Short Stories of Nathaniel Hawthorne*, 501, 505.

Part III: Characterization

Perhaps the clearest encounter with the devil in Hawthorne's fiction is Goodman Brown's meeting with the "fellow-traveler" seated at the foot of an old tree, unmistakably a pre-arranged rendezvous, for he is reproached for being late, hinting at a Faust pact. Shortly thereafter, Goody Cloyse, who had taught Brown his catechism in his youth, screams "The devil," to which the dark figure responds, "Then Goody Cloyse knows her old friend."[58] A similar encounter occurs in "My Kinsman, Major Molineux," when naïve country bumpkin Robin meets a mysterious stranger in the city: "One side of the face blazed an intense red, while the other was black as midnight . . . The effect was as if two individual devils, a fiend of fire and a fiend of darkness, had united themselves to form this infernal visage."[59] In "Ethan Brand" the title character was said to have "conversed with Satan himself in the lurid blaze" of the lime kiln and eventually "became a fiend."[60] Similarly, Roger Chillingworth "was a striking evidence of man's faculty of transforming himself into a devil, if he will only, for a reasonable space of time, undertake a devil's office," and when "there was no more Devil's work on earth for him to do, it only remained for the unhumanized mortal to betake himself whither his Master would find him tasks enough, and pay him his wages duly."[61] In the same work, little Pearl, illegitimate offspring of Hester and Pastor Dimmesdale, was reputed to be "an imp of evil," "a demon offspring," a child "possessed" by an evil spirit that "peeped forth in mockery."[62]

In somewhat the way Chillingworth transforms himself into a devil and becomes unhumanized, Lewis's Professor Weston becomes an Unman by calling the Force of evil into himself completely, and what follows is one of the most vivid descriptions of demon possession in modern literature[63]: "Then horrible things began happening. A spasm like that preceding a deadly vomit twisted Weston's face out of recognition . . . and instantly his whole body spun round as if he had been hit by a revolver-bullet and

---

58. Ibid., "Young Goodman Brown," 248–50.
59. Ibid., "My Kinsman, Major Molineux," 524.
60. Ibid., "Ethan Brand," 477, 482.
61. Hawthorne, *The Scarlet Letter*, 155, 236.
62. Ibid., 86, 91, 89.
63. See D. G. Kehl, "The Cosmocrats: Diabolism in Modern Literature," in John Warwick Montgomery, Editor. *Demon Possession* (1976). For a vivid fictional description of demonic oppression, see Isaac Bashevis Singer, *Satan in Goray* (1963). For a vivid fictional description of demon possession, see James Baldwin, *Go Tell It on the Mountain* (1954).

he fell to the earth, and was there rolling at Ransom's feet, slavering and chattering and tearing up the moss by handfuls."[64] This possessed Un-man becomes a grotesque monster and meets a monster's end, an "It" which Ransom smashes with a stone and hurls into a sea of fire.

Lewis made a significant theological point when he responded to the frequently asked question—whether he believed in the Devil: "Now if by 'the Devil' you mean a power opposite to God and, like God, self-existent from all eternity, the answer is certainly No. There is no uncreated being except God. God has no opposite. No being could attain a 'perfect badness' opposite to the perfect goodness of God . . . The proper question is whether I believe in devils. I do. That is to say, I believe in angels, and I believe that some of these, by the abuse of their free will, have become enemies to God and, as a corollary, to us. These we may call devils . . . Satan, the leader or dictator of devils, is the opposite, not of God, but of Michael."[65] Screwtape and his minions, being fallen angels, would therefore lack omniscience, so his comment that he "saw a train of thought in [a patient's] mind beginning to go the wrong way" would be a blatant lie or an authorial lapse, like the subsequent advice to "look into your patient's mind when he is praying" or to "look carefully into any human's heart."[66] In speaking of love, and denying its possibility, he admits in frustration, "If we could only find out what He is *really* up to! Hypothesis after hypothesis has been tried, and still we can't find out."

In the thirty-one letters, Lewis employs what he called "diabolical ventriloquism" or moral inversion, to provide the perspective of Hell on some twenty issues or topics, such as the church, human nature, prayer, war, existence of devils, the "Law of Undulation," the philosophy of Hell, laughter, the "asphyxiating cloud," humility, time and eternity, gluttony, spiritual pride, the "historical Jesus," "mere Christianity," free will, cowardice and fear, death, and Heaven. The character of Screwtape is revealed largely by implication: he is wily, crafty, self-serving, manipulative, impatient, jealous, envious, avaricious, caustic, condescending, vituperative. He has temper-tantrums and engages in childish name-calling, as when he reacts to the "patient's" love for a Christian girl: "Not only a Christian

64. Lewis, *Perelandra*, 96.
65. Lewis, New Preface, *The Screwtape Letters*, vii. In Letter 7 Screwtape tells Wormwood it is essential to keep his "patient" ignorant of the devils' existence and that predominantly comic devils—in red tights, with horns and pitchfork, in the modern imagination—will be helpful.
66. Ibid., 2, 17, 107.

Part III: Characterization

but such a Christian—a vile, sneaking, simpering, demure, monosyllabic, mouse-like, watery, insignificant, virginal, bread-and-butter miss. The little brute. She makes me vomit."[67] In his anger at learning that Wormwood has lost his "patient" to the "Enemy," Screwtape addresses his underling ironically, caustically, satirically as "my poppet" (a doll or a term of endearment for a child or little girl), "my pigsnie" (a darling), assuring him, "my love for you and your love for me are as like as two peas. I have always desired you, as you (pitiful fool) desired me. The difference is that I am the stronger. I think they will give you to me now, or a bit of you. Love you? Why, yes. As dainty a morsel as ever I grew fat on."[68] Wormwood has failed to bring his "patient" as food to be devoured by the fiends, so he has become food himself. As for the "patient," "he is caught up into that world where pain and pleasure take on transfinite values and all [diabolical] arithmetic is dismayed." He sees not only Them, his friends and all the heavenly beings, but Him: "this animal, this thing begotten in a bed, could look on Him . . ."[69] The Power of Blackness is foiled again.

67. Ibid., 117.
68. Ibid., 171.
69. Ibid., 174–75.

8

Counteractors and Ambivalents in the Power of Blackness

Some characters in the work of Hawthorne and Lewis perpetuate the Power of Blackness, whereas others are victimized by it. Still other characters serve to counteract the Power of Blackness, whereas others come across as ambivalent.

Another affinity shared by Hawthorne and Lewis is their attitude toward and depiction of Puritans and Puritanism, views that could be called ambivalent in each case though perhaps not in the same manner or degree. Diversified conclusions about Hawthorne vis-à-vis Puritanism have been expressed: one critic says, "he was unquestionably a Puritan, or a kind of Puritan"[1]; another says he was "the Rebellious Puritan"[2]; yet another insists, "he was no Puritan. He would have been amazed as well as unhappy at being described as one by some modern scholars. But he was temperamentally attuned to their meanings, and he generally felt himself closer to their view of life than he did to the views of his most liberal contemporaries, who did not, he felt, take the facts of moral experience seriously."[3] Some might label him a Puritan *malgre lui* (a Puritan "in spite of himself") or a "Puritan *manque*" (a "failed" or "defective" Puritan) or an "existential Puritan" or even a "secular Puritan." Herman Melville's comments, noted above, about Hawthorne's "puritan gloom" and "great power of blackness" being derived from a Calvinistic sense of innate depravity and original sin have given rise to what has been labeled

---

1. Stewart, *American Literature and Christian Doctrine*, 15.
2. Moore, *The Rebellious Puritan: Portrait of Mr. Hawthorne*.
3. Waggoner, *Hawthorne: A Critical Study*, 15.

Part III: Characterization

"the Hawthorne Problem," prompting the question of whether Hawthorne actually held those Puritan beliefs or simply made use of them aesthetically in his fiction. For example, Henry James, on the opposite end of the spectrum from Melville, acknowledged that "this capital son of the old Puritans . . . was by race of the clearest Puritan strain," then said further that Hawthorne "had ample cognizance of the Puritan conscience; it was his natural heritage; it was reproduced in him; looking into his soul, he found it there. But *his relation to it was only, as one may say, intellectual; it was not moral or theological. He played with it, and used it as a pigment; he treated it, as the metaphysicians say, objectively* . . . It may be said that when his fancy was strongest and keenest, when it was most itself, then the dark Puritan tinge showed in it most richly."[4]

Perhaps the most nearly valid conclusion to draw about Hawthorne vis-à-vis Puritanism is that he "could neither accept nor disavow"[5] what Brenda Wineapple calls his "Puritan instinct."[6] Hawthorne himself readily admitted, "The spirit of my Puritan ancestors was mighty in me . . ."[7] His opinion of Puritanism and the Puritans seems best summarized in a single word—ambivalence. For example, in "The Custom House," Hawthorne admits to being haunted by his "grave, bearded, sable-cloaked and steeple-crowned progenitor . . . [who] had *all the Puritanic traits, both good and evil.*"[8] Similarly, in *Grandfather's Chair: A History for Youth*, the narrator Grandfather, speaking of the representative Puritan Cotton Mather, tells the children, "It is difficult . . . to make you understand such a character as Cotton Mather's, *in whom there was so much good, and yet so many failings and frailties,*" and later the chair itself concludes: "I have constantly observed that *Justice, Truth, and Love are the chief ingredients of every happy life,*"[9] implying that these traits were lacking in Mather. Consider this description in his story "Alice Doane's Appeal": "In the rear of the procession rode a figure on horseback so darkly conspicuous, so sternly triumphant, that my hearers *mistook him for the visible presence of the fiend himself,* but it was *only his good friend, Cotton Mather, proud of his well-won dignity, as the representative of all the hateful features of his time; the one blood-thirsty*

---

4. James, *Hawthorne*, 45, 5, 46, 80. Emphasis added.
5. Donohue, *Calvin's Ironic Stepchild*, 2.
6. Wineapple, *Hawthorne: A Life*, 61.
7. Hawthorne, *The English Notebooks*, 193.
8. Hawthorne, *The Scarlet Letter*, 9. Emphasis added.
9. Hawthorne, *Grandfather's Chair: A History for Youth*, 104–05, 262.

man, in whom were concentrated those vices of spirit and errors of opinion that sufficed to madden the whole surrounding multitude."[10]

Hawthorne shows a poignant ambivalence toward his Puritan forebears in his historical sketch "Main Street": "... *nor, it may be, have we even yet thrown off all the unfavorable influences, which, among many good ones, were bequeathed us by our Puritan forefathers. Let us thank God for having given us such ancestors,* and let each successive generation *thank Him, not less fervently, for being one step further from them in the march of ages.*"[11] In the modern idiom, Hawthorne seems to be saying, "Thanks for the legacy of Puritanism, but thanks also for the time lapse separation from the Puritans!"

Unmistakably, Hawthorne depicts the Puritans as stern, gloomy, harsh, and bigoted, but he also depicts some, at least a few, as considerate, compassionate, gracious, and kind—but the proportion is skewed toward the former. For example, in *The Scarlet Letter* a key image is that of iron—hard, inflexible, cold—applied first to the "iron-visages" of the old dames muttering heartlessly at that "brazen hussy" Hester Prynne as she is forced to stand in the marketplace with her scarlet badge of shame on her bosom. Significantly, there is one compassionate onlooker, who whispers, "Oh, peace, neighbors, peace! ... [D]o not let her hear you! Not a stitch in that embroidered letter, but she has felt it in her heart."[12] Is this youngest companion, this young wife, the only one to show empathy because the child she holds by the hand is also illegitimate like Pearl? Such a view seems most unlikely, for the narrator indicates that seven years later Hester sees the same faces of that group of matrons—"all save one, the youngest and only compassionate among them, whose burial-robe she had since made."[13] Midway through the novel, the narrator provides a further insight when he ponders the development of a woman who has encountered an experience of peculiar severity: "If she be all tenderness," he says, "she will die. If she survive, the tenderness will either be

---

10. Hawthorne, "Alice Doane's Appeal," *The Complete Short Stories of Nathaniel Hawthorne*, 563–64. Emphasis added. Edward Wagenknecht says of this passage: "Hawthorne's unsparing condemnation of the witchcraft trials in which his ancestors were involved, highly creditable to him as a man, reflects one of his lifelong agonies, but his imputation of primary responsibility to Cotton Mather is unhistorical" (*Nathaniel Hawthorne: The Man, His Tales and Romances*, 189).

11. Hawthorne, "Main Street," *The Snow-Image and Other Twice-Told Tales*, 90.

12. Hawthorne, *The Scarlet Letter*, 51.

13. Ibid., 225.

crushed out of her, or—and the outward semblance is the same—crushed so deeply into her heart that it can never show itself more."[14] In the case of this young wife and mother, the tenderness is apparently crushed out of her not just by the "iron visages" of the matrons, but also by the "iron arm" of law, by the "iron framework" of Dimmesdale's faith, by the "iron framework of reasoning," by the metonymic "iron men and their opinions," by the entirety of "that iron period."[15] Hester, of course, does survive, and her tenderness is not crushed so deeply into her that it is never manifest: ironically, the parishioner counsels her pastor and is strong for him, and she comforts and counsels wronged and wounded women. The narrator surmises that one who has been robbed of her womanhood may regain it only by a "magic touch to effect the transfiguration," and adds, "We shall see whether Hester Prynne were ever afterwards so touched, and so transfigured."[16] The touch to which the narrator refers is apparently the same as that to which Hawthorne himself alludes in a letter to Sophia Peabody; he notes that we are all but mere shadows, not endowed with real life but only with the thinnest substance of a dream—until "that touch creates us—then we begin to be—thereby we are beings of reality, and inheritors of eternity."[17] Though Hawthorne claims to have been transfigured by such a magic touch, Hester by novel's end had not.

The iron image used to characterize Puritans recurs in some of the tales as well, yet with divided sympathy toward them. In "The Gentle Boy," for example, Puritans, characterized by "narrow minds," "uncompromising bigotry," and "brutal cruelty" and seeking to eradicate the Quakers, executed two members of the group. Only two Puritans in the entire community show compassion for the six-year-old Ibrahim, whom Tobias Pearson finds weeping on his father's new-made grave beneath the gallows. Tobias ("the Lord is my good"), who "possessed a compassionate heart, which not even religious prejudice could harden into stone,"[18] and his wife Dorothy care for the boy in their home and later adopt him. The "bigoted Puritans," with "their iron hearts," show only antipathy toward the boy and his adoptive parents, ostracizing them at public worship, even avoiding them on

14. Ibid., 150.
15. Ibid., 51, 72, 113, 149, 181, 238.
16. Ibid., 150.
17. Hawthorne, Letter of 4 October, 1840, *Selected Letters of Nathaniel Hawthorne*, 80.
18. Hawthorne, "The Gentle Boy," *The Complete Short Stories of Nathaniel Hawthorne*, 49.

the path through the woods, where they "passed by on the other side."[19] Only the Pearsons are Good Samaritans, contrasting the parable's priest and Levite, and their counterparts the legalistic Puritans, who, with their "impure hearts," dread contamination, drawing their self-righteous robes about them in sanctimonious, "holier-than-thou" shunning.

John Endicott, stern and imperious, leads an "iron-breasted company" of Puritan soldiers in "Endicott and the Red Cross," brandishes his sword to cut the Red Cross from the banner of the Church of England, demonstrating nationalistic pride. Earlier in the story various examples of retribution of iniquity are mentioned, including a prototype of Hester Prynne, this story appearing in 1838, twelve years before *The Scarlet Letter*: "There was likewise a young woman . . . whose doom it was to wear the letter A on the breast of her gown, in the eyes of all the world and her own children." She had embroidered the letter in scarlet cloth with gold thread, "so that the capital A might have been thought to mean Admirable, or anything rather than Adulteress." This description is followed by the narrator's caveat to the reader who might consider Puritan times "more vicious than our own, when, as we pass along the very street of this sketch, we discern no badge of infamy on man or woman. It was the policy of our ancestors to search out even the most secret sins, and expose them to shame, without fear or favor, in the broadest light of the noonday sun. Were such the custom now, perchance we might find materials for a no less piquant sketch than the above."[20] Perhance indeed! This conclusion corroborates one of Hawthorne's Notebook entries recorded a year before the story appeared: "A man to flatter himself with the idea that he would not be guilty of some certain wickedness, —as, for instance, to yield to the personal temptations of the Devil, —yet to find, ultimately, that he was at that very time committing that same wickedness."[21] Or, to put it another way, "Let the one who is without sin cast the first stone!"

Hardness and coldness are especially conspicuous in "The Man of Adamant," with the subtitle label "An Apologue," that is, a short allegorical tale with a moral, which seems to be that moral sensibility, the heart, the conscience can become increasingly and progressively hardened, petrified, calcified like stone, like adamant (Latin, *adamas*—"the hardest metal," *a*,

---

19. Ibid., 51, 52. Significantly, Hawthorne provides a subtext with the phrase "passed by on the other side" from Luke 10: 31–32, where it is applied to the priest and Levite in the parable of the Good Samaritan.

20. Ibid., "Endicott and the Red Cross," 206.

21. Hawthorne, *The American Notebooks*, 25.

Part III: Characterization

"not" + *daman*, "subdue") through intolerance, obduracy, self-centeredness, and seclusion from others. Richard Digby, "the gloomiest and most intolerant of a stern brotherhood," is so narrow-minded and self-righteous that he believes only he has the plan of salvation, so he reads his Bible to himself, prays to himself, and eventually withdraws by himself to a damp, sepulchral cave, from which not even the gracious, gentle, and compassionate Mary Goffe can persuade this "stony-hearted" monster to repent and drink the water of life from the bright fountain. Years later a young boy and girl discover the cave and in it a statuesque figure resembling a man chiseled from adamant. Digby, who suffers the fate of Ethan Brand and apparently like him committed the Unpardonable Sin, is not identified as a Puritan, but the setting appears to be exactly that of Puritan times—"the old times of religious gloom and intolerance."[22]

Some might argue that the most severe and pervasive indictment of the Puritans appears in "Young Goodman Brown" (discussed above, chapter 7, in relation to witchcraft). Goodman Brown, just three months married to Faith, goes deep into the forest for some guilty purpose but with the naive intention thereafter to cling to his wife's skirts and follow her to heaven. He goes apparently to keep an appointment with a diabolical figure who resembles his own father and who claims to have helped Brown's grandfather lash a Quaker woman through the streets of Salem and brought his father a pitch-pine knot to set fire to an Indian village in King Philip's war. He sees or thinks he sees Goody Cloyse, who taught him his catechism and who claims to have sponsored Brown's grandfather at a witches' meeting. Brown thinks he sees and hears the church minister and deacon, elders and members of the church, ostensibly pious townspeople—and, by the blaze of the torches, his beloved wife. The dark figure solemnly tells them that "evil is the nature of mankind. Evil must be your only happiness," and just as he is about to lay the mark of baptism on their foreheads, Brown admonishes Faith, "Look up to heaven and resist the wicked one," whereupon he staggers against a rock and his cheek is sprinkled with cold dew.

The next morning in Salem village Brown sees the old minister, the deacon, his catechist—and Faith, with her pink ribbons, welcoming him as if nothing has happened. Are the Puritans all hypocrites, pretending to live righteous lives in the village but trafficking with the devil and his minions at night in the forest? Was a glimpse at the "mystery of sin"

---

22. Hawthorne, "The Man of Adamant," *The Complete Short Stories of Nathaniel Hawthorne*, 496.

too overwhelming—"If we say that we have not sinned we make him a liar and his word is not in us"? Or did Brown manifest what some may consider a typical Puritan characteristic—seeing and condemning evil in others but not in himself? The Puritans did believe that "evil is the nature of mankind"—that is, until the divine nature is imputed by grace through faith, with the old Adamic nature remaining in conflict with the New, but certainly not that "evil must be your only happiness," a lie from the father of lies. Brown remains "stern," a common adjective describing the Puritans, distrustful, having lost his "faith," especially in people. He shrinks from the bosom of Faith—but he remains married to her, and he produces a "goodly" number of children and grandchildren, though his dying hour is gloom and no hopeful verse is carved on his tombstone. Is the tale an indictment of the Puritan tendency toward preoccupation with evil and judgmental condemnation of it in others, a predisposition which robs one of love, joy, peace, patience, kindness, goodness, faithfulness, gentleness, self-control—fruit of the Spirit?

The Puritans in "The Maypole of Merry Mount" are "grim," "stern" "men of iron" led by "the severest Puritan of all," "the iron man," "the Puritan of Puritans" whose "visage, frame, and soul seemed wrought of iron"—John Endicott, who turns "his iron frown" upon the wanton revelers and assaults the pagan Maypole, which has been described as "fifty foot of priapic pine." According to the narrator, "as it sank, tradition says, the evening sky grew darker, and the woods threw forth a more somber shadow."[23] Hawthorne's description of the Puritans in this story might serve as his summary view:

> Not far from Merry Mount was a settlement of Puritans, most dismal wretches, who said their prayers before daylight, and then wrought in the forest or the cornfield till evening made it prayer time again. Their weapons were always at hand to shoot down the straggling savage. When they met in conclave, it was never to keep up the old English mirth, but to hear sermons three hours long, or to proclaim bounties on the heads of wolves and the scalps of Indians. Their festivals were fast days, and their chief pastime the singing of psalms. Woe to the youth or maiden who did but dream of a dance! The selectman nodded to the constable; and there sat the light-heeled reprobate in the stocks;

---

23. Ibid., "The Maypole of Merry Mount," 45, 43.

Part III: Characterization

>or if he danced, it was round the whipping-post, which might be termed the Puritan Maypole.[24]

Yet even this story of grim and stern Puritanical retribution ends on a note of compassion when "the iron man was softened" and showed mercy to the newly wed Lord and Lady of the May, each of whom pled altruistically to bear the discipline of his / her spouse. Endicott deals with them gently, casting a garland of roses on their heads, and directing them heavenward, away from the vanities of Merry Mount.

Whereas Hawthorne expressed his ambivalent attitudes toward Puritanism and the Puritans primarily in his fiction, Lewis expressed his only somewhat less ambivalent attitudes toward Puritanism and the Puritans primarily in his expository writing and letters. Hawthorne had an ancestral relation to the Puritans, whereas Lewis had no steeple-crowned progenitor in his lineage. He is quoted as describing himself as a "converted pagan living among apostate Puritans."[25] In *Surprised by Joy*, he wrote, ". . . if in my books I have spoken too much of Hell, and if critics want a historical explanation of the fact, they must seek it not in the supposed Puritanism of my Ulster childhood but in the Anglo-Catholicism of the church at Belsen. I feared for my soul . . . I began seriously to pray and to read my Bible and to attempt to obey my conscience."[26]

Chad Walsh has argued that Lewis had the great advantage of "not being a puritan," but Clyde S. Kilby has taken exception to the illustration Walsh uses to support his argument (that in *The Pilgrim's Regress* John left Puritania for good), noting that Lewis bears a "sympathetic attitude toward the term 'puritan.'"[27] John, who is born in the land of Puritania, chafes at being smacked soundly by his mother and the cook. Dressed in ugly clothes that make him itch all over and taken to see the elderly Steward in his big, dark, ugly stone house, John is told about the Landlord and given a list of all the things he must not do, "but half the rules seemed to forbid things he had never heard of, and the other half forbade things he was doing every day and could not imagine not doing; and the number of the rules was so enormous that he felt he could never remember them all." Then the old man speaks again, through his mask, to warn John of what the Landlord would do to him if he breaks the rules: "He'd take

---

24. Ibid., 43.
25. Kilby, *The Christian World of C. S. Lewis*, 13.
26. Lewis, *Surprised by Joy*, 34.
27. Kilby, *The Christian World of C. S. Lewis*, 193.

you and shut you up for ever and ever in a black hole full of snakes and scorpions as large as lobsters—for ever and ever. And besides that, he is such a kind, good man, so very, very kind, that I am sure you would never *want* to displease him." When John asks if nothing can be done about the snakes and scorpions, the Steward "sat down and talked for a long time, but John could not understand a single syllable," and the Steward assured John that the Landlord was so "extraordinarily kind and good to his tenants [that he] would certainly torture most of them to death the moment he had the slightest pretext."[28]

Surely Hawthorne would have applauded this satiric, ironic caricature of the Puritans—dour parents, dark, foreboding Puritan meetinghouse, Puritan minister with his harsh list of rules and the dire warning of the consequences of not obeying them. Perhaps the masks they all put on symbolize ambiguity and equivocation, on one hand, and downright putative hypocrisy, like that in Salem village, on the other. Yet when the Steward finishes his dire preachment, he removes his formidable mask, has a pleasant chat with John, and gives him a cake. Just as Goodman Brown returns to Salem village, though greatly changed and with his dying hour being gloom, so John returns to Puritania and, with his companion Virtue, approaches the brook "singing and laughing like schoolboys . . . , and they danced more than they walked."[29]

Lewis displayed further ambivalence toward Puritanism in Screwtape's remarks to Wormwood about the diabolical value of negative connotations: ". . . I see few of the old warnings about Worldly Vanities, the Choice of Friends, and the Value of Time. All this, your patient would probably classify as 'Puritanism'—and may I remark in passing that the value we have given to that word is one of the really solid triumphs of the last hundred years? By it we rescue annually thousands of humans from temperance, chastity, and sobriety of life."[30] Lewis comments elsewhere on the misleading negative connotations of the word: "We have come to use the word 'Puritan' to mean what should rather be called 'rigorist' or 'ascetic, ' and we tend to assume that the sixteenth-century Puritans were 'puritanical' in this sense . . . The idea that a Puritan was a repressed and repressive person would have astonished Sir Thomas More and Luther about equally . . . And Puritan

---

28. Lewis, *The Pilgrim's Regress*, 3-4-5.
29. Ibid., 205.
30. Lewis, *The Screwtape Letters*, 51.

theology, so far from being grim and gloomy seemed to err in the direction of fantastic optimism."[31] Lewis said much the same thing in his *English Literature in the Sixteenth Century*: ". . . nearly every association which now clings to the word *puritan* has to be eliminated when we are thinking of the early Protestants. Whatever they were, they were not sour, gloomy, or severe; nor did their enemies bring any such charge against them." He describes the historical development as follows:

> Puritanism, as I have defined it, splits off from general Protestantism in the second half of the sixteenth century . . . Originally coined by certain Anabaptists to describe themselves ['Puritan'] came to be used as a hostile term (though they sometimes accepted it) for those Protestants who believed that the Elizabethan Church was insufficiently reformed and wished to make her more like the Protestant churches on the continent; especially like that of Geneva. The puritans were so called because they claimed to be purists or purifiers in ecclesiastical polity: not because they laid more emphasis than other Christians on 'purity' in the sense of chastity.

Focusing more on Puritan theology, Lewis writes, "All the initiative has been on God's side; all has been free, unbounded grace. And all will continue to be free, unbounded grace. His own puny and ridiculous efforts would be as helpless to retain the joy as they would have been to achieve it in the first place . . .' Works' have no 'merit', though of course faith, inevitably, even unconsciously, flows out into works of love at once. He is not saved because he does works of love; he does works of love because he is saved. It is faith alone that has saved him: faith bestowed by sheer gift . . ."[32]

In his essay titled "False Characterisations," Lewis, discussing English Literature as a subject in schools, remarks: "When the young person in question is an agnostic whose ancestors were Puritans, you get a very

---

31. Lewis, "Donne and Love Poetry in the Seventeenth Century," *Selected Literary Essays*, 116.

32. Lewis, *English Literature in the Sixteenth Century*, 34, 32, 33. Cf. John Calvin's view that "faith alone saves, but the faith that saves is not alone." Later in the same study, Lewis says, "The Puritan party, properly so called, insisted on Calvin's system of church Government as well as on his general theology." He notes that "of course not all Calvinists were puritans . . . We must distinguish a hard core of puritans and a much wider circle of those who were, at varying levels, affected by Calvinism. But a certain severity (however seriously we may take it) was diffused even through that wider circle, in the sense that denunciation of vice became part of the stock-in-trade of fashionable and even frivolous writers" (44, 43).

regrettable state of mind. The Puritan conscience works on without the Puritan theology—like millstones grinding nothing, like digestive juices working on an empty stomach and producing ulcers. The unhappy youth applies to literature all the scruples, the rigorism, the self-examination, the distrust of pleasure, which his forebears applied to the spiritual life, and perhaps soon all the intolerance and self-righteousness."[33] Here Lewis specifies what he apparently considers to be six characteristics of the Puritans—excessive scrupulosity (uneasiness, hesitancy because of conscience), rigidity (hardness, inflexibility), constant self-examination, asceticism, intolerance, self-righteousness—attributes also manifest in a number of Hawthorne's characters.

In an early letter to Arthur Greeves, Lewis refers to his friend's ambivalence toward Puritanism, noting that "both the revulsion from [Puritanism] and attraction back to it are strong elements." Then he specifies four reasons for his own negative feelings: "1. That the system denied pleasures *to others* as well as to the votaries themselves: whatever the merits of *self*-denial, this is unpardonable interference. 2. It inconsistently kept *some* worldly pleasures, and always selected the worst ones—gluttony, avarice, etc. 3. It was ignorant. It could give no '*reason* for the faith that was in it' . . . 4. 'By their fruits ye shall know them.' Have they the *marks* of peace, love, wisdom, and humility on their faces or in their conversation?"[34] There is abundant evidence that Hawthorne would have concurred with Lewis' reasons—and perhaps added others, having dramatized them in his fiction.Both were ambivalent toward the Puritans, at times damning them with faint praise, at other times praising them with a faint damn. Lewis insisted that they were not sour, gloomy, or severe, seeing them as a greatly misunderstood group; Hawthorne saw them as hard and stern, yet recognized both good and evil traits in them, admitting that strong traits of their nature had intertwined themselves with his own, perhaps for both good and ill.

Neither Hawthorne nor Lewis had a close lifelong friendship with a clergyman like Mark Twain's friendship with the Reverend Joseph

33. Lewis, "False Characterisations," *An Experiment in Criticism*, 10.

34. Lewis, Letter of 6 December 1931, *They Stand Together: The Letters of C. S. Lewis to Arthur Greeves*, 432–33. Lewis paraphrases several New Testament verses here—I Peter 3:15, "But sanctify the Lord God in your hearts, and always be ready to give a defense to everyone who asks you a reason for the hope that is in you, with meekness and fear"—Matthew 7:20, "Therefore, by their fruits you will know them"—and Galatians 5:22, "But the fruit of the Spirit is love, joy, peace, longsuffering, kindness, goodness, faithfulness, gentleness, self-control."

Part III: Characterization

Twichell, a Presbyterian minister in Hartford.[35] As with their attitudes toward Puritans and Puritanism, both Hawthorne and Lewis demonstrated ambivalent views of clergymen. Lewis remarked shortly after his conversion, "I was not in the least anticlerical, but I was deeply antiecclesiastical . . . But though I like clergymen as I liked bears, I had as little wish to be in the Church as in the zoo . . . To me, religion ought to have been a matter of good men praying alone and meeting by twos and threes to talk of spiritual matters."[36] Similarly, Hawthorne remarked that he was "to learn that clergymen are made of the same flesh and blood as other people, and perhaps lack one small safeguard which the rest of us possess, because they are aware of their own peccability, and therefore cannot look up to the clerical class for the proof of the possibility of a pure life on earth, with such reverential confidence as we are prone to do." Then he goes on to recall "the innocent faith of my boyhood, and the good old silver-headed clergyman, who seemed to me as much a saint then on earth as he is now in heaven, and partly for whose sake, through all these darkening years, I retain a devout, though not intact nor unwavering respect for the entire fraternity."[37] His tenuous and wavering respect for the clergy is seen further in this comment: "I find my respect for clerical people, as such, and my faith in the utility of their office, decreases daily. We certainly do need a new revelation—a new system—for there seems to be no life in the old one . . . Protestantism needs a new Apostle to convert it into something positive."[38]

---

35. See Fred Kaplan, *The Singular Mark Twain: A Biography*, 221, 238, 245. Twain remarked to his mother, "Puritans are mighty straight-laced, & they won't let me smoke in the parlor, but the Almighty don't make any better people." He said to Livy, his future wife, "[Twichell] prayed fervently for my conversion, & that your love & mine might grow until it was made *perfect* love by the approving spirit of God," and echoing Hawthorne's spiritual tribute to Sophia: "Your love, Livy . . . turned my wandering feet toward the straight gate & the narrow way." Similarly, Ron Powers (*Mark Twain: A Life*, 251) cites Twain's letter to Livy: "Set a white stone—for I have made a friend. It is the Rev. J. H. Twichell . . . I could hardly find words strong enough to tell how much I *do* think of that man."

36. Lewis, *Surprised by Joy*, 233–34. Lewis goes on to acknowledge that he had been "fortunate" in his clerical acquaintances, especially in the Dean of Divinity at Magdalen and the Rector at home in Ireland, who later was the Archbishop of Dublin.

37. Hawthorne, *Our Old Home*, 33–34.

38. Cited in Fick, *The Light Beyond: A Study of Hawthorne's Theology*, 154. Hawthorne also refers to "the difference between the cold, lifeless, vaguely liberal clergyman of our own day, and the narrow but earnest cushion-thumper of puritanical times," concluding that "I prefer the last-mentioned variety of the black-coated tribe."

Both Hawthorne and Lewis pondered and presented in their work a conclave of clerics, a bevy of bishops, a muster of ministers, a parliament of parsons. Hawthorne seemed especially to relish caricaturing the clergy, as in this Notebook entry describing a young clergyman, who was "awkward in his manners, yet it was not an ungentlemanly awkwardness,—intelligent as respects book-learning, but much deficient in worldly tact." The cleric sat most of the day in the bar in order to study character: "sometimes he would endeavor to contribute his share to the general amusement, —as by growling comically, to provoke and mystify a dog; and by some bashful and half-apropos observations."[39] Lewis, for his part, seemed to empathize more with the clergy, for example, defending them against unreasonable expectations from the laity: "The clergy are those particular people within the whole Church who have been specially trained and set aside to look after what concerns us as creatures who are going to live for ever: and we are asking them to do a quite different job for which they have not been trained. The job is really on us, on the laymen."[40]

Yet there is truth in Michael Ward's observation that Lewis was more than ready to find fault with clerics in practice, judging by his fictional portrayals, "nearly all of whom are knaves or fools or weaklings of one kind or another."[41] Almost every one of Lewis's ministers has his share of knavery—deceitfulness, dishonesty, rascality—, foolishness, and weakness, but perhaps the most egregious is the fat apostate Episcopal Bishop Ghost with the cultured voice and "bright clerical smile" in *The Great Divorce*. Of course, the Bishop would label these traits "honest opinions fearlessly followed," not sins. It becomes clear, from his interchange with Dick the White Spirit, that he lost his faith in college, ironically abandoning his belief in a literal Heaven and Hell, in the doctrine of the Resurrection, in the reality of the Supernatural, in the very existence of God, in the need for repentance and forgiveness. He is assuredly one of the most striking, notorious characterizations of an apostate[42] in all of literature,

---

39. Hawthorne, *The American Note-Books*, 193–94.

40. Lewis, *Mere Christianity*, 83. Lewis says that when the laity "ask for a lead from the church most people mean they want the clergy to put out a political programme. That is silly," he says.

41. Michael Ward, in Judith Wolfe and Brendan N. Wolfe, Editors, *C. S. Lewis and the Church*, 75.

42. "Apostasy" is derived from the Greek *apostasia* "to stand away from," "to fall away." The book of Hebrews warns about falling away from the living God because of an evil, unbelieving heart (3:12), and I Timothy 4:1 warns, "The Spirit explicitly says that in later times some will fall away from the faith, paying attention to deceitful

Part III: Characterization

taking his place with the Emperor Julian "the Apostate" (361–63), with Judas Iscariot, with Demas (II Timothy 4:10), with Hymenaeus and Alexander (I Timothy 1:20). He refuses the Spirit's earnest plea to repent and believe, scuttling off ironically to read a paper at a little Theological Society in Hell—on the text of Ephesians 4:13,[43] muttering about how Jesus would have outgrown his earlier views and perhaps gained full stature if he had lived longer and shown more tact and patience.

The Steward, who is the cleric from Puritania in *The Pilgrim's Regress*, is a walking paradox, putatively a "Steward" but apparently the "Keeper" only of a big dark house of stone, making and dispensing interminable lists of rules of things forbidden, along with an occasional cake, appearing kind and full of jokes until he suddenly dons a horrendous mask and warns of how the Landlord will punish disobedience, speaking on and on in a sing-song voice and unintelligible syllables. Later, on his journey, John learns from Wisdom that "the Stewards themselves do not know clearly the meaning of their story: hence, if you ask them how the slaying of the Son should help us, they are driven to monstrous answers . . . And what of the rules? . . . it is idle to make them the arbitrary commands of a Landlord: yet those who do so were not altogether astray, for it is equally an error to think that they are each man's personal choice. . . . every conflict between the rules and our inclinations is but a conflict of the wishes of my mortal and apparent self against those of my real and eternal."[44]

The two prominent Stewards / clerics in *The Pilgrim's Regress* appear as satiric caricatures. Mr. Neo-Angular is motivated by obligation, by duty ("it is my duty according to my office to share my supper with you"); he is rigid and dogmatic ("I should say . . . against half-measures and compromises of all sorts—against any pretense that there is any kind of goodness or decency . . . on this side" of the Canyon); he is prejudicial and whimsical ("I see you are not one of us . . . and you are undoubtedly damned . . . Now let us eat"); he is cynical ("he had explained that the secular virtue of hospitality was worthless, and care for the afflicted a sin if it proceeded from humanitarian sentiment"); he is a Nay-Sayer, a

---

spirits and doctrines of demons."

43. Ephesians 4:13—"Till we all come in the unity of the faith and of the knowledge of the Son of God, unto a perfect man, unto the measure of the stature of the fullness of Christ."

44. Lewis, *The Pilgrim's Regress*, 134–35.

Counteractors and Ambivalents in the Power of Blackness

repudiator ("Go on with your Island, if you like, but do not pretend that it is anything but a part of the land of destruction this side of the canyon").[45]

Mr. Broad, another Steward, is no better. He is captious and judgmental (labeling Mr. Angular as "a little narrow," "a little old-fashioned," Mr. Wisdom as "narrow-minded," and Mother Kirk as "a little out of date"); he seems to be regressing toward apostasy like the Episcopal Ghost ("as I grow older I am inclined to set less and less store by mere orthodoxy [for] so often the orthodox view means the lifeless view, the barren formula"); he seems obsessed with facile sweetness and light ("our common struggle toward the light . . . , the seeking is the finding"); he advocates the study of botany as "a new window on the Infinite," a "key to the mystery"; he repudiates conversion and rebirth ("these sudden conversions and violent struggles don't achieve anything").[46]

The clerics in Hawthorne's satirical, allegorical "The Celestial Railroad" are similar to Lewis's. ". . . The reverend clergy are nowhere held in higher respect than at Vanity Fair . . . In justification of this high praise I need only mention the names of the Rev. Mr. Shallow-deep, the Rev. Mr. Stumble-at-truth, that fine old clerical character the Rev. Mr. This-to-day, who expects shortly to resign his pulpit to the Rev. Mr. That-to-morrow; together with the Rev. Mr. Bewilderment, the Rev. Mr. Clog-the-spirit, and, last and greatest, the Rev. Dr. Wind-of-doctrine."[47] As if the presence and popularity of these apostate clerics were not depressing enough, the narrator observes, with cogent dramatic irony, that "the reader of John Bunyan will be glad to know that Christian's old friend Evangelist, who was accustomed to supply each pilgrim with a mystic roll, now presides at the ticket office,"[48] though some question his identity and allege evidence of an imposture.

In Lewis's self-proclaimed "tall story about devilry," *That Hideous Strength*, it is not surprising to find at least four clerics. Perhaps the most honorific but also the most pathetic is Mr. Jewel (who may be said to live up

---

45. Ibid., 92–93, 95, 93, 96, 97.

46. Ibid., 115, 116–17, 175. Mr. Broad and the Episcopal Ghost are cut from the same clerical cloth. The former espouses the latter's "spirit of sweetness and light and tolerance—and, er, service" (*The Great Divorce*, 42); both, as part of their justification for apostasy, quote the same Scripture—"When I became a man, I put away childish things [I Corinthians 13.11]. These great truths need reinterpretation in every age" (*The Pilgrim's Regress*, 116; *The Great Divorce*, 41).

47. Hawthorne, "The Celestial Railroad," *The Complete Short Stories of Nathaniel Hawthorne*, 301–02.

48. Ibid., 296.

Part III: Characterization

to his name), a canon serving in the collegiate church of Bracton College. When Canon Jewel—elderly, blind, decrepit, and close to weeping—stands to speak against the motion to sell Bragdon Wood, including Merlin's ancient well, to diabolical N.I.C.E. (National Institute of Co-ordinated Experiments), Lord Feverstone rudely interrupts to say, since no one can hear the old man, that if he wishes his views *not* to be heard, that purpose could better be attained by silence. The narrator states that because Canon Jewel was already an elderly man in the days when old men were treated with respect and kindness, "he had never succeeded in getting used to the modern world." Therefore, rather than attempting a reply, "quite suddenly he spread out his hands with a gesture of helplessness, shrunk back, and began laboriously to resume his chair,"[49] as the motion carried.

Another cleric in the work, who presides at the funeral of the murdered Mr. Hingest, is Canon Storey, said to be "isolated both by his faith and by his deafness." Lewis achieves ironic Black Humor with the antiphony of the funeral homily from I Corinthians 15 juxtaposed with the cacophonous voices of workmen shouting outside the chapel: "'Take your bucking great foot out of the light or I'll let you have the whole lot on top of it'; but Storey, unmoved and unaware, replied, 'Thou fool, that which thou sowest is not quickened unless it die.' 'I'll give you one across your ugly face in a moment, see if I don't, ' said the voice again. 'It is sown a natural body; it is raised a spiritual body, ' said Storey."[50] The reader is left to ponder who is the greatest fool—the Canon who drones on totally unaware of his surroundings, oblivious not only of the ironic distractions from outside but also of the incongruity between the words he is reading and the physical / spiritual death of "the proud old unbeliever" or the unbelieving family and congregants present or the carnal Corinthian

---

49. Lewis, *That Hideous Strength*, 28. Earlier Canon Jewel was heard to say "that he would sooner have every tree in the Wood felled to the ground than see it caged in barbed wire" (25).

50. Ibid., 126. Cf. the similar antiphonal juxtapositioning in chapter VIII of Flaubert's *Madame Bovary* (1856), where an agricultural show is going on in the town square, with speeches, awarding of farm prizes, and selling of livestock, while Emma and Rodolphe dally together at the window of a second story council room: "And he seized her hand; she did not withdraw it. 'For good farming generally!' cried the president . . . 'A hundred times I wished to go, and I followed you—I remained.' 'Manures!' 'And I shall remain tonight, tomorrow, all other days, all my life!' . . . 'For a Merino ram!' 'But you will forget me; I shall pass away like a shadow.' . . . 'Porcine race; prizes—equal . . .'" (153–54). There is no evidence that Lewis had read Flaubert, as he apparently nowhere refers to him or his work.

believers, perhaps including the reader, who do not grasp the reality of death and truth of the resurrection.

Two other clerics are both praised by the ominous villain Mr. Wither, who observes that "within religious circles—ecclesiastical circles—types of spirituality of very real value do from time to time arise. When they do, they sometimes reveal great energy. Father Doyle, though not very talented, is one of our soundest colleagues; and Mr. Straik has in him the germs of that total allegiance . . . which is so rare. It doesn't do to be in any way narrow."[51] The most Father Doyle, practically a nonentity, has to recommend him is that he knows Latin. Straik, "the Mad Parson" who considers theology mere "talk—eyewash—a smoke screen—a game for rich men," believes the power of science, especially in the form of N.I.C.E., is bringing the Kingdom of Heaven to earth here and now. "The resurrection of Jesus in the Bible," he insists, "was a symbol," a symbol of "Man Immortal and Man Ubiquitous, . . . Man on the throne of the universe . . . , what all the prophecies really meant," for the resurrection was "neither a historical fact, nor a fable . . . but a prophecy"—of the Real Man—Francois Alcasan, who was guillotined and whose head is now venerated as God—"or a being made by man—who will finally ascend the throne of the universe. And rule forever."[52] Straik is a beneficed parson with no beneficence, a heretical hierophant, an apostate apostle. Screwtape would relish him—with relish!

Screwtape speaks to Wormwood about two clerics of the churches nearest his "patient." One is the Vicar, "who has been so long engaged in watering down the faith to make it easier for a supposedly incredulous and hard-headed congregation that it is now he who shocks his parishioners with his unbelief, not *vice versa*. He has undermined many a soul's Christianity."[53] The other is Father Spike, who vacillates between quasi-Communism and quasi-theocratic- Fascism, between scholasticism and denial of human reason completely, between immersion in politics and rejection of all political systems as equally doomed, all of his positions being linked by hatred. He "cannot bring himself to preach anything which is not calculated to shock, grieve, puzzle, or humiliate his parents and their friends. A sermon which such people could accept would be to him as insipid as a poem which they could scan." But, Screwtape warns, Father Spike "has one fatal defect: he really believes. And this may yet mar

---

51. Ibid., 331.
52. Ibid., 78, 79, 177, 178, 128, 179.
53. Lewis, *The Screwtape Letters*, 82.

Part III: Characterization

all."[54] Such is the array of Lewis's clerics, a spectrum hardly supporting his early claim of his being "not in the least anti-clerical" but most certainly supporting his clerical ambivalence.

Whereas at least ten clerics appear in the fiction of Lewis, no fewer than fifteen appear in the fiction of Hawthorne, perhaps suggesting an obsession with the clergy. In his sketch "The Old Manse," Hawthorne describes a tattered roll of canvas hanging on a wall, on which is the picture of a clergyman —"in wig, band, and gown, holding a Bible in his hand." He tells how as he turned the cleric's face toward the light, "he eyed me with an air of authority such as men of his profession seldom assume in our days. The original had been pastor of the parish more than a century ago, a friend of Whitefield, and almost his equal in fervid eloquence. I bowed before the effigy of the dignified divine, and felt as if I had now met face to face with the ghost by whom, as there was reason to apprehend, the Manse was haunted."[55] The effigy of the dignified divine seemed to haunt not only the old Manse but also the Meister of the Tale.

Hawthorne's clerics occupy a wide-ranging spectrum, from old age to youthfulness, from the highly revered to the disdained, from the devoutly orthodox to the apostate, from Reformed, Calvinistic Episcopalians and Presbyterians to Arminian Methodists to Unitarians, from urban bishops to country parsons, from historical figures to fictional creations, from those who play a major role to those who are barely mentioned.

The Reverend Doctor Harris is a Unitarian clergyman, eighty years old, a "small, withered, infirm, but brisk old gentleman, with snow-white hair, a somewhat stooping figure, but yet with a remarkable alacrity of movement,"[56] whose ghost is said to return regularly to the Athenaeum reading room to peruse the newspaper, whereas a young Episcopal clergyman is one of four stricken with smallpox in "Lady Eleanore's Mantle." In "The White Old Maid," people revere the cleric, a "venerable patriarch, and equally a saint, who had taught them and their fathers the way to heaven for more than the space of an ordinary lifetime. He was a reverend figure, with long, white hair upon his shoulders, a white beard upon his breast, and a back so bent over his staff that he seemed to be looking downward continually, as if to choose a proper grave for his

---

54. Ibid., 83–84.

55. Hawthorne, "The Old Manse," *Mosses from an Old Manse*, 21–22.

56. Hawthorne, "The Ghost of Doctor Harris," *The Complete Short Stories of Nathaniel Hawthorne*, 565.

weary frame."⁵⁷ Contrasting this patriarch is the wayward and deceived old Puritan apostate, who, "yielding to the speculative tendency of the age ... had gone astray from the firm foundation of an ancient faith, and wandered into a cloud region, where everything was misty and deceptive, ever mocking him with a semblance of reality..."⁵⁸ Some clerics are stern and severe but sincere and well-intentioned but misunderstood, like Parson Thumpcushion, so named

> from the very forcible gestures with which he illustrated his doctrines. Certainly, if his powers as a preacher were to be estimated by the damage done to his pulpit furniture, none of his living brethren, and but few dead ones, would have been worthy even to pronounce a benediction after him. Such pounding and expounding the moment he began to grow warm, such slapping with his open palm, thumping with his closed fist, and banging with the whole weight of the great Bible, convinced me that he held, in imagination, either the Old Nick or some Unitarian infidel at bay, and belabored his unhappy cushion as proxy for those abominable adversaries.⁵⁹

Other clerics are faithful, hard-working parsons who labor long for little, like Robin Molineux's father, "settled on a small salary, at a long distance back in the country"⁶⁰ or the faithful rector who presides at the strange service when the "wedding knell" is tolled. Others appear sensitive and well-balanced, like the Rev. Doctor Mather Byles, "whose Presbyterian scruples [did] not keep him from the entertainment,"⁶¹ who is able to laugh heartedly with fits of merriment that to some may not befit his cloth. Still others arouse suspicion, like "the good old minister [of Salem village] taking a walk along the graveyard to get an appetite for breakfast and meditate his sermon,"⁶² from whom Goodman Brown shrinks upon his return to the village, or Father Hooper, who refuses to remove the black veil he wears.

Surely one of the most fascinating and arresting clerics is the "traveling preacher of great fame among the Methodists, ... a tall, thin figure in rusty black," who comes riding up to the group of people on the Stamford

57. Ibid., "The White Old Maid," 186–87.
58. Ibid., "The Christmas Banquet," 357.
59. Ibid., "Passages from a Relinquished Work," 413.
60. Ibid., "My Kinsman, Major Molineux," 526.
61. Ibid., "Howe's Masquerade," 123.
62. Ibid., "Young Goodman Brown," 255.

Part III: Characterization

road, informing "the seven vagabonds" who had intended to make their way together to the camp-meeting in Stamford, that the meeting had already broken up. The itinerant minister, dressed ominously in black and riding westward, seems to symbolize fixed destiny and perhaps death, as the group disperses, continuing as true vagabonds spiritually, "sundered at once to the four winds of heaven."[63]

Two of Hawthorne's clerics are historical figures, the most prominent being Roger Williams (1603–1683), graduate of Pembroke College, Cambridge, who arrived in Boston in 1631. He soon distinguished himself for his outspoken beliefs in freedom of conscience, separation from the Church of England, and separation of church and state. Tried for heresy and sedition, he fled to Narragansett Bay, where he established a colony at Providence and is credited with establishing the First Baptist Church in America. He makes a brief appearance in "Endicott and the Red Cross," bearing a letter, via Governor Winthrop, from King Charles of England, stating that the King and Archbishop Laud plan to send a governor-general, who will assume authority in New England and institute a form of the English Episcopacy. Williams is described as "an elderly gentleman, wearing a black cloak and band, and a high-crowned hat, beneath which was a velvet skull-cap, the whole being the garb of a Puritan minister. This reverend person bore a staff that seemed to have been recently cut in the forest, and his shoes were bemired as if he had been traveling on foot through the swamps of the wilderness. His aspect was perfectly that of a pilgrim, heightened also by an apostolic dignity."[64] Williams urges restraint lest the people be unduly stirred up and boldly asserts that Endicott's words would not be suitable even for a private chamber, much less the public street, but Endicott orders him to be silent, makes full disclosure, then brandishes his sword to cut the Red Cross from the English banner. Hawthorne establishes a significant subtext and reveals his extensive knowledge of Williams' character and life—his clothing, his staff cut from the forest and shoes bemired from walking through the swampy wilderness, his aspect of a "pilgrim," his "apostolic dignity," his "mild visage," the fortitude of his bold reproach of Endicott, his attempt to be a peacemaker.[65]

---

63. Ibid., "The Seven Vagabonds," 181.

64. Ibid., "Endicott and the Red Cross," 206.

65. For an extended fictional treatment of Roger Williams, see Mary Lee Settle's excellent novel *I, Roger Williams: A Fragment of Autobiography*.

Counteractors and Ambivalents in the Power of Blackness

According to one report, when Roger Williams arrived in Boston in 1631, he was invited to serve as Assistant Minister of the Boston Church while the pastor, Rev. John Wilson, returned to England to get his wife. The Rev. Mr. Wilson (1591–1667) had come to Massachusetts with John Winthrop in 1630 and was the first pastor of the Boston church, a highly influential cleric known for his balance of strict orthodoxy and gracious compassion. He is referred to more than twenty times in four major scenes in *The Scarlet Letter*. The first is when Hester is on the platform of ignominy, being urged by Governor Bellingham and Rev. Mr. Wilson to reveal the father of her child. The second scene is in the Governor's mansion, when the officials must decide whether to remove little Pearl from her mother. The third occurs when Dimmesdale is on the scaffold in the middle of the night, and the venerable Father Wilson, having come from the death-chamber of Governor Winthrop, passes by. Finally, again described as a "venerable" clerical brother, Wilson tries to support the tottering Dimmesdale during the Election Day procession, but is repelled by the young clergyman. Wilson is referred to a final time in the Conclusion, when he is mentioned as one of Chillingworth's executors.

Hawthorne's ambivalence is again evident in his depiction of Wilson. On one hand, he is described as "the reverend and famous John Wilson, the eldest clergyman of Boston, a great scholar, like most of his contemporaries in the profession, and withal a man of kind and genial spirit." Yet the narrator adds that his kind, genial spirit "had been less carefully developed than his intellectual gifts, and was, in truth, rather a matter of shame than self-congratulation with him."[66] He sternly warns Hester not to transgress beyond the limits of Heaven's mercy. In the later scene, Wilson is described as "the venerable pastor . . . whose beard [was] white as a snow-drift," as "the not unkind old minister," the litotes, perhaps leaving a modicum of uncertainty or doubt about his kindness. Similarly, when he first appears "he looked like the darkly engraved portraits which we see prefixed to old volumes of sermons; and *had no more right than one of those portraits would have to step forth, as he now did, and meddle with a question of human guilt, passion, and anguish.*" Perceptive readers may remember the key verb "meddle" later when Dimmesdale asks Chillingworth, "But who are thou, *that meddlest in this matter?—that dares thrust himself between the sufferer and his God?*"[67] Could Hawthorne be sug-

---

66. Hawthorne, *The Scarlet Letter*, 61, 64.

67. Ibid., 99, 104, 61, 126. Emphasis added. Litotes is a rhetorical device that expresses an understatement whereby something is stated by negation of its contrary.

Part III: Characterization

gesting that Pastor Wilson and the adamant Puritan leaders are guilty, though in a lesser degree, of the same violating sin of which Chillingworth is guilty?

Unmistakably, the two most prominent clerics in Hawthorne's work are the Rev. Mr. Hooper, central figure in "The Minister's Black Veil," and the Rev. Arthur Dimmesdale, a central figure in *The Scarlet Letter*. Parson Hooper, an erudite bachelor of about thirty, abruptly hides his face by donning a black veil, symbol of secret sin, and refuses to remove it even at the urging of his betrothed, deacons, pious members of his congregation, and a fellow-minister, the Rev. Mr. Clark.[68]

Great ambivalence and dramatic irony pervade Hawthorne's depiction of Dimmesdale. Outwardly, publicly, ostensibly, he is a "godly pastor," "a true priest, a true religionist, with the reverential sentiment largely developed, and an order of mind that impelled itself powerfully along the track of a creed, and wore its passage continually deeper with the lapse of time." Not only had he "achieved a brilliant popularity in his sacred office" but his parishioners "reverenced" him, "venerated" him, even "deemed the young clergyman a miracle of holiness [and] fancied him the mouthpiece of Heaven's messages of wisdom, and rebuke, and love. In their eyes, the very ground on which he trod was sanctified." "He stood . . . on the very proudest eminence of superiority, to which the gifts of intellect, rich lore, prevailing eloquence, and a reputation of whitest sanctity, could exalt a clergyman in New England's earliest days, when the professional character was of itself a lofty pedestal." When he spoke "it was as if an angel, in his passage to the skies, had shaken his bright wings over the people for an instant, —at once a shadow and a splendor, —and had shed down a shower of golden truths upon them . . . Were there not the brilliant particles of a halo in the air about his head? So etherealized by spirit as he was, and so apotheosized by worshipping admirers, did his footsteps . . . really tread upon the dust of earth?" "An erudite clergyman" "whose scholar-like renown still lived in Oxford, [he was] considered by his more fervent admirers as little less than a heaven-ordained apostle, destined, should he live and labor for the ordinary term of life, to do as great deeds for the now feeble New England Church as the early Fathers had achieved for the infancy of the Christian faith."[69]

---

68. Parson Hooper and his black veil will be discussed more fully in chapter 10, vis-à-vis the veils in *The Blithedale Romance* and Orual's white veil in Lewis's *Till We Have Faces*.

69. Ibid., 48, 113, 130, 175, 131, 227, 228, 144, 110.

Such pervasive veneration, even to the point of deifying a fallen hypocrite who has committed adultery with a member of his congregation, leads not only to ambivalence but also to recurring dramatic irony: Hester, the reader, and ultimately Hester's husband, Roger Chillingworth, know the truth of the clergyman's guilt even as the parishioners continue to reverence and worship him. Dimmesdale himself is seriously convicted and conflicted, longing to speak out in confession: "I your pastor, whom you so reverence and trust, am utterly a pollution and a lie," but his remorse is overcome by cowardice; he remains a "remorseful hypocrite," making a "mockery of penitence" and a "vain show of expiation." Rather than being putatively "childlike," with his words affecting the people "like the speech of an angel," he is *childish*, too craven to speak the truth and admit his culpability. Governor Bellingham, with cogent dramatic irony, early enjoins him, "the responsibility of this woman's soul lies greatly with you," but the pastor later pleads ironically with his parishioner Hester, his "better angel," "Be thou strong for me . . . Advise me what to do."[70]

The ambivalence and irony are cogently expressed by paradox and oxymoron. Dimmesdale accurately describes himself as "the *polluted priest*." Hester charges Chillingworth, ". . . you cause him to *die daily a living death*." And in the climactic scene when Dimmesdale openly confesses his sin and kisses little Pearl, "a spell was broken." The cleric delivers his most powerful homily: ". . . He is merciful! He hath proved his mercy, most of all, in my afflictions. By giving me this burning torture to bear upon my breast! By sending yonder dark and terrible old man, to keep the torture always at red-heat! By bringing me hither, to die *this death of triumphant ignominy* before the people! Had either of these agonies been wanting, I had been lost forever! Praised be His name! His will be done!"[71]

Dimmesdale's confession has elicited some surprisingly diversified conclusions. For example, Agnes McNeill Donohue summarily condemns him for "his dying words of incomparable spiritual pride" and for his alleged selfishness in giving no assurance of God's mercy to Hester:

70. Ibid., 132, 136, 133, 135, 136, 62, 185, 180.
71. Ibid., 179, 156, 233. Emphasis added. All of the characters in the novel are oxymoronic: not only is Dimmesdale the "polluted priest," "homiletical hypocrite," and "tarnished angel," but Chillingworth is the "diabolical doctor," "hypocritical Hippocrates," "violated violator," and "unhumanized mortal," just as Hester is the "sister of mercy" needing mercy, possessing the "taint of deepest sin in the most sacred quality of human life," little Pearl is the "angelic imp," "nymph child," and child in need of a father, both earthly and heavenly, and the Puritan community, rendering "unjust justice," are judges in need of judgment.

Part III: Characterization

". . . he dies damned, proclaiming his own election . . ."[72] Similarly, Edward H. Davidson sees only eternal damnation for the minister; William Dillingham interprets his confession as ironic; and William B. Nolte discounts the confession entirely because, in his view, it costs Dimmesdale "absolutely nothing."[73] Others have seen the minister and his confession more honorifically. For example, Edward Wagenknecht has said, "A self-called 'polluted priest,' he is still a faithful pastor, and he cannot bring himself to disillusion those who believe in him and to whom his ministry, besides being vastly more humane than that of most of his associates, and even more effective because of the anguish consequent upon his sin, has been—make no mistake about it—nearly ideal."[74] Only somewhat less positive is Hyatt H. Waggoner, who notes that Dimmesdale "first descends from his original position as a saintly guide and inspiration of the godly to the position he occupies during the greater part of the novel as very nearly the worst of the sinners in his hypocrisy and cowardice, then reascends by his final act of courageous honesty to a position somewhere in between his reputation for light and his former reality of darkness."[75] Perhaps closer to Hawthorne's own implied view is Darrel Abel's observation that Dimmesdale rejected Hester's plan of escape by elopement because he was aware that it would be spiritually fatal to them both: "He evaded this death of the soul by the grace of God, who granted him in his death hour the strength to confess and deliver himself from the untruth which threatened his spiritual extinction."[76]

There seems to be scant reason to take a jaundiced view of the minister's dying confession. He honestly admits that he and Hester forgot their God and sinned against Him, that they mutually violated their reverence for each other, and that God is merciful, a mercy abundantly proven by his torturous afflictions and by God's sending the "dark and terrible" Chillingworth, more sinning than sinned against, to keep the torture ever at red-heat. The arresting paradox of *God* sending the diabolical, vengeful Chillingworth is supported by the Psalmist's assertion that

72. Donohue, *Hawthorne: Calvin's Ironic Stepchild*, 60.

73. Davidson, "Dimmesdale's Fall," *New England Quarterly*, 36 (1963), 358–70; Dillingham, "Arthur Dimmesdale's Confession," *Studies in Literary Imagination* , Vol. 2, No. 1 (1969), 21–26; Nolte, "Hawthorne's Dimmesdale: A Small Man Gone Wrong," *New England Quarterly*, 32 (1965), 168–86.

74. Wagenknecht, *Nathaniel Hawthorne: The Man, His Tales and Romances*. 88.

75. Waggoner, *Hawthorne: a Critical Study*, 149.

76. Abel, *The Moral Picturesque: Studies in Hawthorne's Fiction*, 187.

God makes "even the wrath of men to praise Him" (Psalm 76:10) and the Apostle Paul's reminder of the sovereignty of God—He "causes all things to work together for good to those who love God, to those who are called according to His purpose" (Romans 8:28). Dimmesdale recognizes that he would have been lost forever if the afflictions had been missing. He dies a death of oxymoronic "triumphant ignominy," openly accepting the divine, sovereign will and praises God with his last breath. Is the reader to discount the words of a dying man and the reconciling kiss of little Pearl, which broke the alienating spell?

In the novel's Conclusion, Hawthorne, in typical "multiple choice" fashion, offers several theories for the reader to consider, including the possibility that the manner of the minister's death was intended to be a parable to teach that "we are sinners all alike," the need to discern "the Mercy which looks down," and to "repudiate more utterly the phantom of human merit, which would look aspiringly upward." Finally, the narrator adds, this version of the cleric's story may only be "an instance of that stubborn fidelity with which a man's friends—and especially a clergyman's—will sometimes uphold his character, when proofs, clear as the mid-day sunshine on the scarlet letter, establish him a false and sin-stained creature of the dust."[77] Though he was not particularly fond of this novel, Jack Lewis, with his own extensive pondering of various clerics, would most likely concur with this view.

---

77. Hawthorne, *The Scarlet Letter*, 235.

Part IV

Companion Pieces

9

Culpa—Happy or Sad?: *Perelandra* and *The Marble Faun* (*Transformation*)

THE PARALLELS, THE CONSANGUINITIES, between Jack Lewis and Nat Hawthorne include not just their personal backgrounds, lifestyles, and worldviews, not just common themes and motifs, and not just similar characterization but also strikingly similar works, some of which can be profitably examined as companion pieces. In some cases, a particular work was only imagined or envisioned by one but written by the other.

Several of Hawthorne's prospective vignettes in his Notebook seem to anticipate several of Lewis's works. For example, in September of 1836 Hawthorne pondered this idea: "To picture the predicament of worldly people, if admitted to paradise,"[1] and six years later he wrote: "To sit at the gate of Heaven, and watch persons, as they apply for admittance, some gaining it, others being thrust away."[2] One could almost imagine that these vignettes were the basis of Lewis's *The Great Divorce*, what he called his "imaginative supposal," his dream of a *Refrigerium* or a holiday from Hell, his "fantasy" with a moral—that "evil can be undone, but it cannot 'develop' into good. Time does not heal it . . . If we insist on keeping Hell (or even Earth) we shall not see Heaven: if we accept Heaven we shall not be able to retain even the smallest and most intimate souvenirs of Hell."[3] Lewis as narrator, along with teacher George MacDonald, does stand not at the gate of Heaven but in the Valley of the Shadow of Life and observes at least sixteen Ghosts from the Valley of the Shadow of Death as they are

---

1. Hawthorne, *The American Notebooks*, 18.
2. Ibid., 236.
3. Lewis, "Preface," *The Great Divorce*, viii–ix.

confronted by Solid People (six named), who attempt to convince them to repent and choose Life, but only the man with a red lizard of lust on his shoulder consents to be changed, the hideous lizard being forcibly, painfully removed and transformed into a flying stallion like Perseus.

Another such example is this 1835 vignette—"An old volume in a large library,—every one to be afraid to unclasp and open it, because it was said to be a book of magic,"[4] which anticipates Lewis's account of Lucy Pevensie's discovery and opening of the Magic Book of spells in *The Voyage of the "Dawn Treader."*[5] Still other works have parallels in subject matter, theme, imagery, and tone, such as Hawthorne's 1844 sketch "The Intelligence Office," its Orwellian setting a combination employment office and lost-and-found, with Big Brother in the form of a manipulative Supreme Intelligence Officer, who possesses the records of every wish, desire, and activity of every person, vis-a-vis Lewis's *That Hideous Strength*, which presents a sinister, Orwellian, dystopian organization of technocrats—the National Institute for Co-ordinated Experiments—dramatizing a central idea in Lewis's *The Abolition of Man*, that objective morality is essential to our humanity.

Two quite different works which can be profitably examined as companion pieces address the same complex theological issue: Lewis's *Perelandra* (1943), the second of his space trilogy, and Hawthorne's *The Marble Faun* (British title *Transformation*) (1860), a work much admired by Lewis as being "very good indeed [with] a lot about painting in it & some fine descriptions of Italian scenery."[6] *Perelandra* is Lewis's "Paradise Retained," working out, he said, "a *supposition*. ('Suppose, even now, in some other planet there were a first couple undergoing the same that Adam and Eve underwent here, but successfully')."[7] In another letter Lewis referred to the Fall: "I believe it resulted from a free act of sin & cd. have been avoided. If God created any other rational animals in some other part of the universe, perhaps they did *not* fall. One may imagine . . ."[8] And imagine he certainly did! Transported to Perelandra (Venus) is Dr. Elwin Ransom to support Tinidril, the Green Lady Queen, in overcoming the diabolical attacks from the Bent One,

---

4. Hawthorne, *The American Notebooks*, 14.
5. Lewis, *The Voyage of the "Dawn Treader,"* Chapter X, "The Magician's Book."
6. Lewis, Letter of 28 October 1917, *The Collected Letters of C. S. Lewis*, III, 340.
7. Ibid., Letter of 29 December 1958, 1004.
8. Ibid., Letter of 3 May 1954, 466.

Culpa—*Happy or Sad?*: Perelandra *and* The Marble Faun (Transformation)

supported by Ransom's old nemesis Edward Rolles Weston, who represents Scientism. Lewis remarked to his friend Arthur Greeves, "the idea is that Venus is at the Adam-and-Eve stage: i.e. the first two rational creatures have just appeared and are still innocent. My hero arrives in time to prevent their 'falling' as *our* first pair did."[9] Ransom, Lewis said, "plays the role of Christ not because he allegorically represents him . . . but because in reality every real Christian is really called upon in some measure to *enact* Christ. Of course Ransom does this rather more spectacularly than most."[10]

In yet another letter Lewis wrote, "I've got Ransom to Venus and through his first conversation with the 'Eve' of that world: a difficult chapter. I hadn't realized till I came to write it all the *Ave-Eve* business. I may have embarked on the impossible. This woman has got to combine characteristics which the Fall has put poles apart—she's got to be in some ways like a Pagan goddess and in other ways like the Blessed Virgin. But if one can get even a fraction of it into words it is worth doing."[11] The following excerpt demonstrates that Lewis succeeded in getting much more than a mere fraction of it into words, proving that it was well worth doing:

> There was no category in the terrestrial mind which would fit her. Opposites met in her and were fused in a fashion for which we have no images. One way of putting it would be to say that neither our sacred nor our profane art could make her portrait. Beautiful, naked, shameless, young—she was obviously a goddess: but then the face, the face so calm that it escaped insipidity by the very concentration of its mildness, the face was like the sudden coldness and stillness of a church when we enter it from a hot street—that made her a Madonna. The alert, inner silence which looked out from those eyes overawed [Ransom]; yet at any moment she might laugh like a child, or run like Artemis or dance like a Maenad.[12]

Strikingly similar in imagery, allusion, ironic paradox, and tone is Hawthorne's description of Hester Prynne as she stands on the scaffold in

9. Ibid., Letter of 23 December 1941, II, 504.

10. Ibid., Letter of 29 December 1958, III, 1005. Ransom plays a sacrificial role in the tale and, in his struggle with the Un-Man, suffers a serious injury in his heel, echoing the words of Yahweh to Satan in Genesis 3:15—"I will put enmity between you and the woman, and between your seed and her seed; he shall bruise you in the head, and you shall bruise him in the heel."

11. Ibid., Letter of 9 November 1941, II, 496.

12. Lewis, *Perelandra*, 64.

the market-place: "Had there been a Papist among the crowd of Puritans, he might have seen in this beautiful woman, so picturesque in her attire and mien, and with the infant at her bosom, an object to remind him of the image of Divine Maternity, which so many illustrious painters have vied with one another to represent; something which should remind him, indeed, but only by contrast, of that sacred image of sinless motherhood, whose infant was to redeem the world. Here, there was the taint of deepest sin in the most sacred quality of human life . . ."[13] Could Lewis's depiction of Tinidril be indebted to Hawthorne's depiction of Hester? It seems unlikely, though the parallels are striking. Both images are said to defy portraiture by "illustrious painters." Both stress the meeting and fusing (or balancing) of opposites. Both emphasize sacred and profane beauty. Both describe a Madonna or Divine Maternity, though one is pristinely innocent and unfallen whereas the other is patently fallen, tainted with "deepest sin in the most sacred quality of human life." Each has picturesque beauty and a numinous quality, "a mixture of awe," like that of a deity, Tinidril being compared to Artemis (Roman Diana), goddess of chastity and patroness of unmarried girls, associated with healing and purification, goddess of bountiful nature and harvest, of fertility and childbirth, moon goddess, virgin huntress of wild creatures, as well as to a Maenad, a female devotee and priestess of Dionysus (Roman Bacchus, god of wine and revelry) engaging in wild, orgiastic rites. Interestingly, the two writers arrive at similar descriptions of their respective women, though approached from opposite perspectives—Hawthorne describing a "fallen," unfaithful wife, an adulteress in her hour of abject ignominy, but fused with sacred, divine maternity, Lewis describing an "unfallen," faithful wife, an innocent queen in her triumphant hour of temptation and testing, but fused with profane associations and pagan myth.

It should be no surprise that Lewis repeatedly specified *Perelandra* as his favorite of all his books. To one correspondent he wrote, "It is always nice to hear of anyone really enjoying *Perelandra*. I don't think the pleasure on my part is merely vanity. I enjoyed that imaginary world so much myself that I'm glad to find anyone who has been there and liked it as much as I did . . ." To another he said, "Thanks for your kind words. *Perelandra* is my favourite too." To a third he said, "*Perelandra* is much the best book I've written." Another time he said he liked *Till We Have Faces* and *Perelandra*

---

13. Hawthorne, *The Scarlet Letter*, 53.

Culpa—*Happy or Sad?*: Perelandra *and* The Marble Faun (Transformation)

best, and again, speaking comparatively, he wrote, "On my own view *Perelandra* is worth 20 Screwtapes."[14]

Perhaps one of the reasons Lewis so much enjoyed and valued *Perelandra* and, as noted above, Hawthorne's *The Marble Faun* (*Transformation*), in addition to the exotic settings and imagery of both novels, is that each addresses and grapples with a deep theological issue. In pondering the aftermath and effects of sin, both writers considered that age-old question of whether the Fall could be called *Felix Culpa* ("Happy Fault"), *Felix Peccatum Adae* ("Fortunate Sin of Adam"), for, it is argued, if there had been no Fall, no sin, no fault, then there would have been no grace, no Incarnation, no redemption. The Roman Catholic Easter Liturgical hymn "Exultet" includes these lines: "O truly needful sin of Adam, which was blotted out by the death of Christ! O happy fault, that merited so great a Redeemer!"

The belief is ordinarily traced to Augustine, who writes in his *Enchiridion* (a term that comes from the Greek word for "handbook"), God "judged it better to bring good out of evil, than not to permit any evil to exist . . . He designed that His unmerited mercy should shine forth the more brightly in contrast with the unworthiness of its objects . . . As He foresaw that man would make a bad use of his free-will, that is, would sin, God arranged His own designs rather with a view to do good to man even in his sinfulness, that thus the good will of the Omnipotent might not be made void by the evil will of man, but might be fulfilled in spite of it."[15]

---

14. Lewis, Letter of 24 April 1958, Letter of 18 October 1963, Letter of 10 April 1946, Letter of 6 December 1960, Letter of 4 July 1955, *The Collected Letters of C. S. Lewis*, III, 939–40, 1467, 1564, 1214, 627.

15. Augustine, *Enchiridion on Faith, Hope, and Love*, XXVII, CIV, 33–34, 122. In his discussion of God's foreknowledge and predestination, John Calvin cites and praises this version of Augustine's statement: "Let us confess with the greatest benefit, what we believe with the greatest truth, that the God and Lord of all things, who made all things very good, both foreknew that evil was to arise out of good, and knew that it belonged to his most omnipotent goodness to bring good out of evil, rather than not permit evil to be, and so ordained the life of angels and men as to show in it, first, what free will could do; and, secondly, what the benefit of his grace and his righteous judgment could do" (*Institutes of the Christian Religion*, Volume II, 232). Few systematic theologians address the issue of *Felix Culpa* , an exception being Stephen Charnock, who writes: "God's wisdom is seen in bringing good to the creature out of sin . . . God, by an act of infinite wisdom, brings good out of [sin] to the creature, as well as glory to his name. . . He willed the permission of sin, as an occasion to bring forth mystery of the incarnation and passion of our Saviour . . . The redemption of man in so excellent a way, was drawn from the occasion of sin . . . the highest good hath been brought forth by the greatest wickedness . . . Without the wisdom of God permitting sin to enter into the world, some attributes of God had not been experimentally known, so some graces could not have been exercised

Similarly, in *Of True Religion*, Augustine writes: "Out of our sin, which our nature committed in the first sinful man, the human race is made the great glory and ornament of the world, and is so properly governed by the provisions of divine providence that the art of God's ineffable healing turns even the foulness of sin into something that has a beauty of its own."[16] Further, in *The City of God*, he wrote: "God foresaw the defeat which the Devil would suffer at the hands of a descendant of Adam, and with the help of divine grace, and that this would be to the greater glory of the saints . . . God preferred not to use His own power, but to leave success or failure to the creature's choice. In this way, God could show both the immense evil that flows from the creature's pride and also the even greater good that comes from His grace."[17]

Thomas Aquinas, who lived nearly nine hundred years after Augustine, also wrote of *Felix Culpa*: "If evil were completely excluded from things, much good would be rendered impossible. Consequently it is the concern of Divine Providence, not to safeguard all beings from evil, but to see to it that the evil which arises is ordained to some good . . . By permitting the existence of evil in the world, the divine goodness is more emphatically asserted in the good, just as is the divine wisdom when it forces evil to promote good . . . God allows evil to happen in order to bring a greater good therefrom . . . O fortunate crime which merited such and so great a redeemer!"[18]

The theme recurs in much literature through the years, for example in Edmund Spenser's *The Faerie Queene*, a favorite work of both writers, which dramatizes the idea that falling is often prelude to rising: "Ay me, how many perils doe enfold / The righteous man, to make him daily fall? / Were not, that heavenly grace doth him uphold, / And stedfast truth acquite him out of all."[19] Similarly, John Milton echoes the theme in *Paradise Lost*:

> O goodness infinite, goodness immense!
> That all this good of evil shall produce,
> And evil turn to good; more wonderful
> Than that which by creation first brought forth

. . ." (*The Existence and Attributes of God*, I, 535–37).

16. Augustine, *Of True Religion*, 48–49.
17. Augustine, *The City of God*, 321.
18. Aquinas, *Aquinas' Shorter Summa Theologica*, 159–60.
19. Spenser, *The Faerie Queene*, I, VIII, 1.

Culpa—*Happy or Sad?*: Perelandra *and* The Marble Faun *(Transformation)*

> Light out of darkness! Full of doubt I stand,
> Whether I should repent me now of sin
> By me done and occasioned, or rejoice
> Much more, that much more good thereof shall spring,
> To God more glory, more good will to men
> From God, and over wrath grace shall abound.[20]

The poet seems to be pondering the Apostle Paul's forthright words to the Romans: "What shall we say then? Shall we continue in sin, that grace may abound? God forbid. How shall we, that are dead to sin, live any longer therein?"[21] Lewis noted that Milton's version of the Fall is essentially that of Augustine, which, he says, "is that of the Church as a whole . . . Though God has made all creatures good He foreknows that some will voluntarily make themselves bad and also foreknows the good use which He will then make of their badness . . . At the end of the poem Adam is astonished at the power 'that all this good of evil shall produce . . .' [Satan] is allowed to do all the evil he wants and finds that he has produced good. Those who will not be God's sons become His tools."[22]

The pervasive recurrence of the "Fortunate Fall" concept in *belles-lettres* is demonstrated perhaps no more cogently than its appearance in James Joyce's seemingly unintelligible novel *Finnegan's Wake*, which Joseph Campbell and Henry Morton Robinson have called "a mighty allegory of the fall and resurrection of mankind."[23] The "fall" is a recurring image and motif: Lucifer's fall, angels' fall, Eve's fall, Adam's fall, Humpty Dumpty's fall, the fall of Rome, the fall of Newton's apple, the Wall Street crash, the setting sun, rainfall, Finnegan's fall from a ladder, fall from grace. Recurring throughout the 628-page book are such phrases as "O foenix culprit," "phaymix cuppluts," "O ferax cupla," "Felix Day," "O happy fault," "O felicitous culpability," "O fortunous casualitas" et al.[24]

---

20. Milton, *Paradise Lost*, XII, 469–78.
21. Romans 6:1–2.
22. Lewis, *A Preface to Paradise Lost*, 67–68.
23. Campbell and Robinson, *A Skeleton Key to Finnegan's Wake*, 3.
24. Joyce, *Finnegan's Wake*, 23, 606, 27, 202, 263, 175. Joyce's novel, first published in 1939, perhaps offers a nod to Augustine ("the ruah of Ecclectiastes of Hippo," 38) but unlikely a nod to Lewis in his reference to "the climbing boys at his Eagle and Child" (59), a central Oxford pub since 1650, where the Inklings regularly met from 1939 until 1962. Lewis was obviously acquainted with *Finnegan's Wake*, referring to Joyce's use of imaginary names and his term "*silvamoonlake*" in a passage one-third of the way through the novel (Letter of 11 July 1963, *The Collected Letters of C. S. Lewis*, III, 1440).

Though Lewis does not address "the fortunate fall" explicitly in "The Fall of Man" (*The Problem of Pain*), his comments do anticipate *Perelandra*: ". . . if there are other rational species than man, existing in some other part of the actual universe, then it is not necessary to suppose that they also have fallen," and he alludes to the good of the Incarnation, necessitated by the Fall: "In fact, of course, God saw the crucifixion in the act of creating the first nebula. The world is a dance in which good, descending from God, is disturbed by evil arising from the creatures, and the resulting conflict is resolved by God's own assumption of the suffering nature which evil produces."[25]

If the world is a dance in which the good created by God was disrupted by creaturely evil and the resultant conflict was resolved by that greatest miracle of all—the Incarnation—then the Great Dance, which concludes *Perelandra*, is an superb metaphor for the perfect pattern of happiness, joy, peace, and unity in which all creatures play a strategic role. As Lewis expressed it in *Mere Christianity*, "The whole dance, or drama, or pattern of this three-Personal life is to be played out in each one of us: or (putting it the other way round) each of us has got to enter that pattern, take his place in that dance. There is no other way to the happiness for which we were made."[26]

One of the voices at the Great Dance says, "In the Fallen World He prepared for Himself a body and was united with the Dust and made it glorious for ever. This is the end and final cause of all creating, and the sin whereby it came is called Fortunate . . ." Weston argues before Tinidril, the Green Lady, "He [Ransom] has not told you that it was this breaking of the commandment which brought Maleldil to our world and because of which He was made man. He dare not deny it." Ransom initially feels daunted by the argument: "The unfairness of it all was wounding him like barbed wire. Unfair . . . unfair. How could Maleldil expect him to fight against this, to fight with every weapon taken from him, forbidden to lie and yet brought to places where truth seemed fatal? It was unfair!" Shortly thereafter his impulse of rebellion turns to sudden doubt: "How if the enemy were right after all? *Felix peccatum Adae*. Even the Church would tell him that good came of disobedience in the end." Weston, who subsequently became the "Un-man," tempted the woman to disobey Maleldil's command not to stay on the fixed land, not to dwell there but

---

25. Lewis, *The Problem of Pain*, 84–85.
26. Lewis, *Mere Christianity*, 176.

Culpa—*Happy or Sad?*: Perelandra *and* The Marble Faun (Transformation)

always to return to the floating lands. When the evil spell of Weston is broken, however, Ransom delivers a forceful argument against the Fortunate Fall: "Of course good came of it. Is Maleldil a beast that we can stop His path, or a leaf that we can twist His shape? Whatever you do, He will make good of it. But not the good He had prepared for you if you had obeyed Him. That is lost for ever. The first King and first Mother of our world did the forbidden thing; and He brought good of it in the end. But what they did was not good; and what they lost we have not seen. And there were some to whom no good came nor ever will come." Then Ransom turns to Weston and challenges him to tell all—what good came to *him* if *he* rejoices that Maleldil became a man, what joys does *he* have, and what profit did *he* have when he made Maleldil and death "acquainted."

Later, Malacandra (Mars) tells Ransom, "... two creatures of the low worlds, two images of Maleldil ... step up that step at which your parents fell, and sit in the throne of what they were meant to be. It was never seen before. Because it did not happen in your world, a greater thing happened, but not this. Because the greater thing happened in Thulcandra [Earth], this and not the greater thing happens here." As Ransom stands looking at the sleeping Lady he longs to have seen "the great Mother of his own race thus, in her innocence and splendour. 'Other things, other blessings, other glories, ' he murmured. 'But never that. Never in all worlds, that. God can make good use of all that happens. But the loss is real.'"[27] The loss indeed is real; that truth cannot be gainsaid. It would seem that for Lewis, then, the Fall was both "unfortunate," because the disobedience resulted in undeniable, unspeakable, inexplicable loss, and "fortunate," because it resulted in great good—the Incarnation, Grace, and Redemption. In a 1958 letter Lewis wrote: "... what results from the Fall is not bad [not only bad?]—e.g. the Redemption results from it."[28]

Debate over the Fortunate Fall is no less prominent and perhaps even more extensive and intense in Hawthorne's *The Marble Faun* (British title: *Transformation*), which Lewis highly recommended to his friend Arthur Greeves. The novel, Hawthorne's longest, is set in Rome, not on floating islands of a pristine planet like Perelandra, although at one point the two American visitors felt "as if they had been thrown together on a desert island. Or, they seemed to have wandered, by some strange chance, out of the common world ..." One of the two Americans, a copyist painter, is

---

27. Lewis, *Perelandra*, 215, 120–21, 197, 152.
28. Lewis, Letter of 27 June 1958, *The Collected Letters of C. S. Lewis*, III, 959.

Hilda, repeatedly described as a "daughter of the Puritans," who claims to be "a poor, lonely girl, whom God has set here in an evil world, and given her only a white robe, and bid her wear it back to Him, as white as when she put it on." Her compatriot is Kenyon, a sculptor, a devout man who freely asserts that "Providence is infinitely good and wise"; though "the ways of Providence are utterly inscrutable . . . it doeth all things right! His will be done!" Similar to Lewis's description of Christianity as a hall with doors opening into various rooms[29] is Kenyon's analogy: "Christianity is a grand Cathedral, with divinely pictured windows. Standing without, you see no glory, nor can possibly imagine any; standing within, every ray of light reveals a harmony of unspeakable splendours!"[30] Lewis must have read this passage with great approbation!

A third character is the mysterious Miriam, also an artist, rumored variously to be the daughter and heiress of a great Jewish banker, a German princess, the offspring of a South American planter, and the lady of an English nobleman. The titular character, Donatello, a young Italian, is said to resemble the Faun of Praxiteles—"neither man nor animal, and yet no monster, but a being in whom both races meet, on friendly ground . . . , not supernatural, but just on the verge of Nature, and yet within it." He is "a singularly wild creature . . . [with] a great deal of animal nature in him; as if he had been born in the woods, and had run wild, all his childhood, and were as yet but imperfectly domesticated." Miriam surmises that "the Faun had no conscience, no remorse, no burthen on the heart, no troublesome recollections of any sort . . ." In his pristine innocence he is, in effect, a prelapsarian Adam, in what Miriam calls "this great mystery . . . , the story of the Fall of Man." But, in stark contrast to Lewis's triumphant Tinidril, this "Adam falls anew, and Paradise, heretofore in unfaded bloom, is lost again, and closed forever, with the fiery swords gleaming at its gates." When Miriam is stalked by a mysterious Model—"Spectre of the Catacomb," an "ill-omened" "Man-Demon" (rather like Lewis's demonic Un-man), an "ominous shadow," "some unspeakable evil," a "dark adversary," a "pertinacious Demon"[31]—the fawning Donatello, thinking Miriam's eyes bade him do so, casts the wretch off the precipice of the Tarpeian Rock. The victim is alleged to be a Capuchin monk named Antonio.

---

29. Lewis, *Mere Christianity*, xv-xvi.
30. Hawthorne, *The Marble Faun*, 373, 54, 362, 399, 466, 208, 413, 258, 306.
31. Ibid., 10, 13, 104, 13–14, 434, 204, 30–31, 93, 32, 140, 171, 108, 148.

Culpa—*Happy or Sad?*: Perelandra *and* The Marble Faun (Transformation)

Donatello's nefarious crime, though motivated by love, has a profound effect on all the characters, for, as the narrator states, "Every crime destroys more Edens than our own!" For example, Hilda, who witnesses the act, is so beset by guilt that this "daughter of the Puritans" seeks peace in a confessional in St. Peter's. For Donatello, the crime effects his "transformation" —"the glad Faun of [Kenyon's] imagination and memory [was] now transformed into a gloomy penitent . . ." To Kenyon "the growth of a soul" he imagined he witnessed in Donatello "seemed hardly worth the heavy price that it had cost, in the sacrifice of those simple enjoyments that were gone forever. A creature of antique healthfulness had vanished from the earth; and, in his stead, there was only one other morbid and remorseful man, among millions that were cast in the same indistinguishable mould." Earlier, Kenyon remarks to Donatello that "'as we grow older . . . [we] lose somewhat of our proximity to Nature. It is the price we pay for experience. . . .' 'A heavy price, then!'" Donatello responds.[32] Loss of innocence, the price to pay for experience, is a heavy price indeed! For further evidence, consult William Blake's *Songs of Innocence* and *Songs of Experience*, where "the modest Rose puts forth a thorn: / The humble Sheep a threatening horn." But does the prickly thorn then produce a bloom and the threatening wolf beget a lamb? Is the heavy price for experience worth it? Does good come from the weighty "transformation" Donatello undergoes? Is the Fall fortunate? These are the key questions raised by the novel, the same questions raised in Lewis's *Perelandra*, though in that novel Lady Eve does not fall, and Paradise is not lost.

Kenyon feels "that there was something lost, or something gained (he hardly knew which) that set the Donatello of today irreconcileably [sic] at odds with him of yesterday." What was lost seems all too clear, but what was gained, besides the rescue of Miriam from "the dark adversary"? Later, the narrator states that "in the black depths, the Faun had found a soul, and was struggling with it towards the light of Heaven." Still later, Kenyon tells Miriam, "Out of his bitter agony, a soul and intellect (I could almost say) have been inspired into him." Miriam, who earlier tells Hilda that because she (Hilda) has no sin nor any conception thereof she is "terribly severe" and needs "a sin to soften" her, wishes to tell Donatello that she (Miriam) "most wretched, who beguiled him into evil, might guide him to a higher innocence than that from which he fell." It is Kenyon who assures Miriam that Donatello is "one whom a terrible

---

32. Ibid., 212, 393–94, 250.

misfortune has begun to educate; it has taken him, and through your agency, out of a wild and happy state, which, within circumscribed limits, gave him joys that he cannot elsewhere find on earth."[33]

Subsequently, it is Miriam who speaks of Donatello's "growing intellectual power and moral sense . . . [for] a soul is being breathed into him; it is the Faun, but advancing towards a state of higher development." In her conversation with Kenyon, Miriam asks more forthrightly, "Was the crime—in which he and I were wedded—was it a blessing in that strange disguise? Was it a means of education, bringing a simple and imperfect nature to a point of feeling and intelligence, which it could have reached under no other discipline?" But at this point Kenyon demurs: "You stir up deep and perilous matter, Miriam . . . I dare not follow you into the unfathomable abysses, whither you are tending." Miriam says she delights "to brood on the verge of this great mystery . . . Was that very sin—into which Adam precipitated himself and all his race—was it the destined means by which, over a long pathway of toil and sorrow, we are to attain a higher, brighter, and profounder happiness, than our lost birthright gave? Will not this idea account for the permitted existence of sin, as no other theory can?" Kenyon, however, is appalled by this argument: "It is too dangerous, Miriam! I cannot follow you! . . . Mortal man has no right to tread on the ground where you now set your feet!" Miriam tells Kenyon to ask Hilda her view: "At least, she might conclude that Sin—which Man chose instead of Good—has been so beneficently handled by Omniscience and Omnipotence, that, whereas our dark Enemy sought to destroy us by it, it has really become an instrument most effective in the education of intellect and soul."[34] Miriam argues that perhaps the great omniscient, omnipotent God has so "beneficently handled" events that the sin which the dark enemy intended to use to destroy mankind would become the most effective instrument in the education of the minds and souls of humans. Again, Lewis must have read this assertion with great interest, for just over eighty years later he wrote that Milton's Satan hoped to pervert any good which God attempted but instead "was allowed to do all the evil he [wanted] and [found] that he [had] produced good. Those who will not be God's sons become His tools."[35] Are Milton and Hawthorne and Lewis saying that the Dark Enemy and sin are servants of God and good *malgre lui*?

33. Ibid., 217, 268, 209, 283, 321.
34. Ibid., 380, 434–35.
35. Lewis, *A Preface to Paradise Lost*, 68.

Culpa—*Happy or Sad?*: Perelandra *and* The Marble Faun (Transformation)

Kenyon later expresses his "perplexity" to Hilda: "Sin has educated Donatello, and elevated him. Is Sin, then—which we deem such a dreadful blackness in the Universe—is it, like Sorrow, merely an element of human education, through which we struggle to a higher and purer state than we could otherwise have attained? Did Adam fall, that we might ultimately rise to a far loftier Paradise than his?" But Hilda, daughter of the Puritans, responds negatively: "Oh, hush . . . This is terrible; and I could weep for you, if you indeed believe it. Do not you perceive what a mockery your creed makes, not only of all religious sentiment, but of moral law, and how it annuls and obliterates whatever precepts of Heaven are written deepest within us? You have shocked me beyond words!" Perhaps surprisingly, especially in view of all he said earlier, Kenyon recoils and retracts, admitting, "I never did believe it"; he asks Hilda's forgiveness, and he enjoins her to be his guide, counselor, and "inmost friend," pleading with her to guide him home,[36] much as Dimmesdale asked Hester, his "better angel," to "be strong" for him and to "advise [him] what to do,"[37] perhaps to guide him *away* from home. Kenyon's words are also reminiscent of Hawthorne's words to Sophia in many of his letters.

The question of which character is correct and which view is Hawthorne's has been much contested and debated in the criticism. Hyatt H. Waggoner, for example, concludes that Kenyon is much more of a spokesman for Hawthorne than is Miriam and that Hilda's perspective echoes his wife Sophia's "buoyant faith [which was] a needed counterbalance to [Hawthorne's] own dark questionings."[38] Similarly, Richard H. Brodhead concludes that "Kenyon's pronouncements on Donatello's case have about them that sententious gravity that tempts a reader to label them the Author's Message," yet it is Hilda who has the last word on the issue.[39] Agnes McNeill Donohue has noted that ". . . Kenyon speaks with a religious authority that is a curious blend of belief in the fortunate fall and Calvinist dogma," adding that "it seems to be Hawthorne's voice and reflects his own spiritual confusion and crisis of belief." She also states that because "Hilda has effectively damned Miriam and Donatello by refusing even to listen to the concept of the fortunate fall, . . . her hope in the final

---

36. Hawthorne, *The Marble Faun*, 460–61. Agnes McNeill Donohue dismisses Kenyon as "a whining, humbling Puritan schoolboy who wants to go home" (*Hawthorne: Calvin's Ironic Stepchild*, 294).
37. Hawthorne, *The Scarlet Letter*, 185, 180.
38. Waggoner, *Hawthorne: A Critical Study*, 213.
39. "Introduction," *The Marble Faun*, xix-xx.

sentence ["Hilda had a hopeful soul, and saw sunlight on the mountain-tops"] is based only upon the fact that she is a moral imbecile."[40]

Arlin Turner reflects the ambiguity of the issue in his comment that "the theme underlying the novel [is] that sin affords an otherwise impossible depth of insight into the meaning of life, and at the same time isolates the sinner from human associations,"[41] a view similar to Lewis's idea that the Fall is both "fortunate" and "unfortunate." Roy R. Male argues that "almost every page of the book indicates that without sin and suffering, moral growth rarely, if ever, results" and concludes that the tragic vision of Hawthorne's fiction lies in the fact that "in this imperfect world some rise by sin and some fall by virtue."[42] Yet another view is that the question is essentially unanswerable, ultimately an answer even being unnecessary: "Hawthorne's reason for introducing it [the fortunate fall] is probably to have it rejected and thereby to set the limits of what can be known about the archetypal situation he treats. Whether Donatello is better for having fallen and having renewed himself than he would have been had he stayed innocent is essentially an unanswerable question. And it is a question that does not need to be answered. For Hawthorne man has fallen; man does have the capacity to sin in his nature; and in treating the human condition as he viewed it, Hawthorne does not need to go beyond those postulates."[43]

Both Hawthorne and Lewis would seem to concur that although the Sovereign Deity is assuredly not the author of evil, he is able to bring good from it. Leonard J. Fick argues that there is nothing "to justify the belief that sin is the cause, rather than the occasion, of good. The actual cause of [Donatello's] soul's growth is the man himself, cooperating with God's grace; the sin provides him with an opportunity for initiating this growth . . . Hawthorne's position is clear: sin can, in the Providence of God be the *occasion*, not the *cause*, of good."[44] Hilda learns, on her visit to St. Peter's, that "there was access to the Divine

---

40. Donohue, *Hawthorne: Calvin's Ironic Stepchild*, 294–95. Barbara Wineapple says that "one can almost hear him [the narrator] snicker" at the final statement. She also states summarily that "Hilda is a prig" (*Hawthorne: A Life*, 325), countering Mark Van Doren's comment that "it is one of Hawthorne's minor triumphs that he saves Hilda from seeming to be a prig" (*Nathaniel Hawthorne: A Critical Biography*, 228).

41. Turner, *Nathaniel Hawthorne: An Introduction and Interpretation*, 107.

42. Male, *Hawthorne's Tragic Vision*, 175, 177.

43. Stubbs, "*The Marble Faun*: Hawthorne's Romance of the Adamic Myth," in J. Donald Crowley, Editor. *Nathaniel Hawthorne: A Collection of Criticism*, 110.

44. Fick, *The Light Beyond: A Study of Hawthorne's Theology*, 120–21.

Culpa—*Happy or Sad?*: *Perelandra* and *The Marble Faun* (Transformation)

Grace for every Christian soul,"[45] but there seems to be no evidence that the Faun has yet learned that lesson or yet experienced that grace.

Surely no work of *belles lettres* has ever treated the issue of *felix culpa* more extensively, more cogently, and more engagingly than do these two novels.[46] Hawthorne and Lewis each perceptively refers to the crucial doctrine of grace and its role, echoing the Apostle Paul: "Where sin abounded, grace abounded much more" (Romans 5:20). Hawthorne's narrator states that Hilda realizes that "there was access to the Divine Grace," and Lewis often referred to Grace, especially in his letters, noting, for example, that four of his "fallen," rebellious characters— "Eustace, Edmund, Jane, and Mark[—]are all meant to be recipients of Grace."[47] "Grace," *charis*, means so much more than the common definition, "unmerited favor." (It is actually favor *against* merit, for not only did humans *not deserve* redemption and eternal life but *deserved* eternal damnation.) It denotes God's undeserved favor that miraculously transforms the neg-

45. Hawthorne, *The Marble Faun*, 356.

46. It should be noted that implications of the Fortunate Fall appear in other works by Hawthorne as well. For example, Dimmesdale, by the "black trouble of the soul" achieved great power in his sacred office. "His intellectual gifts, his moral perceptions, his power of experiencing and communicating emotion, were kept in a state of preternatural activity by the prick and anguish of his daily life' (*The Scarlet Letter*, 130). In fact, as time went on, "a spirit as of prophecy had come upon him" as mightily as it did upon the old prophets of Israel . . . ; it was as if an angel, in his passage to the skies, had shaken his bright wings over the people for an instant, —at once a shadow and a splendor, —and had shed down a shower of golden truths" upon the people (226–27). As with Dimmesdale, the Rev. Mr. Hooper in "The Minister's Black Veil" ironically has greater power after he dons his black veil, symbol of secret sin: "A subtle power was breathed into his words . . . , [making it] greatly the most powerful effort that [his congregants] had ever heard from their pastor's lips" (*The Complete Short Stories of Nathaniel Hawthorne*, 33). Hyatt H. Waggoner has said that "My Kinsman, Major Molineux" "is perhaps the only story Hawthorne ever wrote in which there is a fall that is clearly fortunate" (*Hawthorne: A Critical Study*, 210). Perhaps this is true, for, as the gentleman tells Robin at the end of the tale, "perhaps, as you are a shrewd youth, you may rise in the world without the help of your kinsman . . ." (*The Complete Short Stories of Nathaniel Hawthorne*, 530). Though "Roger Malvin's Burial" does conclude "in a reunion with God and man after isolation . . . , whatever 'rise' there is here is a very sad one, [and] the vision of life it implies remains tragic" (Waggoner, 210).

47. Letter of 17 January 1953, *The Collected Letters of C. S. Lewis*, III, 282. Eustace Scrubb, an obnoxious boy who appears in *The Voyage of the "Dawn Treader*," has to be "un-dragoned." His cousin Edmund Pevensie betrayed his siblings to the White Witch in *The Lion, the Witch, and the Wardrobe*. Mark Studdock is a sociologist who is drawn into involvement with the diabolical N.I.C.E. in *That Hideous Strength*. Jane, Mark's wife, is a graduate student in English literature at Bracton College. Mark experiences "undeception" in his journey toward Christian conversion, rejoining Jane at the end of the novel.

ative into the positive, the unpleasing into the pleasing. Perhaps Lewis's most vivid example of this quality of grace is not just the removal of the lizard of lust from the shoulder of a man in *The Great Divorce* but the transformation of that hideous red lizard into a beautiful flying horse. In a letter Lewis said, "The metamorphosis of the lizard into the stallion was meant to symbolise perfect sublimation, after painful struggle and agonising surrender, not by ordinary psychological law but by supernatural Grace."[48] According to both writers, the Fall was "unfortunate" because it brought devastation and death, a plight which only supernatural Grace could remedy, but it was "fortunate" in that it occasioned the Incarnation and abounding Grace, which alone could transform the negative into the positive, the unpleasing into the pleasing, death into life. It transformed sin into the servant of goodness.[49]

---

48. Lewis, Letter of 13 February 1958, *The Collected Letters of C. S. Lewis*, III, 920. Redemption, Lewis wrote, "is not like teaching a horse to jump better and better but like turning a horse into a winged creature . . . it is not mere improvement but Transformation," a key word echoing Hawthorne's use (*Mere Christianity*, 216, 218).

49. Speaking of evading the presence of God, Lewis said, "Out of this evil comes a good" (*Letters to Malcolm: Chiefly on Prayer*, 75). "All the good in us comes from Grace," he wrote (Letter of 3 August 1953, *The Collected Letters of C. S. Lewis*, III, 355).

10

The Black Veil and the White: "The Minister's Black Veil," *The Blithedale Romance*, *Till We Have Faces*

OTHER WORKS BY HAWTHORNE and Lewis can be construed as companion pieces by virtue of their images and symbols. In two of Hawthorne's works—the early story "The Minister's Black Veil" (1835) and the later novel *The Blithedale Romance* (1852)—and in Lewis's novel *Till We Have Faces* (1956), the recurring image of the veil becomes symbolic and even metaphoric. Although there is no explicit evidence that Lewis was familiar with any of Hawthorne's short stories, for he never refers to any of them in his letters, diary, or essays, it is hard to believe he was not, given his great enthusiasm for two of the novels and his stated intention "to read all Hawthorne."[1] Lewis's familiarity with *The Blithedale Romance* is well documented by the numerous marginal notations (over eighty—in the form of vertical marks in margins, underlining, crossing out, writing over, and occasional marginal notations) in his copy of the novel (Edinburgh: William Paterson, 1885) housed in the Marion E. Wade Center at Wheaton College.

In an early Notebook entry Hawthorne contemplated "an essay on the misery of being always under a mask. A veil may be needful, but never a mask. Instances of people who wear masks in all classes of society, and never take them off even in the most familiar moments, though sometimes they may chance to slip aside."[2] Hawthorne himself apparently felt the needfulness of a veil, for in commenting on his guarded reticence he

---

1. Lewis, Letter of 29 November 1916, *They Stand Together: The Letters of C. S. Lewis to Arthur Greeves*, 153.

2. Hawthorne, *The American Note-Books*, 29-30.

said, "So far as I am a man of really individual attributes I veil my face," not being one of those authors "who serve up their own hearts, delicately fried, with brain sauce, as a titbit [sic] for their beloved public." Along with this veil of reserve, he often donned the veil he refers to earlier in the same piece—"a veil woven of intermingled gloom and brightness."[3] Lewis more clearly rejected facial barriers, noting that the idea of *Till We Have Faces* "was that a human being must become real before it can expect to receive any message from the superhuman . . . , being for good or ill itself, not any mask, veil or *persona*."[4]

Both writers imply a distinction between the veil and the mask, with the former having the more honorific connotation and even the more positive denotation. The mask is "invested with something at once of profound mystery and of the shameful, since anything that is so modified as to become 'something else' while still remaining the thing that it was, must inevitably be productive of ambiguity and equivocation . . . Secrecy tends towards transfiguration: it helps what-one-is to become what-one-would-like-to-be"[5] or what-one-would-like-to-be-thought. The mask is a covering intended to conceal identity, representing something one is not, a pretense, a disguise, a fabrication, a grotesque, sometimes humorous, false face. Poe's story is "Masque of the Red Death" not "Veil of the Red Death," and, of course, nuns "take the veil," not the mask.

References to masks appear a dozen times in *Till We Have Faces*, seven of which apply to the bird-masks worn by priests, especially Arnom, new priest of Ungit. Orual, who in narrating the story, presents her case against the gods, remarks that Arnom's "voice [was] strange out of the mask" and notes that "if he is still the Priest when he puts on his mask, perhaps he becomes a god while he wears it."[6] Later, as Queen she has her maid stitch her "a hood or mask of fine stuff, but such as could not be seen through, [having] two eye-holes and covered with the whole helmet . . . but," she says, "the mask made [her] look very dreadful, as a ghost might look." When she slays an enemy from Phars, she wept hard but kept her head well down so Bardia, captain of the guard and her loyal friend, would not see the tears dripping from under the mask.[7] The other two references to

---

3. Hawthorne, "The Old Manse," Preface, *Mosses from an Old Manse*, 44, 2.

4. Letter to Dorothea Conybeare, Cited in Hooper, *C. S. Lewis: A Companion & Guide*, 252.

5. Cirlot, *A Dictionary of Symbols*, 205.

6. Lewis, *Till We Have Faces*, 270, 107.

7. Ibid., 215, 216, 220.

the mask in Lewis's novel apply ironically to Psyche: when she is taken away to be sacrificed, Orual sees her as appearing like a painted, gilded, and be-wigged temple girl, "her eyes peering out of the heavy, lifeless mask, which they had made of her face, . . . [a] painted and gilded horror to poison [Orual's] last look at her."[8] Thus the mask in Lewis's novel is variously lifeless, secretive, restrictive, strange, alienating, portentous, formidable, ominous, dreadful, horrific.

The mask is referenced just twice in Hawthorne's *The Blithedale Romance*. In the first case, the narrator Miles Coverdale remarks that Zenobia is merely the lady's public name, "a sort of mask in which she comes before the world, retaining all the privileges of privacy—a contrivance, in short, like the white drapery of the Veiled Lady, only a little more transparent." Interestingly, the mask is here distinguished from the veil as being slightly more transparent, not opaque like Lewis's masks. The second reference is applied to Hollingsworth by Coverdale, who feels "as if the whole man were a moral and physical humbug; his wonderful beauty of face . . . might be removeable [sic] like a mask."[9] Thus the mask in Hawthorne's novel is secretive but less opaque than the veil, private, contrived, removable, deceptive, spectral.

Clearly, then, the veil is the predominant image and symbol in all three works. The veil "signifies the concealment of certain aspects of truth or of the deity."[10] The major function of the veil is to cover for the purpose of concealing, protecting, or enhancing the face. Its intent is to hide the real nature of something, with the ultimate result, whether intentional or not, of separating, alienating, estranging. A major motif in each of the three works is that of *concealing* and *revealing*, or *not revealing*. Significantly, the word *reveal* is derived from the Latin verb *revelare—re*, "back," plus *velum*, "veil"; "reveal" literally means "to draw back the veil" or perhaps "to cover again *with* a veil." A key issue in each of the three works is whether the veil will, in fact, be drawn back to reveal who or what is hidden.

Hawthorne's "The Minister's Black Veil" deals with the Reverend Mr. Hooper, who appears at his church one Sunday with a black crepe veil covering his face and refuses to remove it for the rest of his life, even at the urging of a delegation from his church, his fiancée Elizabeth, and a fellow clergyman present at Parson Hooper's death. Suggesting an

8. Ibid., 80-81.
9. Hawthorne, *The Blithedale Romance*, 42, 107.
10. Cirlot, *A Dictionary of Symbols*, 359.

historical basis, Hawthorne included a note referring to another clergyman, Joseph Moody of York, Maine, who had accidentally killed a friend and wore a veil until his death, apparently hiding his face in ignominy and penance, but Hawthorne notes that Hooper's veil has a different import. The author designates the story as a parable, the moral apparently being that every person hides secret sin (also the subject of the parson's sermon the very day he dons the veil), for Hooper asks Elizabeth, ". . . if I cover it [his face] for secret sin, what mortal might not do the same?" and in his dying moments he says, ". . . lo! on every visage a Black Veil."[11] In the story's nine pages the veil is referenced sixty-five times, with forty-one of those specifying the veil as *black*, along with such adjectives as "gloomy," "dismal," "awful," "terrible," "horrible," and "dreadful" (the latter term used by Orual to describe her mask).

Hawthorne is intent on stressing the symbolic role of the veil, for the narrator refers to it as a "mysterious emblem," "now an appropriate emblem" (at the funeral of a young lady), "his mysterious emblem"; from the perspective of the congregants it is "the symbol of a fearful secret between him and them"; and Hooper himself refers to it as "a type and symbol," "a sign," a "material emblem," and "the symbol beneath which [he] lived."

Another image or gesture repeated throughout the story is Parson Hooper's melancholy smile behind the veil, a faint, sad smile that flickered and glimmered faintly, even lingering on the lips of his corpse. Why is this clergyman constantly smiling behind his "double fold of black crepe" as his congregants recoil in mystery, suspicion, perturbation, and dread? Surely, like the ironic laughter in so many of Hawthorne's stories, what he often calls cachinnation, the parson's simper, unlike the Cheshire Cat's perpetual grin, is not due to whimsical silliness but rather to the ironic incongruity Hooper perceives between his overpowering awareness of secret sin and the congregants' seeming unawareness of it,

---

11. Hawthorne, "The Minister's Black Veil," *The Complete Short Stories of Nathaniel Hawthorne*, 36, 39. In his review of Hawthorne's *Twice-Told Tales*, Edgar Allan Poe praised "The Minister's Black Veil" as "a masterly composition" but concluded that "the *moral* put into the mouth of the dying minister will be supposed to convey the *true* import of the narrative; and that a crime of dark dye (having reference to the 'young lady'), has been committed, is a point which only minds congenial with that of the author will perceive." This interpretation might serve to explain two accounts—one of "a superstitious old woman" who reported that when the minister bent over the young lady's coffin and his veil hung down from his forehead, the corpse had slightly shuddered, the other a couple who fancy that they had seen the minister and the maiden's spirit walking hand in hand.

between their honorific perception of him and his own sense of guilt, between the uncondemning external appearance and the damning internal condemnation of his conscience.

Of particular importance in the story are the effects of the Parson's wearing of the veil and his refusal to take it off. If it was initially a moving object lesson of sorrow for sin, penance for secret sin, and even a sign of penitence for great guilt, ironically giving him a subtle power in his preaching, his adamant refusal to remove the veil has numerous dire effects. For example, "it threw its obscurity between him and the holy page as he read the Scriptures," and it "lay heavily on his uplifted countenance" when he prayed. For Puritans, who valued the Holy Scriptures and prayer so much, what could be worse? Further, the veil seemed to dim the light of the candles at the wedding, and it separates Hooper from the community of mankind and, most tragically, from Elizabeth, his beloved fiancée, enveloping "the poor minister, so that love or sympathy could never reach him." It "separated him from cheerful brotherhood and woman's love, and kept him in the saddest of all prisons, his own heart, and still it lay upon his face, as if to deepen the gloom of his darksome chamber, and shade him from the sunshine of eternity."[12] What seemed initially to be a sincere, legitimate attempt to objectify his innermost conviction of personal guilt and to graphically illustrate the universality of secret sin became an unrelenting obsession, a deleterious *idée fixe*, a hopeless monomania. Perhaps Hawthorne was presenting Parson Hooper as synecdoche, a trope in which a part signifies the whole, for the purpose of indicting the Puritans for their alleged obsession and preoccupation with sin and guilt. Eminent Puritan clergy, such as John Owen, Richard Baxter, Thomas Watson, John Flavel et al. would undoubtedly have counseled Parson Hooper with the Holy Writ that his veil obscured: "Thou hast placed our iniquities before Thee, our secret sins in the light of Thy presence." As Moses says in this prayer, no one can hide his sins from the Almighty, for "the eyes of the Lord are in every place, watching the evil and the good." Further applicable is this passage from a psalm by David: "Who can understand his errors? Cleanse me from secret [hidden] faults. Keep back thy servant also from presumptuous sins; Let them not have dominion over me. Then I shall be blameless, And I shall be acquitted of great transgression."[13] According to the Psalmist, a simple prayer of

---

12. Ibid., 32, 34, 37, 38.
13. Psalm 90:8, Proverbs 15:3, Psalm 19:12-13.

repentance will bring forgiveness and cleansing—even to a minister with a black veil, which he could then remove.

Miles Coverdale, in Hawthorne's *The Blithedale Romance*, remarks to Zenobia that "it is really impossible to hide anything, in this world, to say nothing of the next,"[14] a key statement applicable to all three works being considered here. Hawthorne based the novel on his brief stay at utopian, reformist Brook Farm in West Roxbury, Massachusetts, for about eight months in 1841. The novel, like Lewis's *Till We Have Faces,* employs a first-person narrator, the only one of Hawthorne's novels to do so. The narrator is Miles Coverdale, a reclusive minor poet who describes his role as resembling that of the Chorus in a classic play. One critic describes him as "a Hawthorne manqué [and] the most intriguing and important character in the novel"[15]; another says he is melancholy and distrustful . . . , a caviling poet [and] perpetual loner, a prurient bachelor who . . . believes he can best hold himself together by holding himself apart"[16]; yet another summarily labels him "an ass."[17] It may be valid to call him a hypocrite, as someone does, that is, a stage actor wearing a mask and pretending to be someone he is not, living up to his name—*Coverdale* in *Blithedale*—perhaps "covering" more in "happy valley" than he uncovers.

The other major characters include Hollingsworth, originally a blacksmith, currently "a modern philanthropist" intent on the reformation of criminals, an aspiration that results in his "prolonged fiddling upon one string, such multiform presentation of one idea!" Like Aylmer, Hooper, Ethan Brand, Rappaccini, and others, he has, according to Coverdale, "completely immolated himself to that one idea of his." Thus "he was not altogether human," the narrator says; "this is always true of those men who have surrendered themselves to an over-ruling purpose . . . They have no heart, no sympathy, no reason, no conscience. They will keep no friend, unless he make himself the mirror of their purpose; they will smite and slay you, and trample your dead corpse under foot

---

14. Hawthorne, *The Blithedale Romance*, 157.

15. Donohue, *Hawthorne: Calvin's Ironic Stepchild*, 114.

16. Wineapple, *Hawthorne: A Life*, 247. Wineapple also refers to this work as "a psychological roman a clef," that is, a novel in which actual persons are presented as fictional, in this case, Coverdale and Hawthorne, perhaps Zenobia and Margaret Fuller, perhaps Priscilla and Hawthorne's sister Louisa and perhaps his wife Sophia.

17. Van Doren, *Hawthorne*, 190. Van Doren concludes that "Miles Coverdale not only tells his story badly—so badly that when he is not forcing scenes he is suppressing them altogether, with the result that we do not know what the story is—but sports and luxuriates in the role of spectator until we lose patience with him . . ."

...."[18] Hollingsworth's monomania for reformation leads to, or is motivated by, his overweening egotism, described variously as "terrible," "all-devouring," "dark, self-delusive," "huge." To Coverdale, he is "a wretch," having "a heart of ice." To Zenobia, he is "but a monster! A cold, heartless, self-beginning and self-ending piece of mechanism!" "You are a better masquerader," she tells him, "than the witches and gipsies [sic] yonder, for your disguise is a self-deception."[19]

If Hollingsworth's "veil" is self-deception and his philanthropic project, Zenobia's is her pseudonym, "her public name [which is] a sort of mask in which she comes before the world, retaining all the privileges of privacy . . ." She is a dark-haired beauty with "as much native pride as any queen would have known what to do with," a person of "pride and pomp," of "pride and strength," a prelapsarian Eve, an enchantress with a magnificent flower in her hair as a talisman, a "sorceress . . . fair enough to tempt Satan with a force reciprocal to his own." When Coverdale encounters Zenobia in the forest before the night of her suicide by drowning, she warns him, "When you next hear of Zenobia, her face will be behind the black-veil; so look your last at it now—for all is over!"[20] Essentially she exchanges one veil for another, the veil of secrecy and deception for the veil of death, echoing Shelley's words from *Prometheus Unbound*: "Death is the veil which those who live call life: / They sleep, and it is lifted."[21]

Coverdale learns near the end of the novel that Priscilla, the "pale, large-eyed little woman," is Zenobia's half-sister and the mysterious Veiled Lady. She is manipulated and victimized by the diabolical Professor Westervelt, who uses her in his magical exhibitions, requiring her to wear a silvery veil, which is touted as "an enchantment, having been dipt . . .with the fluid medium of spirits." Is she a genuine prophetess, a seeress with spiritual intimations, or a charlatan behind that magic veil? Zenobia relates the legend of "The Silvery Veil," essentially a microcosm of the novel. Like a myth or folk tale, it relates how a skeptical young gentleman aspires to solve the mystery of the Veiled Lady. She tells him

---

18. Hawthorne, *The Blithedale Romance*, 56, 63, 78, 159, 88-89. The description of Hollingsworth's lack of heart, sympathy, reason, and conscience echoes the similar description of the Old Inspector in The Custom House Introduction to *The Scarlet Letter*—"My conclusion was that he had no soul, no heart, no mind; nothing, as I have already said but instincts . . ." (17).

19. Hawthorne, *The Blithedale Romance*, 202, 197.

20. Ibid., 42, 47, 46, 48, 115, 49, 69, 194, 204.

21. Shelley, *Prometheus Unbound*, III, 3, 114-15.

Part IV: Companion Pieces

that her lips are forbidden to reveal the secret behind the veil, but she offers a condition—agree to meet her virgin lips where her breath stirs the veil and she will be his with never more a veil between them. When he refuses, imagining the lips of a dead girl, the jaws of a skeleton, or a monster's mouth, she makes another offer—he may lift the veil but she will thereafter be his evil fate with never more a taste of happiness. Preferring to lift the veil first, he forcibly grasps it, flings it upward, then casts it to the floor—and catches a fleeting glimpse of a pale, beautiful face, which then disappears, leaving him to mourn and long for it evermore. In the legend's coda, the pale, mysterious maiden vanishes, then attaches herself to a sympathetic woman in a group of visionary people seeking better lives. The sympathetic woman subsequently meets a bearded man in the woods, who offers her a silvery veil, which he calls "a spell" and "a powerful enchantment," instructing her to throw the veil over the head of a secret foe, stamp her foot, and cry out, "Arise, Magician, here is the Veiled Lady," whereupon he will rise up through the earth to seize her and make her safe. The sympathetic woman subsequently finds the pale, shadowy maiden among the visionary group seeking better lives, throws the veil over the maiden's head, stamps her foot, and invokes the dark Magician, who had bartered away his soul like Faust and now seizes the Veiled Lady to be his bond-slave forever. Zenobia concludes her legend by performing the magic ritual, flinging silver gauze over the head of Priscilla, who, making no attempt to remove the veil, promptly faints.[22]

Ten chapters later, the villainous Westervelt presents a discourse about a new era that would unite all souls in a one-world brotherhood, after which he presents the Veiled Lady, "enveloped in a long veil of silvery whiteness," saying she "beholds the Absolute" and boasting that no one but himself could persuade her to lift the veil or rise out of her chair. At that point, Hollingsworth, who had mounted the platform, bids the Veiled Lady to come to him, assuring her safety, whereupon she casts off the veil, utters a shriek, and flees to Hollingsworth and escapes the dark Magician's power. Later, at the grave of Zenobia, however, Coverdale notes that the happiness in Priscilla's "fair and quiet countenance" is "veiled."[23]

Hyatt H. Waggoner sees Priscilla as Hawthorne's "redemptive character, whose love will save Hollingsworth if anything can. She is, despite the veil thrust upon her in her role as the Veiled Lady, the only major

22. Hawthorne, *The Blithedale Romance*, 73, 185, 122-23.
23. Ibid., 214.

character who does not either wear a veil by choice or manifest spiritual and intellectual pride. She is the only character motivated consistently by love."[24] In point of fact, Priscilla is motivated much of the time by fear for her safety, by longing to escape the manipulative power of Westervelt, by desire to establish relationships with the group, and by wishing to cast off the restrictive veil. She "redeems" no one, not even herself, being too passive, too effete, too victimized, too shrinking. Coverdale "confesses" in the final chapter (which appeared in the first edition but not in the manuscript) that he was in love with Priscilla, but this is no great revelation, for the perceptive reader will recall that in chapter XXII, he then stated: "Priscilla! I love her best—I love her only!—but with shame, not pride. So dim, so pallid, so shrinking . . ."[25] One needs only to compare and contrast Priscilla with Orual or Phoebe or Hilda to recognize her passivity and effeteness.

With nearly thirty references to the Veiled Lady and at least thirty-five other references to the veil, which is an archetype expanding to metaphor, the novel deals with re-veiling more and revealing less, with hiding more and showing less, with covering more and exposing less. Perhaps Hawthorne is suggesting that because the veil separates and isolates individuals, removal of the veil is a significant prerequisite to any success of utopian reform and community of brotherhood and sisterhood: how can we meet face to face in community till we have faces?

In another application of the veil image, Hawthorne ponders that in Nature "there is far more of the picturesque, more truth to native and characteristic tendencies, and vastly greater suggestiveness, in the back view of a residence, whether in town or country, than in its front. *The latter is always artificial; it is meant for the world's eye, and is therefore a veil and a concealment. Realities keep in the rear . . .*"[26] The veil, he suggests, is artificial, often concealing the realities of Nature, the picturesque, the truth.

Another application presents the veil in a less pejorative, more ambiguous sense. In one of the conversations on the role of women, Coverdale states that "in the better order of things, Heaven grant that the ministry of souls may be left in charge of women! The gates of the

---

24. Waggoner, *Hawthorne: A Critical Study*, 202.

25. Hawthorne, *The Blithedale Romance*, 179.

26. Ibid., 147-48. Emphasis added. Gwendolyn Brooks expresses a similar idea in "a song in the front yard": "I've stayed in the front yard all my life. / I want a peek at the back / Where it's rough and untended and hungry weed grows. / A girl gets sick of a rose" (Brooks, *Selected Poems*, 6).

Blessed City will be thronged with the multitude that enter in, when that day comes! The task belongs to woman. God meant it for her." (Lewis marked this passage in his copy of the novel.) Coverdale continues: "He has endowed her with the religious sentiment in its utmost depth and purity, refined from that gross, intellectual alloy, with which every masculine theologian—*save only One, who merely veiled Himself in mortal and masculine shape, but was, in truth, divine*—has been prone to mingle it."[27] Hawthorne perceives the Incarnation as a mere veil of the truly divine. Surely Lewis would have relished Hawthorne's unequivocal assertion of the Incarnation—which Lewis called "the Grand Miracle," the "very center of Christianity"—and the divinity of Christ.

Hawthorne, for his part, would surely have appreciated Lewis's *Till We Have Faces*, especially for its extensive use of the veil image (over forty-five references). Lewis's novel, subtitled *A Myth Retold*, is Lewis's retelling of the story of Cupid and Psyche from the *Metamorphoses* or *The Golden Ass* of Apuleius (Lucius Apuleius Platonicus). Whereas Hawthorne functioned as myth-maker in creating the myth of the Veiled Lady, Lewis functioned as myth-user in reinterpreting an old extant myth. In various letters, Lewis stated that he considered it his best book: "I think it much my best book but not many people agree."[28] Again he wrote: " . . . that book, which I consider far and away the best book I have written, has been my one big failure both with the critics and with the public."[29] Apparently many readers found the novel opaque, difficult to understand, very different from his other fiction. Lewis, however, perhaps relished it so much because it represents his most extensive effort to relate Christian truth by means of classical myth or to relate myth from a Christian perspective,[30] because his future wife, Joy Davidman, reportedly offered him criticisms and valuable advice during a weekend stay at The Kilns,[31]

---

27. Hawthorne, *The Blithedale Romance*, 127.

28. Lewis, Letter of 7 August 1957, *The Collected Letters of C. S. Lewis*, III, 873.

29. Ibid., Letter of 26 August 1960, III, 1181.

30. Few novels have been so successful in presenting Christian truth by using classical myth. Critical opinion of Lewis's novel has changed somewhat in recent years, becoming more positive and honorific. Another outstanding novel which effectively uses Greek myth vis-à-vis realism is John Updike's *The Centaur*, published in 1963, the year of Lewis's death. One wonders how Lewis might have responded to Updike's masterful juxtaposing of the noblest Centaur and George Caldwell, general science teacher at Olinger High School, sometimes within the same sentence.

31. The novel is dedicated to Joy Davidman, who perhaps played a greater role in writing the novel than has been realized.

The Black Veil and the White

and because the story and its themes had captivated Lewis as early as 1922, when he was twenty-four and an undergraduate at Oxford. In a diary entry for 7 May of that year he wrote: "Sat in the garden, writing a passage for a new version of 'Psyche' in blank verse, not without some success . . ." On 23 November of that year he noted: "After lunch I went out for a walk up Shotover, thinking how to make a masque or play of Psyche and Caspian." Again on 9 September of 1923 he wrote: "My head was full of my old idea of a poem on my own version of the Cupid and Psyche story in which Psyche's sister would not be jealous, but unable to see anything but moors when Psyche showed her the Palace. I have tried it twice before, once in couplet and once in ballad form."[32]

Thinking that most readers would probably not know or remember the myth of Psyche and Cupid, Lewis wisely included a note at the end of the book,[33] summarizing the story, along with his central alterations. In both Roman and Greek legend, Psyche, personification of the soul, was a king's daughter whose exquisite beauty aroused the jealousy of Venus / Aphrodite, who ordered her son Eros / Cupid to arouse Psyche's love for a worthless mortal, but Cupid fell in love with her himself and carried her off to an sumptuous palace, where he visited her only at night. Rather like Hawthorne's Veiled Lady, Cupid "veiled" himself to hide his identity by visiting Psyche only in the dark. He warned her never to seek to look upon his face, but her jealous sisters goaded her curiosity, causing her to light a lamp while Cupid was sleeping, and a drop of hot oil fell on him, whereupon he awoke, was angry, rebuked her, and disappeared. Wholly distraught, Psyche wandered everywhere in search of her lover, eventually appearing in the temple of Aphrodite, who imposed upon her three tasks meant to be impossible, but with the secret aid of Cupid she accomplished them, was reconciled with Aphrodite, forgiven by and united with Cupid, and apotheosized and immortalized by Jupiter / Zeus.

---

32. Lewis, *All My Road Before Me: The Diary of C. S. Lewis*, 31, 142, 266. In several letters to Jocelyn Gibb, managing director of Geoffrey Bles, his publisher, Lewis made recommendations of art work for the dust jacket, mentioning sculpture from the Temple of Aphaia on the island of Aegina. One wonders if he knew of "The Story of Cupid & Psyche" by del Salaio in the Fitzwilliam Museum in Cambridge, or for that matter Antonio Canova's great sculpture "Cupid & Psyche" in the Louvre or works by Raphael, Fragonard, David, Burne-Jones, Rodin, Munch, Sargent, Dulac, and others.

33. Lewis wisely insisted that the note should come at the end of the book: " . . . it *must* come at the end, not (like a preface) at the beginning" (Letter of 27 April 1956, *The Collected Letters of C. S. Lewis*, III, 745).

Part IV: Companion Pieces

In a letter Lewis explains his changes to the story: "My version of Cupid & Psyche. Apuleius got it all wrong. The elder sister (I reduce her to one) couldn't *see* Psyche's palace when she visited her. She saw only rock & heather. When P. said she was giving her noble wine, the poor sister saw & tasted only spring water. Hence her dreadful problem: 'is P. mad or am I blind?' As you see, tho' I didn't start from that, it is the story of every nice, affectionate agnostic whose dearest one suddenly 'gets religion', or even every luke warm [sic] Christian whose dearest gets a Vocation. Never, I think, treated sympathetically by a Christian writer before. I do it all thro' the mouth of the elder sister."[34]

Psyche's elder half-sister Orual, called Maia by Psyche, relates the story, her complaint against the gods, inquiring why they dealt unjustly with her, why they gave her Psyche to love and then took her away, why the story they relate is false (saying the sisters *saw* the palace and were jealous of Psyche), why they hid or veiled the truth, why holy places must be dark places—essentially spitting in her face. The novel, much like Hawthorne's *The Blithedale Romance*, deals with veiling and unveiling, hiding and revealing, covering and exposing.

At least four individuals wear veils. The first is Orual's stepmother, who comes to the bridal chamber as "thickly veiled" as Orual and her sisters, who take off the new Queen's veil, revealing her beautiful but terrified face. Another is the judge who adjudicates Orual's complaint against the gods, his person "covered from crown to toe in sweepy black," his face heavily veiled, symbolizing the obscuring of truth. Psyche herself, named Istra in her native Glome, is represented in her temple by an image wearing a black veil: "The thing that marred [the image] was a band or scarf of some black stuff tied round the head of the image so as to hide its face—much like my own [Orual's] own veil, but that mine was white."[35] The priest explains the ritual to Orual: when Istra completes the

---

34. Ibid., Letter of 2 April 1955, III, 590. The blind insensitivity of Orual parallels the experience of Diggle the dwarf in Lewis's *The Last Battle*, published in the same year as *Till We Have Faces* (1956). Instead of beautiful sky, trees, and flowers, the dwarfs "see" only a "pitch-black, poky, smelly, little hole of a stable." Instead of fresh, damp, aromatic violets that Lucy holds to his nose, Diggle smells "a lot of filthy stable-litter" with a thistle in it. Instead of the glorious feast prepared by Aslan, the dwarfs perceive only "the sort of things you might find in a stable"—hay, a bit of an old turnip, and raw cabbage head. Instead of rich red wine they taste only "dirty water out of a trough that a donkey's been at." Imprisoned in their own minds, they are "so afraid of being taken in that they can not be taken out" (*The Last Battle*, 144–47). Fortunately, Orual's eyes are opened, and she sees the real thing.

35. Lewis, *Till We Have Faces*, 243, 12, 289.

hard tasks she becomes a goddess and they take off her black veil during spring and summer, but when harvest comes and the god flies away, they veil her again all winter, the veil symbolizing Istra's / Psyche's separation, alienation from Cupid.

It is Orual who is most often veiled; she is Lewis's Veiled Queen as Priscilla is Hawthorne's Veiled Lady, but for quite different reasons and with different effects. She covers her face with a veil for at least six different reasons. First and initially, the veil symbolizes her attempt to hide her perceived ugliness. When the priest of Ungit (Aphrodite or Venus) asks, "Are the young women to be veiled or unveiled?" the King, father of Psyche and Orual, laughs and replies, "Do you think I want my queen frightened out of her sense? Veils of course. And good thick veils too," and Orual notes, ". . . I think that was the first time I clearly understood that I am ugly." Later, as Queen of Glome, she, still veiled, encounters Prince Trunia of Phars, who says he never lets a pretty girl pass without a kiss, to which Orual replies: "'You've good eyes if you can see beauty in this face,' . . . turning it on him to make sure he saw the blank wall of the veil." Here the veil again hides and imposes a formidable wall of separation. Later still, after the death of the loyal guard Bardia, whom she had loved, veiled Queen Orual visits the widow, Ansit, and, sensing jealousy, pulls aside her veil and cries, "Look, look, you fool! . . . Are you jealous of this?"[36]

Though Orual's father, King Trom, initially demanded "good thick veils," later when he sees her veiled, he shouts, "Now, girl, what's this? Hung your curtains up, eh? Were you afraid we'd be dazzled by your beauty? Take off that frippery!" Orual's veil is hardly a showy display of cheap, tawdry, gaudy apparel! After the King's death, Orual has a dream in which her father appears and when she starts to put on her veil, he says, "None of that folly, do you hear?"[37] He realizes *sub specie aeternitatis* how foolish and futile it is to attempt to hide one's natural features.

Orual also wears the veil for secrecy. She remarks that, like all the country women, she had gone "bareface," but on her two journeys up the Mountain to find Psyche, she "had worn a veil because [she] wished to be secret. [She] now determined that [she] would go always veiled [and] kept this rule, within doors and without, ever since." She wears the veil to hide her identity, to be unknown, but after some years, when she is Queen, a new thought occurs to her: "My veil was no longer a means to be unknown.

---

36. Ibid., 11, 191, 262.
37. Ibid., 181, 274.

Part IV: Companion Pieces

It revealed me; all men knew the veiled Queen. My disguise now would be to go barefaced; there was hardly anyone who had seen me unveiled. So, for the first time in many years, I went out barefaced; showed that face which many had said, more truly than they could know, was too dreadful to be seen. It would have shamed me no more to go buff-naked."[38] Such irony would surely have appealed to Hawthorne: the veil, worn for years as a means of being unknown, has become her distinguishing feature, revealing immediately who she is, so her new "disguise" is to go barefaced.

Another motivation for wearing the veil grew out of one of its effects: its intriguing mystery. Wild stories spread about what the veil hid, surely nothing so mundane as the face of an ugly woman, but rather a beauty so dazzling that if men saw it the world would go mad, or a beauty so exquisite that Ungit was jealous and would blast her if she went barefaced, or something monstrously frightening, or perhaps no face at all, just emptiness behind the veil. The mystery of not knowing what was behind the veil, as in the case of Hawthorne's Veiled Lady, created awe. "The upshot of all this nonsense was that I became something very mysterious and awful." The awe leads to another effect and accompanying motivation—fear. The Queen of the territory of Essur "was manifestly terrified by my veil," Orual says, "and by the stories she had heard of me."[39]

Still another effect of the veil and motivation for wearing it is the sense of strength and power it gives. Orual specifies that her strength lay in two things—The Fox and Bardia as counselors and her veil. Because her face was invisible "people began to discover all manners of beauties in [her] voice." In one of her confrontations with her father the King, Orual says, "To see his face while he could not see mine seemed to give me a kind of power." "It's hard if I'm scolded both for my face and for hiding it," she says to her father, "putting no hand to the veil." She concludes, "He never struck me, and I never fear him again. And from that day I never gave back an inch before him."[40] The veil not only evoked fear in others but also removed fear in herself.

After the initial imposition of the veil by the King, Orual herself chooses to wear the veil (with at least six references to her donning it, re-veiling), but at times she chooses to take it off (at least six references to her veil being taken off—before Psyche, when she ate, before Ansit, and

38. Ibid., 180, 278.
39. Ibid., 228-29, 239.
40. Ibid., 227-28, 181-82.

when the veil and all her clothes are torn from her before the judge). Often Orual refers to what is behind her veil, what she calls "endless sleights and contrivances behind my veil," her weeping behind the veil (contrasting Rev. Mr. Hooper's perpetual smiling), and, of course, her common "bareface"[41] (contrasting Psyche's "young boldface" and "brightface"). Orual learns that she "could mend [her] soul no more than [her] face [unless] the gods helped." But why did they not help? She finishes writing her complaint against the gods, and when her case is heard she comes to realize that, ironically, the complaint was itself the answer.[42]

The key idea of the novel is a framed in a question: "How can they [the gods, supernatural beings] meet us [mortals, humans] face to face [*tete-a-tete*, head-to-head, in private, intimate interchange] till we have faces [become real, without veils, masks, or *personae*]?"[43] In her final paragraph, Orual expresses another key truth she has learned: "I know now, Lord, why you utter no answer. You are yourself the answer. Before your face questions die away. What other answer would suffice?" Mortals are to seek the face of God—"Seek the Lord and His strength; *seek His face continually*"[44]—and come to meet Him face-to-face, with all veils removed. But how, specifically, is one to remove the veil? Lewis gives some indication, for example, in *Letters to Malcolm: Chiefly on Prayer*, where he equates "unveiling" with prayer and confession: "For it is by the Holy Spirit that we cry 'Father.' *By unveiling, by confessing our sins and 'making known' our requests*, we assume the high rank of persons before Him. And He, descending, becomes a Person to us."[45] The Apostle Paul in speaking of Moses, who wore a veil when he descended from Mt. Sinai so the Israelites might be protected from the sight of glory fading, states that "to this day whenever Moses is read, a veil lies over their heart; but *whenever a man turns to the Lord, the veil is taken away* . . . and we all,

---

41. Lewis preferred the title *Bareface*, but "the publishers wouldn't have that because they said people wd. think it promised a book about Red Indians!" (Letter of 15 March 1958, *The Collected Letters of C. S. Lewis*, III, 924).

42. Lewis, *Till We Have Faces*, 266, 282, 294.

43. Ibid., 294.

44. Psalm 105:4. Emphasis added.

45. Lewis, *Letters to Malcolm: Chiefly on Prayer*, 21. Emphasis added. In the next paragraph, Lewis clarifies and qualifies his statement: "But I should not have said 'becomes.' In Him there is no becoming. He reveals Himself as Person: or reveals that in Him which is Person."

with unveiled face behold as in a mirror the glory of the Lord, are being transformed into the same image from glory to glory . . ."⁴⁶

Lewis said in a letter to Clyde S. Kilby that "Psyche is an instance of the *anima naturaliter Christiana* making the best of the Pagan religion she is brought up in and thus being guided (but always 'under the cloud', always in terms of her own imagination or that of her people) towards the true God. She is in some ways like Christ not because she is a symbol of Him but because every good man or woman is like Christ. What else could they be like? But of course my interest is primarily in Orual."⁴⁷

With his primary interest being in Orual, note how Lewis ends the novel. Whereas Hawthorne's Coverdale adds a final chapter or coda in which he "confesses" his love for Priscilla, Lewis's Orual "ends" her narrative by dying in mid-sentence⁴⁸: "Long did I hate you [Lord], long did I fear you. I might—" Arnom, priest of Aphrodite, has the final word, having saved Orual's manuscript, noting that Orual's head must have fallen forward on the document as she died, making the markings illegible. As the reader is challenged earlier to judge between Orual and the gods, so at the end the reader is left with the challenge of completing the sentence, with Orual's implied intention. Could it be: "I might yet requite [make repayment, make amends for] all the wrong and injuries I have done"? Or perhaps: "I might yet repent, believe, and be saved"? Either or both of these possibilities seem to be in the spirit of what Lewis said in a letter: "Psyche has a vocation and becomes a saint. Orual lives the practical life and *is, after many sins, saved*."⁴⁹ In any event, in her dying moment, unlike that of Parson Hooper, her veil is gone—and she can meet face-to-face with the Lord because she has a baldface, a boldface, a brightface at last!

---

46. II Corinthians 3:13, 15-16, 18. Emphasis mine. Interestingly, the Greek word translated "transformed" in verse 18 is the verb *metamorphoo*, source of *metamorphosis*, which appears in Apuleius's title *Metamorphoses*.

47. Lewis, Letter of 10 February 1957, *The Collected Letters of C. S. Lewis*, III, 830. The Latin phrase is borrowed from *Apologeticus* of Tertullian (160-240): "O witness of the soul naturally Christian" or "soul by nature Christian."

48. Orual at one point intended to drown herself as Hawthorne's Zenobia did, but she heeds the god, who urges her to "die before you die. There is no chance after," meaning "the death of our passions and desires and vain opinions" (279, 281).

49. Lewis, Letter of 7 August 1957, *The Collected Letters of C. S. Lewis*, III, 874.

11

Allegory to the 3rd Power: "The Celestial Railroad" and *The Pilgrim's Regress*

HAWTHORNE AND LEWIS SHARED an intense ambivalence toward allegory, at once admiring its value when used responsibly by writers and understood properly by readers but also rejecting and even deprecating it for its dangers of limitation and misapplication. The term itself is derived from the Greek *allos*, "other" or "else," plus *agoreuein*, "to speak in an assembly" or *agora*, "marketplace"—literally "to speak of 'other' in public assembly," hence a story that characterizes an abstract idea in terms of a concrete image. Images, objects, persons, places, events, or actions represent abstract ideas.

Lewis himself provided some of the best definitions of *allegory*. For example, in a 1958 letter he argues that the Narnia Chronicles and *Perelandra* are not allegories at all: "By an allegory I mean a composition (whether pictorial or literary) in wh. immaterial realities are represented by feigned physical objects e.g. . . . in Bunyan, a giant represents Despair."[1] In another letter Lewis distinguishes *allegory* from *myth*: ". . . a good myth (i.e. a story out of which ever varying meanings will grow for different readers and in different ages) is a higher thing than an allegory (into which one meaning has been put). Into an allegory a man can put only what he already knows; in a myth he puts what he does not yet know and cd not come to know in any other way."[2] His most extensive discussion of *allegory* appears in his seminal work *The Allegory of Love: A Study in Medieval Tradition*, first published in 1936, three years after *The Pilgrim's*

---

1. Letter of 29 December 1958, *The Collected Letters of C. S. Lewis*, III, 1004.
2. Ibid., Letter of 21 September 1956, 788.

Part IV: Companion Pieces

Regress: An Allegorical Apology for Christianity, Reason and Romanticism. He states, "It is of the very nature of thought and language to represent what is immaterial in picturable forms . . . ; you can start with an immaterial fact, such as the passions which you actually experience, and can then invent *invisibilia* to express them. If you are hesitating between an angry retort and a soft answer, you can express your state of mind by inventing a person called *Ira* with a torch and letting her contend with another invented person called *Patientia*. This is allegory . . ." He then proceeds to distinguish between allegory and symbolism or sacramentalism, noting that "the difference can hardly be exaggerated": "the allegorist leaves the given—his own passions—to talk of that which is confessedly less real, which is a fiction. The symbolist leaves the given to find that which is more real . . . Symbolism is a mode of thought, but allegory is a mode of expression."[3] Accordingly, it is clear that Bunyan's Mr. Worldly-Wiseman represents one, single concept—worldly wisdom—just as Hawthorne's Mr. Smooth-it-away and Lewis's Mr. Virtue each stands for one idea, whereas an object like the veil in the work of Hawthorne and Lewis, as noted above, can—and does—suggest any number of different ideas.

On another occasion, Lewis noted that *allegory* is "one of those words which needs defining in each context where one uses it" and referred to "the extreme danger, in individual cases, of applying allegorical interpretations."[4] In the same context he expressed his recurring frustration at individuals who inveterately insist on interpreting works like his Narnia Chronicles and Space Trilogy as allegories: "I am also convinced that the wit of man *cannot* devise a story in wh. the wit of some other man cannot find an allegory."[5]

Hawthorne demonstrates some of the same ambivalence toward allegory. On the one hand, he wrote an unpublished collection that he called "Allegories of the Heart." As Richard Harter Fogle points out, "allegory is organic to Hawthorne, an innate quality of his vision. It

---

3. Lewis, *The Allegory of Love: A Study in Medieval Tradition*, 44–45, 48.

4. Similar dangers arose with allegorical interpretations of Scripture, apparently arising as early as the fifth century BC, with Philo later as the major proponent, the allegorizing continuing with Origen, Jerome, and Augustine. The practice was questioned by Thomas Aquinas and ultimately rejected by the Reformers.

5. Lewis, Letter of 10 December 1956, *The Collected Letters of C. S. Lewis*, III, 816. Lewis repeated the assertion in almost the same words in a Letter of 19 August 1957 (Ibid., 876). In another letter he says that "a strict allegory is like a puzzle with a solution" whereas "a great romance is like a flower whose smell reminds you of something you can't quite place" (Ibid., Letter of 11 September 1958, 971).

is his disposition to find spiritual meaning in all things natural and human. This faculty is an inheritance from the Puritans, who saw in everything God's will . . . Hawthorne without his allegory is hard to imagine."[6] Perhaps, as Lewis cautioned, it is necessary to define the term in each context in which it is used, for it would seem that much of what Fogle would label "allegory" might better be labeled "symbol." Arlin Turner has pointed out that Hawthorne seems to have considered allegory a drawback, remarking that his books "might have won him greater reputation but for an inveterate love of allegory, which is apt to invest his plots and characters with the aspect of scenery and people in the clouds, and to steal the human warmth of his conceptions." He wrote to his publisher friend James T. Fields, "Upon my honor, I am not quite sure that I entirely comprehend my own meaning, in some of those blasted allegories."[7]

There is no way of knowing if any of these negative views of allegory, which Hawthorne expressed in 1854, may have been influenced by the views of his friend Melville, whose *Moby Dick,* published in 1851 and dedicated to Hawthorne, includes the demur that ignorant landsmen "might scout at Moby Dick as a monstrous fable, or *still worse and more detestable, a hideous and intolerable allegory.*"[8] Neither is there a way of knowing if any of Lewis's negative views of allegory were in any way influenced by the views of his friend J. R. R. Tolkien, who wrote in his Foreword to *The Fellowship of the Ring,* "I cordially dislike allegory in all its manifestations and always have done so since I grew old and wary enough to detect its presence. I much prefer history, true or feigned, with its varied applicability to the thought and experience of readers. I think that many confuse 'applicability' with 'allegory'; but the one resides in the freedom of the reader, and the other in the purposed domination of the author."[9]

Just as Hawthorne and Lewis shared a markedly ambivalent view of allegory, they also shared an intense admiration of John Bunyan and his great allegory *The Pilgrim's Progress.* His sister Elizabeth recalled that

---

6. Fogle, *Hawthorne's Fiction: The Light & the Dark,* 7, 41.

7. Turner, *Nathaniel Hawthorne: An Introduction and Interpretation,* 69.

8. Melville, *Moby Dick,* 204. Emphasis added. It is interesting to note that Ishmael, Melville's narrator, earlier refers to John Bunyan and his great allegory: "Bear me out in it, thou great democratic God! who didst not refuse to the swart convict, Bunyan, the pale, poetic pearl" (114).

9. Tolkien, Foreword, *The Fellowship of the Ring,* 7.

Hawthorne, from age six, during visits to his grandmother's house, would lie on the carpet or sit silently most of an afternoon in a large chair, engrossed in reading *The Pilgrim's Progress*. James R. Mellow notes that Hawthorne recalled reading Shakespeare and *The Pilgrim's Progress* on rainy days in Maine. Mellow adds, ". . . his two favorite books of these earlier years were Spenser's *Faerie Queene* and Bunyan's *Pilgrim's Progress*, which he read and reread (and frequently alluded to) throughout his life."[10] According to Arlin Turner, Hawthorne "knew *The Pilgrim's Progress* virtually by heart, he once said, and he referred to it more often than any other literary work."[11]

It is clear that Hawthorne was so familiar with Bunyan's work that it seemed to become second nature to him, as reflected by his many allusions to it in all of his novels and several of his short tales, most often in the form of similes or metaphors. For example, in describing the light that glimmered out of Chillingworth's eyes, Hawthorne uses this simile: the light was "like one of those gleams of ghastly fire that darted from Bunyan's awful doorway in the hill-side, and quivered on the pilgrim's face."[12] Hawthorne apparently assumes that the reader is as familiar with Bunyan's work as he is; otherwise the comparison would not be nearly as effective. In this example, as with others, Hawthorne could be said to use a *remez*, a Semitic term denoting "hinted meaning," a shorthand manner of hearkening back to something that needs no further elaboration because the reader will know the source and context.[13] Similarly, Hawthorne described the lime-kiln in "Ethan Brand" as follows: ". . . it resembled nothing so much as the private entrance to the infernal regions, which the shepherds of the Delectable Mountains were accustomed to show to pilgrims."[14] In *The House of the Seven Gables*, Clifford whispers to Hepzibah, "Come, come; make haste, or he [Judge Pyncheon] will start up, like Giant Despair in pursuit of Christian and Hopeful, and catch us yet!"[15] Coverdale, in *The*

10. Mellow, *Nathaniel Hawthorne in His Times*, 21.

11. Turner, *Nathaniel Hawthorne; An Introduction and Interpretation*, 124.

12. Hawthorne, *The Scarlet Letter*, 119.

13. For insights into the common use of the *remez* in Jewish literature and in the Gospels, I am indebted to Doug Greenwald.

14. Hawthorne, "Ethan Brand," *The Complete Short Stories of Nathaniel Hawthorne*, 474. In his tale "The Hall of Fantasy," Hawthorne uses this *remez*: ". . . in the observatory of the edifice is kept that wonderful perspective glass, through which the shepherds of the Delectable Mountains showed Christian the far-off gleam of the Celestial City. The eye of Faith still loves to gaze through it" (*The Complete Short Stories of Nathaniel Hawthorne*, 291).

15. Hawthorne, *The House of the Seven Gables*, 220.

Blithedale Romance, remarks, "I see in Hollingsworth an exemplification of the most awful truth in Bunyan's book of such;—from the very gate of Heaven, there is a by-way to the Pit!"[16] Even in *The Marble Faun*, both the country-fair in Perugia and the carnival in Rome, with its frolicking and mysterious apparitions of revelers and masqueraders, are reminiscent of Bunyan's Vanity Fair.

From all indications, Lewis was equally as familiar with *The Pilgrim's Progress* as Hawthorne was. In a letter to his father in 1916, when he was eighteen, Lewis wrote of returning again to Bunyan's allegory: "I am reading at present, what do you think? Our own friend 'Pilgrim's Progress'. It is one of those books that are usually read too early to appreciate, and perhaps don't come back to. I am very glad however to have discovered it. The allegory of course is obvious and even childish, but just as a romance it is unsurpassed, and also as a specimen of real English." Later in the same year he wrote to Arthur Greeves that he had read *Pilgrim's Progress* again and was "awfully bucked [elated]."[17]

Though Lewis did not use recurrent *remezim* in works of fiction, he did often hearken back to *The Pilgrim's Progress* in letters, with the obvious assumption that his correspondent would be aware of the source and context. For example, in a letter to Arthur Greeves, he describes his walking tour in Derbyshire, where the limestone mountains, "owing to the paleness of the rock and the extreme clarity of the rivers, [are] *light* instead of somber—sublime yet smiling—*like the delectable mountains*."[18] On another trip he calls the area "*Perfect Pilgrims Progress Country*,"[19] and in still another letter he tells his correspondent that he needs her prayers "because I am *(like the pilgrim in Bunyan) traveling across 'a plain called Ease*.'"[20] Whereas Hawthorne pondered "what were the contents of the burden of Christian in the Pilgrim's Progress [because] he must have been taken for a peddler traveling with his pack,"[21] Lewis pondered whether a person totally ignorant of any religion would be able to say *what* the burden on Christian's back was or *who* Giant Despair was."[22]

16. Hawthorne, *The Blithedale Romance*, 215.

17. Lewis, Letter of 3 November 1916, Letter of 15 November 1916, *The Collected Letters of C. S. Lewis*, I, 247, 254.

18. Ibid., Letter of 23 April 1935, II, 160. Emphasis added.

19. Ibid., Letter of 11 April 1940, II, 387. Emphasis added.

20. Ibid., , Letter of 5 June 1951, III, 123. Emphasis added.

21. Hawthorne, *The American Notebooks*, 23.

22. Lewis, Letter of 18 August 1940, *The Collected Letters of C.S. Lewis*, II, 439.

Part IV: Companion Pieces

Lewis presents another perspective of Bunyan and his work in his essay "The Vision of John Bunyan," which he first read on the BBC, then published it in *The Listener* in 1962, thereafter including it in *Selected Literary Essays* (1969). In the essay Lewis puts *The Pilgrim's Progress* in the category of books which, "while didactic in intention, are read with delight by people who do not want their teaching and may not believe that they have anything to teach." He notes that its strengths are its "enthralling narrative" and "genuinely dramatic dialogue." He also mentions some perceived weaknesses—for example, at times "the speakers step out of the allegorical story altogether. They talk literally and directly about the spiritual life. The great image of the Road disappears. They are in the pulpit. If this is going to happen, why have a story at all? Allegory frustrates itself the moment the author starts doing what could equally well be done in a straight sermon or treatise. It is a valid form only so long as it is doing what could not be done at all, or done so well, in any other way." These are astute observations, but readers must draw their own conclusions not only about Bunyan's work but also about Hawthorne's "The Celestial Railroad" and Lewis's *The Pilgrim's Regress*, when these criteria are applied (for example, note Lewis's expository excess in the house of Wisdom section, chapters eight though twelve).

Hawthorne's "The Celestial Railroad" was first published in *The Democratic Review* (1843), reprinted in pamphlet form, and then collected in *Mosses from an Old Manse*. Lewis's *The Pilgrim's Regress*, reportedly written during a two-week stay with Arthur Greeves in Ireland, was published exactly ninety years (to the month—May, 1933) after Hawthorne's work. In a letter to Greeves, Lewis wrote, "It is yours by right—written in your house, read to you as it was written, and celebrating (at least in the most important parts) an experience which I have more in common with you than anyone else,"[23] referring, he said later, to the private meaning he gave to the word "Romanticism." He wisely agreed to delete "*Pseudo-Bunyan's Periplus*" from the original title, acknowledging the needless obscurity of "periplus" ("peripatetic" or "itinerant," "to walk about from place to place"). Responding to a correspondent, he wrote, "I don't wonder that you got fogged in *Pilgrim's Regress*. It was my first religious book and I didn't then know how to make things easy. I was not even trying to very much, because in those days I never dreamed I would become a 'popular' author and hoped for no readers outside a small 'highbrow'

---

23. Ibid., Letter of 25 March 1933, II, 104. Lewis dedicated the book to Arthur Greeves.

circle. Don't waste your time over it any more."[24] To be sure, attentive time spent on the work is not wasted, but Lewis's correspondent was assuredly not the last to be "fogged" by it.

For his part, Hawthorne, commenting in a letter to Sophia, remarks that to his horror he encountered a clerical contemporary and concludes, "The Celestial Railroad must have given him a pique; and, if so, I shall feel as if Providence had sufficiently rewarded me for that pious labor."[25] Unless Hawthorne is simply being "ironic," as some are always quick to say, in his reference to feeling "rewarded for that pious labor," the comment surely illuminates his serious intent. Hawthorne's view is quite clear, as evidenced from his journal, where he commented on the difference "between the cold, lifeless, vaguely liberal clergyman of our own day, and the narrow but earnest cushion thumper of puritanical times." "On the whole" he went on to affirm, "I prefer the last-mentioned variety of the black-coated tribe."[26]

Though both Hawthorne and Lewis were stimulated, inspired, motivated by the same author and work, they wrote quite different, quite disparate, works. Hawthorne's is a short tale of fewer than a dozen pages; Lewis's is a lengthy tome of several hundred. Hawthorne's is simple and easy to follow (he "knew how to make things easy"); Lewis's is a complex, philosophical, allusive discourse couched in allegorical terms. (There is no discursive "periplus" in Hawthorne's story, though there are "mephitic gases" that intoxicate the brain, along with "an omnigenous erudition.") Hawthorne's is an ironic reversal of Bunyan, focusing on the decline from the time of Christian's pilgrimage to that of the present; Lewis's is an attempt to explain the part which joy, the dialectic of desire, *Sehnsucht* played in his conversion.

For all their differences, however, the two works are also quite similar in other ways. For example, both are highly satirical, sometimes caustically so. Hawthorne holds up to forceful ridicule the new liberalism in religion, education, politics, science, and social affairs and philosophies, including Transcendentalism, represented by the Giant Transcendentalist, a "huge miscreant," an "ill-proportioned figure, considerably more like a heap of fog and duskiness," who shouts "in so strange a phraseology" that no one knew what he meant or "whether

---

24. Ibid., Letter of 19 January 1953, III, 282–83.
25. Hawthorne, *The American Note-Books*, 459.
26. Mellow, *Nathaniel Hawthorne in His Times*, 246.

to be encouraged or affrighted."[27] Lewis satirizes the entire modernist movement, cerebral men represented by the North (Mr. Sensible, Mr. Neo-Angular, Mr. Neo-Classical, Mr. Humanist), emotive men represented by the South (Mr. Broad), various philosophies now deemed false and inadequate, Freudian psychology, and others. Hyatt H. Waggoner correctly notes that Hawthorne's "satire [is] aimed not at Bunyan but at religious modernists of Hawthorne's day . . . The ending is hard on the religious liberals of Hawthorne's day. Mr. Smooth-it-away, the modernist preacher who serves as the speaker's guide and who believes that Hell 'has not even a metaphorical existence,' refuses at the last moment to enter the Celestial City."[28]

Both works also make effective use of wit and humor.[29] For example, in Hawthorne's version of Vanity Fair, the innumerable lecturers who aid the eminent divines "diffuse such a various profundity in all subjects of human or celestial science, that any man may acquire an omnigenous erudition without the trouble of even learning to read." Further, there is a "species of machine for the wholesale manufacture of individual morality," and Mr. Smooth-it-away smilingly asserts that when Bunyan's shepherds assured Christian that the door in the hillside was a byway to hell it was a joke, referring actually to "a smokehouse for the preparation of mutton hams." Much of the humor is black, as when the narrator describes Mr. Smooth-it-away adamantly denying the existence of hell even as its smoke rises from its crevices and "he felt its fiery tortures raging within his breast . . . a smoke-wreath [issuing] from his mouth and nostrils, while a twinkle of lurid flame darted out of either eye, proving indubitably that his heart was all of a red blaze."[30]

---

27. Hawthorne, "The Celestial Railroad," *The Complete Short Stories of Nathaniel Hawthorne*, 301.

28. Waggoner, *Hawthorne: A Critical Study*, 18.

29. There is wit and humor in Bunyan's work also, though, of course, the tone is quite serious. Talkative, who Lewis says is not allowed to talk very much, the son of Say-well in the town of Prating-row, responds as follows when Faithful asks him what one thing they should found their discourse upon: "What you will: I will talk of things heavenly, or things earthly; things moral, or things evangelical; things sacred, or things profane; things past, or things to come; things foreign, or things at home; things more essential, or things circumstantial, provided that all be done to our profit" (Bunyan, *The Pilgrim's Progress*, 112).

30. Hawthorne, "The Celestial Railroad," *The Complete Short Stories of Nathaniel Hawthorne*, 302, 305, 304, 306.

Allegory to the 3rd Power: "The Celestial Railroad" and The Pilgrim's Regress

Lewis also uses a great deal of wit and humor. For example, near the beginning, when John is in the woods attempting unsuccessfully to enjoy the woods as a true Romantic (there was the grass and there were the trees—but what was he to *do* with them?) and then attempting to imagine a picture of the Island in his mind, he opens his eyes and sees a laughing brown girl (the source of much criticism for alleged implicit racism) of about his own age, with no clothes on. The chapter ends, "And John rose and caught her, all in haste, and committed fornication with her in the wood." The next chapter, titled "Ichabod" ("Where is the Glory?" or "The Glory is Departed"), begins: "After that John was always going to the wood."[31] At least temporarily he exchanges his desire to be a sensuous Romantic for his desire as a sensual romantic.

In explaining to John how science works, Mr. Enlightenment tells him, "Hypothesis, my dear young friend, establishes itself by a cumulative process; or, to use popular language, if you make the same guess often enough it ceases to be a guess and becomes a Scientific Fact." Similarly, when John asks Reason, a barren virgin, if there is such a place as the Island or only a feeling in his mind, she says, "I cannot tell you ... because you do not know." "But you know," says John, to which Reason replies, "But I can tell you only what *you* know. I can bring things out of the dark part of your mind into the light part of it. But now you ask me what is not even in the dark part of your mind." Sometimes the humor comes from description, as in this example: "In this valley the year came on with seven-leagued boots." Later the guide Slikisteinsauga (the name itself is hilarious) describes the dragon that sits on the northern isthmus as "cold, costive, crustacean." A *crustaceous* dragon evokes humor in its own right (having a hard crust or shell like a crab, shrimp, lobster or barnacle, living in the water and breathing through gills), but a *constipated* dragon? Now that conjures an interesting image—even in the figurative sense of "uncommunicative" or "stingy."

Hawthorne's story and Lewis's longer narrative both seem to be based on the assumption that readers will be well acquainted with Bunyan's allegory. Hawthorne alludes directly to Bunyan eight times and to Christian four times in the story; Lewis quotes Bunyan at the beginning of Book Seven: "Some also have wished that the next way to their Father's house were here that they might be troubled no more with either Hills or Mountains to go over; but the way is the way, and there's an end"—a statement which could serve most appropriately as an epigraph for Hawthorne's story.

---

31. Lewis, *The Pilgrim's Regress*, 13, 22, 58, 129, 183.

Part IV: Companion Pieces

Hawthorne's story and Lewis's narrative have both been called parodies of Bunyan's allegory. A parody, originally and literally "a song sung beside," is a work which satirically imitates another, but in both of these cases the ridicule is directed not at the author or subject matter of the original work but at ironic distortions of original concepts and beliefs, actually implying a flattering tribute to both the author and subject. Hyatt H. Waggoner is technically correct in calling Hawthorne's story "a pastiche [French word for *parody*] on *Pilgrim's Progress*," but the current negative connotations, and even the denotations, of *pastiche* ("inept, confused borrowing, or a jumbled hodgepodge") are misleading in this context. Hawthorne's tale has been variously called an allegorical fable, a strained allegory, an allegory of an allegory, an adaptation, a travesty, a parable of modern spiritual accommodation. Lewis's narrative has been called "an allegorical autobiography," "an allegory of demystification," "a relentlessly analytical, systematic allegory." Lewis himself referred to *The Pilgrim's Regress* as "a kind of Bunyan up to date."[32] Both works could be called sequels to Bunyan's allegory.

The two works adopt the dream vision framework used in Bunyan's allegory and in such other works as *The Romance of the Rose*, Chaucer's *The Book of the Duchess*, *The House of Fame*, and *The Parliament of Fowls*, Langland's *The Vision of Piers Plowman*, and the Gawain poet's *The Pearl*. Other examples include Keats's *The Fall of Hyperion*, Lewis Carroll's *Alice in Wonderland*, Edward Bellamy's *Looking Backward*, Mark Twain's *A Connecticut Yankee in King Arthur's Court* (Hank Morgan, machine-shop foreman, has hideous dreams after he is knocked cold by a blow on the head)—and, of course, Lewis's own *The Great Divorce*. Bunyan's dreamer is Bunyan himself, having "lighted on a certain place, where was a den" (the gaol [jail] where he was incarcerated), who becomes the detached narrator describing the pilgrimage of Christian (originally "Graceless"), who flees the City of Destruction bound for Mt. Sion (Zion), the Celestial City.

Hawthorne's dreamer / unreliable narrator is on a trek, not a bona fide "pilgrimage," literally not "in good faith," but, as he says, a trip "to gratify a liberal curiosity." Rather than Christian or even a counterpart, he most resembles Bunyan's character named Ignorance, as David E. Smith has suggested.[33] This character in Bunyan's allegory, "a very brisk lad" from the country of Conceit, accompanies Christian and Hopeful

---

32. Lewis, Letter of 17 January 1933, *The Collected Letters of C. S. Lewis*, II, 94.
33. Smith, *John Bunyan in America*, 61.

Allegory to the 3rd Power: "The Celestial Railroad" and The Pilgrim's Regress

just long enough to debate about the way of salvation: "Would you have us trust to what Christ in his own person has done without us?" Ignorance asks. "This conceit would loosen the reins of our lust, and tolerate us to live as we list: for what matter how we live if we may be justified by Christ's personal righteousness from all, when we believe it?" Christian replies: "Ignorance is thy name, and as thy name is, so art thou . . . Ignorant thou art of what justifying righteousness is, and as ignorant how to secure thy soul through the faith of it from the heavy wrath of God. Yea, thou also art ignorant of the true effects of saving faith in this righteousness of Christ . . ."[34] Ignorance reappears at the conclusion, seeks admission at the Gate of the City, but is denied because he has no certificate, then is bound hand and foot and carried through the air to the byway to Hell in the side of the hill. Hawthorne's narrator, aboard a steam ferryboat on the River of Death, learns that he is not to be transported to the Celestial City—but when the cold waters spray him, he awakens from his dream "with a shiver and a heartquake."[35]

Lewis's narrator is, like Bunyan's, a non-participant dreamer, recounting the story of John, who leaves his native Puritania in search of the (exotic) Island in the West. After his long peripatetic journey, John learns that his beloved Island is in fact the Mountains or the other side of the Mountains near Puritania and not, in truth, an Island at all. He is told by the Guide that, ironically, "the way to go on . . . is to go back," to "regress" to the Home of the Landlord in those mountains, the way of relearning and repentance.

Bunyan's Christian meets or briefly encounters approximately eighty characters in the course of his pilgrimage, including such figures as Mr. Worldly-Wiseman from the town of Carnal-Policy, Mr. Legality from the village of Morality, Mr. By-ends from the town of Fair-speech, Giant Despair and his wife Diffidence, Turn-away from the town of Apostasy, Little-faith from the town of Sincere, and others. He visits or passes through approximately thirty-six places, including the Slough of Despond, the Hill called Difficulty, the Valley of Humiliation, Vanity Fair, the Delicate Plain called Ease, Doubting Castle, the Delectable Mountains, Enchanted Ground, the Country of Beulah, the Valley of the Shadow of Death, and ultimately the Celestial City.

---

34. Bunyan, *The Pilgrim's Progress*, 162, 188–89.

35. Hawthorne, "The Celestial Railroad," *The Complete Short Stories of Nathaniel Hawthorne*, 306.

Part IV: Companion Pieces

Christian faces many formidable adversaries, the greatest being Apollyon,[36] whom Christian valiantly battles for over half a day, finally wounding him with his two-edged sword. Ironically, Apollyon appears in Hawthorne's version as the chief engineer of the train thought to be on its way to the Celestial City. When the narrator (Ignorance?) learns this he exults "with irrepressible enthusiasm," shouting "Bravo, bravo! . . .This shows the liberality of the age; this proves, if anything can, that all musty prejudices are in a fair way to be obliterated. And how will Christian rejoice to hear of this happy transformation of his old antagonist!"[37] What a cogent example of dramatic irony this statement is, for the reader knows that such is definitely not the case! Further ironic in Hawthorne's story is the reference to Prince Beelzebub[38] (not in Bunyan's version or Lewis's), who, because of "the principle of mutual compromise,"[39] is now the keeper of the wicket gate, rather than Good Will, who opened the gate for Christian.

Christian, accompanied by Faithful and Hopeful, is further helped along the way by Evangelist, who directs him to the Wicket Gate (in Hawthorne's story Evangelist is reputed to preside at the ticket office, now offering square pieces of pasteboard rather than the mystic roll of parchment), Interpreter (who taught Christian how grace can clear away the dust of original sin from the heart, but whose house in Hawthorne's story is now a tavern of long standing), Help, Good Will, Watchful (porter at the lodge), and the Shepherds of the Delectable Mountains.

In Hawthorne's story the narrator (Ignorance?) is accompanied by Mr. Smooth-it-away, one of the largest stockholders of the railroad company. At the place where Christian's burden fell from his back when he encountered the Cross, Christian is confronted by Mr. Live-for-the-world, Mr. Hide-sin-in-the-heart, and Mr. Scaly-conscience—all from the town

---

36. Apollyon is the Greek name, meaning "Destruction," of the angel of the bottomless pit, Abaddon. Note Revelation 9:11—"And they had as king over them the angel of the bottomless pit, whose name in Hebrew is Abaddon, but in Greek he has the name Apollyon."

37. Hawthorne, "The Celestial Railroad," *The Complete Short Stories of Nathaniel Hawthorne*, 297.

38. The name Beelzebub is a compound of "*Baal*," Canaanite god of fertility, and "*zebub*" for "fly" or "poisonous insect." In the synoptic gospels Jesus is accused by the Pharisees of casting out demons with the power of their ruler (Satan): "He is possessed by Beelzebul," and "He casts out the demons by the ruler of the demons" (Mark 3:22. Cf. Matthew 12:24, Luke 11:15). Cf. William Golding's novel *Lord of the Flies* (1954).

39. Hawthorne, "The Celestial Railroad," *The Complete Short Stories of Nathaniel Hawthorne*, 296–97.

of Shun-repentance. They all extol the advantages of having their burdens (sins) "snugly deposited in the baggage car" to be delivered to their owners at journey's end, rather than having to carry them onerously on their backs. These characters are but four of over thirty figures that Ignorance encounters on his curiosity trek, others including Mr. Take-it-easy, who gives up on his journey to the Celestial City, complaining that there is "no fun going on, nothing to drink, and no smoking allowed, and a thrumming of church music from morning till night," concluding, "I would not stay in such a place if they offered me house room and living free." Also conspicuously absent are Mr. Greatheart, said to have "grown preposterously stiff and narrow in his old age," having gone off to the Celestial City "in a huff." The charming young ladies of Palace Beautiful (Miss Prudence, Miss Piety, and Miss Charity) are now "old maids, every soul of them—prim, starched, dry, and angular," not one of them reportedly having altered the fashion of her gown since the time of Christian's pilgrimage.[40] How old-fashioned, how retrograde, how out of touch with reality they are!

Ignorance passes at least twenty places on his trek, including the Slough of Despond (a quagmire which has been filled in with old books of morality and philosophy, as well as tracts, sermons, essays, and commentaries of Scripture), the station house (at the site of the Wicket Gate), Hill Difficulty (a tunnel now runs through it, the materials having been used to fill up the Valley of Humiliation, where inflammable gas lights the passage), the lurid caverns at the mouth of the infernal region (its existence derogated by Mr. Smooth-it-away, who points out that it is the crater of a half-extinct volcano, now equipped with forges to manufacture railroad iron), the cavern of the cruel giants Pope and Pagan (now replaced by Giant Transcendentalism), and, of course, Vanity Fair.

In Bunyan's allegory Vanity Fair, in the town of Vanity, was established by Beelzebub, Apollyon, and Legion, selling such merchandise as "houses, lands, trades, places, honours, preferments, titles, countries, kingdoms, lusts, pleasures, and delights of all sorts, as whores, bawds, wives, husbands, children, masters, servants, lives, blood, bodies, souls, silver, gold, pearls, precious stones, and what not."[41] It is difficult to imagine how Vanity Fair in Hawthorne's story could be any worse, but it is

---

40. Ibid., 296, 300, 297, 298–99.

41. Ibid., 125. Cf. William Makepeace Thackeray's novel *Vanity Fair: A Novel Without a Hero* (1847–48). It was Trollope's view that the novelist's business is to "preach his sermons with the same purpose as the clergyman ...[to] make virtue alluring and vice ugly, while he charms his readers instead of wearying them."

Part IV: Companion Pieces

more delusive, more deceptive. It is the "great capital of human business and pleasure" where purchasers make foolish bargains—for example, a fortune expended for the purchase of diseases, crowns of laurel and myrtle and paltry wreaths, with thousands selling their happiness for a whim and others selling their birthrights for messes of pottage, piping hot. A considerable difference is that "almost every street has its church . . . and the reverend clergy are nowhere held in higher respect than at Vanity Fair." Esteemed clergy include the Rev. Mr. Shallow-deep, the Rev. Mr. Stumble-at-truth, the Rev. Mr. Bewilderment, the Rev. Mr. Clog-the-spirit, the Rev. Dr. Wind-of-Doctrine, and the Rev. Mr. This-today, who is resigning his pulpit to the Rev. Mr. That-tomorrow.[42] Passing reference is made to the persecution of Christian and the martyrdom of Faithful: they were beaten, smeared with dirt, and put in a cage, then tried by Judge Hategood, with witnesses Envy, Superstition, and Pickthank, and jurors Mr. Blind-man, Mr. No-good, Mr. Malice, Mr. Love-lust, Mr. Live-loose, Mr. Heady, Mr. High-mind, Mr. Enmity, Mr. Liar, Mr. Cruelty, Mr. Hate-light, and Mr. Implacable. No Vanity Fair per se appears in Lewis's allegory, though in the country of the Spirit of the Age, presided over by Mr. Mammon, John is clapped in fetters by Sigismund Enlightenment, son of old Mr. Enlightenment.

In Lewis's allegory, John encounters approximately forty-six figures, including such opponents as Mr. Enlightenment and his son Sigismund Enlightenment, Old Mr. Halfways and his daughter Media Half-ways and son Gus Halfways, the Clevers, Glugly, Mr. Mammon, Master Parrot, the Giant, the three Pale Men (Mr. Neo-Angular, Mr. Neo-Classical, Mr. Humanist), Mr. Broad, the witch in Luxuria, and the dragons. Figures who assist or guide him are the Steward, his companion Mr. Virtue, Reason, (and her two sisters Philosophy and Theology), Mr. Sensible (and his servant Drudge), Mr. Wisdom and his daughter Contemplation, History the hermit, Guide Slikissteinsauga, and of course Mother Kirk, daughter-in-law of the Landlord. John passes or visits about twenty places, including the Steward's house, the woods, the city of Claptrap, the city of Thrill, the city of Eschropolis, the country belonging to the Spirit of the Age, the pit in the side of the hill, Mr. Sensible's House, Land of the Tough-minded, the House of Wisdom, Wisdom's Valley (said to be marked on the old maps as the Valley of Humiliation), and significantly the precipitous Grand Canyon (called *Peccatum Adae*, "Adam's sin"). Mother Kirk assists

---

42. Lewis, *The Pilgrim's Regress*, 301-02.

Allegory to the 3rd Power: "The Celestial Railroad" and The Pilgrim's Regress

John and his companion Virtue in crossing the chasm by diving into the river at the bottom, then discovering that the Mountains are, in fact, the Eastern Mountains of Puritania. To alter the old proverb, "The longest way round is the only way home": progress by learning to regress.

Bunyan's Christian and his friend Hopeful cross the River of Death and are met by two shining ones, "ministering Spirits," who help them up the mighty hill to the Celestial City, where a great company of the heavenly host come out to welcome them. In Hawthorne's story, the two pilgrims, Mr. Stick-to-the-right and Mr. Foot-it-to-heaven, who have been ridiculed, scorned, belittled, and laughed at throughout their pilgrimage, are greeted by "a multitude of shining ones [who] had assembled on the other side of the river, to welcome two poor pilgrims, who were just emerging from its depths."[43] Mark Van Doren effectively summarizes Hawthorne's story, noting that it "exposes the error of those who think that Heaven and Hell are no more, that evil is a superstition, and that the good life is a comfortable train trip made with no difficulty at all. The Valley of the Shadow of Death is conquered, these folks think, because they have piped its vapors into gas lamps. Vanity Fair is the whole of this new world, and nobody knows it."[44]

Certainly all three of these works—Bunyan's, Hawthorne's, and Lewis's—cogently dramatize the conclusion Lewis made about Bunyan's allegory: "that the choice of ways at any cross-road may be more important than we think and that short cuts may lead to very nasty places."[45] That truth is no tenuous dream from which we awaken.

---

43. Hawthorne, "The Celestial Railroad," *The Complete Short Stories of Nathaniel Hawthorne*, 305.
44. Van Doren, *Hawthorne: A Critical Biography*, 129.
45. Lewis, "The Vision of John Bunyan," *Selected Literary Essays*, 153.

12

Four Loves and Seven Gables: *The Four Loves* and *The House of the Seven Gables*

IT SEEMS ESPECIALLY APROPOS to conclude this discussion of the affinities between Jack Lewis and his American cousin, Nat Hawthorne, by considering Hawthorne's *The House of the Seven Gables* vis-à-vis Lewis's *The Four Loves*. One could easily get the impression, were it not for the obvious contretemps (in the literal sense of that word—"opposite," "against," or "opposing" time, specifically the one-hundred-and-nine-year separation of publication dates), that Hawthorne set about writing his 1851 novel as a dramatization of Lewis's 1960 treatise about the four kinds of love.

Lewis was just eighteen when he wrote to his friend Arthur Greeves about "the most glorious novel (almost) that I have ever read. I daresay you have read it already or at any rate you must have hearded [sic] it praised too often to need my advice. It is Nathaniel Hawthorne's 'House with the Seven Gables' [sic]." Then he adds several reasons why he so much loved the novel: "I love the idea of a house with a curse! And although there is nothing supernatural in the story itself there is a brooding sense of mystery and fate over the whole thing. Have you read it?"[1] A week later he writes to Greeves,

> Although by experience I am somewhat shy of recommending books to other people I think I am quite safe in earnestly advising you to make 'the Gables' your next purchase. By the way I shouldn't have said 'mystery', there is really no mystery in the proper sense of the word, but a sort of feeling of fate & inevitable

---

1. Lewis, Letter of 22 November 1916, *They Stand Together: The Letters of C. S. Lewis to Arthur Greeves*, 152.

horror as in 'Wuthering Heights'.[2] I really think I have never enjoyed a novel more. There is one lovely scene where the villain—Judge Phycheon [sic]—has suddenly died in his chair, all alone in the old house, and it describes the corpse sitting there as the day wears on and the room grows darker—darker—and the ticking of his watch. But that sort of bald description is no use! I must leave you to read that wonderful chapter to yourself. There is also a very good 'story in a story'—curiously resembling the Cosmo[3] one tho' of course not so openly impossible. I intend to read all Hawthorne after this. What a pity such a genius should be a beastly American![4]

It is clear that Lewis admired Hawthorne's novel primarily for its Gothic[5] elements, such as the dark, dreary, weather-beaten, oppressive, foreboding house itself (resembling Poe's House of Usher and anticipating the Compson and Sutpen houses in Faulkner, Ephraim Cabot's elm-shaded farmhouse in O'Neill's *Desire Under the Elms*, and others). In addition, there is the mysterious portrait of Colonel Pyncheon, a secret spring and compartment behind the picture containing a legal document, rumor of a buried fortune, a reputedly magic looking-glass, ghostly music, a strange black grimalkin (an old female cat) prowling the premises, a mysterious crime, old wizard Maule's prophetic curse that God would give Colonel Pyncheon and his male descendants blood to drink, the corpse of Judge Jeffrey Pyncheon, like his kinsman thirty years before, sitting lumpishly in

---

2. Emily Bronte's *Wuthering Heights*, which appeared in 1847, is set in a farmhouse on a Yorkshire moor, deals with three generations, involves revenge and intrigue, a supernatural visitant, villainy and passion. Lewis especially noted Catherine's comment: "I am Heathcliff and he is I." (Lewis, Letter of 22 October 1959, *The Collected Letters of C. S. Lewis*, III, 1097).

3. Cosmo von Wehrstahl appears in George MacDonald's *Phantastes*, chapter xiii. A reclusive student at the University of Prague, he lives by himself in one of the highest houses in the city. He purchases an old mirror, which proves to be enchanted when a woman all in white appears briefly each day. Having fallen in love with the mysterious woman, Cosmo agrees to break the magic mirror to set her free, whereupon she finds him dead, his hand pressed to his side, blood welling from between his fingers. *Phantastes* was published in 1858, seven years after *The House of the Seven Gables*.

4. Lewis, Letter of 29 November 1916, *They Stand Together: The Letters of C. S. Lewis to Arthur Greeves*, 153.

5. Gothic fiction was introduced and reputedly named by Horace Walpole in 1764, with his *Castle of Otranto, A Gothic Story*, and popularized by such works as Ann Radcliffe's *The Mysteries of Udolpho* (1786), Charles Brockden Brown's *Wieland* (1798), Mary Shelley's *Frankenstein* (1818), William Godwin's *Caleb Williams* (1868), Wilkie Collins's *Moonstone* (1868), and others.

the same oaken elbow-chair with a crimson stain on its shirt bosom, his eyes wide open, a fly buzzing on his nose, his watch ticking in his cold, stiff hand. Further demonstrating Hawthorne's penchant, shared by Lewis, for the image of a corpse sitting in solitude is this 1849 entry in his Notebook: "The sunbeam that comes through a round-hole in the shutter of a darkened room, where a dead man sits in solitude."[6]

It would seem, however, that the Gothic trappings, along with pervasive guilt symbolizing original sin, the prolonged effects of evil action, and the dead weight of the past on the present are only part of what so attracted Lewis to the novel. Another major theme of the novel is the redemptive, transforming power of multiform love.

Hawthorne himself, like Lewis, expressed a preference for *The House of the Seven Gables* over *The Scarlet Letter*, which he said lacked sunshine, calling it "positively a hell-fired story, into which I found it almost impossible to throw any cheering light."[7] When Hawthorne read the manuscript to his wife Sophia, upon whom the novel's Phoebe is said to be based, she wrote to her mother: "There is unspeakable grace and beauty in the conclusion, throwing back upon the sterner tragedy of the commencement an ethereal light, and a dear home-loveliness and satisfaction."[8] Modern critics, however, disagree with Hawthorne, Sophia, and Lewis in assessing the two novels, particularly the conclusion of *House*.

Lewis made relatively few markings in his copy of Hawthorne's *The House of the Seven Gables* (housed in the Marion E. Wade Center at Wheaton College). Other than the ostensible tea stains on pages 24 and 25 and a corrected typographical error, his typical underlining with a vertical mark in the margin is infrequent but significant. Not surprisingly, he marked this key statement in chapter xxi: ". . . no great mistake, whether acted or endured, in our mortal sphere, is ever really set right"—for such rectitude is rendered impossible because of "Time, the continual vicissitude of circumstances, and the invariable inopportunity of death." Hawthorne is careful to note that this truth would be "a very sad one but for the higher hopes which it suggests,"[9] the "higher hopes" apparently referring to grace, faith, hope, and joy. Another key passage which Lewis marked was this one in chapter xvii, when Clifford, on his abortive

---

6. Hawthorne, *The American Notebooks*, 293.
7. Stewart, *Nathaniel Hawthorne: A Biography*, 97.
8. Mellow, *Nathaniel Hawthorne in His Times*, 355.
9. Hawthorne, *The House of the Seven Gables*, 272.

Four Loves and Seven Gables: The Four Love *and* The House of the Seven Gables

train ride with Hepzibah, tells her that the electric telegraph should be consecrated for lovers to send their heartthrob messages from Maine to Florida with such words as these—"I love you more than I can!"[10] Clearly, Lewis was impressed both with Hawthorne's expression of the truth that humans can never "set right" the great mistakes made in this mortal life without "the higher hopes" and with the assertion that we must "love more than we can." Some forty years after he first read Hawthorne's novel, Lewis had occasion to express his views of the four varieties of love.[11]

Lewis was persuaded by his publisher to write a brief description or blurb (a laudatory advertisement or summary, usually appearing on a book dust jacket)[12] for his book *The Four Loves*. The blurb, which appeared on the dust jacket of the original 1960 English edition, is cited here, in part, to provide a brief summary:

> The four loves are, of course, Affection, Friendship, Eros, and Charity. They have often been dealt with separately by authors as different as Ovid, St. Bernard and Stendhal: and usually one or other of them is treated as the only love worth much consideration. Dr. Lewis is more a map-maker than a partisan. He marks frontiers and trade-routes and tries to do justice to all.
>
> Three quotations used by the author indicate the principles that govern his survey: from St. John, 'God is Love', from Donne, 'That our affections kill us not, nor dye' and from Denis de Rougemont, 'Love ceases to be a demon when he ceases to be a god.'[13]

Like Lewis, Hawthorne expressed concern about the vitality and possible death of love, on one occasion using the metaphor or analogy

---

10. Ibid., 231.

11. In 1958 the Episcopal Radio-TV Foundation of Atlanta invited Lewis to record his talks on the Four Loves; it was these talks which formed the basis of his book *The Four Loves*.

12. The term "blurb" was coined around 1910 by F. G. Burgess, for "self-praise, to make a noise like a publisher."

13. Lewis, Letter of 14 October 1959, *The Collected Letters of C. S. Lewis*, III, 1091. See Ovid's *The Art of Love*, St. Bernard of Clairvaux's *On Loving God*, and Stendhal's (Marie-Henri Beyle) *On Love*. Note I John 4:8, 16—"The one who does not love does not know God, for God is love . . . And we have come to know and have believed the love which God has for us. God is love, and the one who abides in love abides in him." John Donne's "A Litany," xxvii—"That our affections kill us not, nor die, / Hear us, weak echoes, O thou ear, and cry." Denis de Rougemont's *Love in the Western World*: "In ceasing to be a god, [Eros] ceases to be a demon," Book vii, chapter 5, "Eros Rescued by Agape." Lewis referred to this latter idea as early as 1942: "Treat 'Love' as a god and you in fact make it a fiend" (Letter of 6 March 1942, *The Collected Letters of C. S. Lewis*, II, 511).

of a tree's leaves and roots: "Caresses, expressions of one sort or another, are necessary to the life of the affections, as leaves are to the life of a tree. If they are wholly restrained, love will die at the roots."[14] Similarly, Lewis uses the metaphor or analogy of fruit trees and a garden: "It is no disparagement to a garden to say that it will not fence and weed itself, nor prune its own fruit trees, nor roll and cut its own lawns. A garden is a good thing but that is not the sort of goodness it has. It will remain a garden, as distinct from a wilderness, only if someone does all those things to it."[15] According to Hawthorne, just as a tree's leaves must remain healthy and its roots well watered and nourished without restraint, so human affections must be stimulated physically and verbally—or love will die. According to Lewis, just as fruit trees and a garden must be cultivated, pruned, and weeded, or the garden will become a wilderness, so natural loves must be tenderly, sensitively cared for, with Divine Grace coming down like rain and sunshine—or love will die.

In view of these analogies, it is not surprising that a key, recurring image in Hawthorne's novel is the garden behind the old Pyncheon house, standing in stark contrast to the desolate, decaying, accursed house. Phoebe, the morning after her arrival, peeped down from her chamber window at the tall white double rosebush, which looked "as if it had been brought from Eden that very summer," along with other species of flowers growing there "in a wilderness of neglect."[16] The rose, alluded to more than twenty times in the novel, is the emblem of Venus and symbol of love and the beloved. Significantly, it is in the garden where Phoebe first meets Holgrave, the daguerreotypist, who has been pruning, trimming, weeding, and cultivating the flowers and vegetables, along with a pear tree and three damson trees.[17] The recurrent roses function not just as a symbol but as metonymy,[18] for Phoebe is described as "a young rosebud of a girl," "such a flower was Phoebe," "as if the garden flower were the sister of the household maiden," "the rosy girl," "the blooming girl"; "the

---

14. Hawthorne, *The American Note-Books*, 565.

15. Lewis, *The Four Loves*, 116.

16. Hawthorne, *The House of the Seven Gables*, 68–69. Note that the Pyncheon garden has become "*a wilderness of neglect*," an image anticipating Lewis's description.

17. The damson tree is a Damascus plum tree, a Eurasian, rosaceous tree cultivated from ancient times for its blue-black plums.

18. Metonymy is a "substitute meaning," an object closely associated with a word being used for the word itself.

flower of Eden has bloomed ... in this old, darksome house today."[19] Thus the rose, which is associated with Phoebe, comes to represent the girl herself and the love that she both manifests and evokes.

If one were to read Hawthorne's novel after reading Lewis's treatise on the four loves, it may appear that the novel was written to demonstrate and dramatize each of the four loves. Lewis describes affection (*storge*) as domestic love, especially that between and among parents and offspring. Affection, he says, is the humblest, most modest, broadest, most widely diffused of the loves, most instinctive, least discriminating, least finical (finicky, overly fussy, fastidious, particular or exacting). He says that affection "is an affair of old clothes, and ease, of the unguarded moment, of liberties which would be ill-bred if we took them with strangers." Note how Clifford Pyncheon in his old-fashioned dressing gown of faded damask, repeatedly falling asleep in his cushioned chair, illustrates Lewis's description. "Affection," Lewis adds, "is responsible for nine-tenths of whatever solid and durable happiness there is in our natural lives."[20] Note how Clifford, starved for love, cries out, "I want my happiness! ... Many, many years have I waited for it! It is late! It is late! I want my happiness!"[21] Rather than love and its accompanying happiness, he has received a legacy of hatred, animosity, ascerbity, and a nefarious accusation—by his own kinsman—of a crime he did not commit.

Affection is amply illustrated by Phoebe, whose name means "the shining one," and her cousin Hepzibah, whose name itself evokes *storge*, for not only was the Hebrew Hepzibah the mother of Manasseh, king of Judah (II Kings 21:1), but it was the symbolic name for Jerusalem (Isaiah 62:4), meaning "my delight is in her"—that is, Yahweh's delight will be in her when she is restored from desolation. Hawthorne writes, "The two relatives—the young maid and the old one—found time ... *to make rapid advances towards affection and confidence.*" "*Towards Phoebe ... she was affectionate—far tenderer than ever before*, in their brief acquaintance ..." When the old maiden lady steps forward and kisses Phoebe, the narrator asks, "How came there to be *so much love in this desolate old heart*, that it could afford to well over thus abundantly?" Phoebe, deeply affected by the gesture, says to her cousin, "*If you begin to love me, I am glad!*"

---

19. Hawthorne, *The House of the Seven Gables*, 106, 129, 131, 196, 268.
20. Lewis, *The Four Loves*, 43, 53.
21. Hawthorne, *The House of the Seven Gables*, 141.

Hepzibah later says to Phoebe, "Bear with me; *for I love you, Phoebe*, though I speak so roughly!"[22]

Similarly, mutual affection is illustrated between Phoebe and Clifford: "Phoebe gave him an *affectionate regard, because he needed so much love, and seemed to have received so little*." "There was *something very beautiful in the relation that grew up between this pair, so closely and constantly linked together* . . . [Clifford's] *sentiment for Phoebe*, without being paternal, was *not less chaste than if she had been his daughter*." Hawthorne makes it clear repeatedly that Phoebe shows affection for both Clifford and Hepzibah. For example, when she is preparing to return to her country village, "the tears were in Phoebe's eyes; a smile, *dewy with affectionate regret*, was glimmering around her pleasant mouth . . . How had Hepzibah—grim, silent, and irresponsive to her overflow of cordial sentiment—*contrived to win so much love?*"[23]

Clifford and Hepzibah also show mutual affection: "There is *nothing but love here*, Clifford," Hepzibah tells her brother when he returns to the old house after being released from prison; "*nothing but love! You are at home!*" Lewis speaks of the "love of home, of the place we grew up in . . . of all places fairly near these and fairly like them . . . , of familiar sights, sounds and smells."[24] Hepzibah has been "elevated by *the strong and solitary affection of her life*"; she has devoted herself to her brother, "*whom she had so loved—so admired for what he was, or might have been—and to whom she had kept her faith, alone of all the world . . .*" She was "ready to do her utmost; and *with affection enough*, if that were all, to do a hundred times as much! . . . How patiently did she *endeavor to wrap Clifford up in her great, warm love*, and make it all the world to him, so that he should retain no torturing sense of the coldness and dreariness without!" But, the narrator asks, "how could he love to gaze at her"—wrinkled, yellow, melancholic, an old turban on her head? "*Did he owe her no affection for so much as she had silently given?*" "He owed her nothing," the narrator answers, for "*we must heap up our heroic and disinterested love . . . so much the more, without a recompense.*"[25] Lewis's response would likely be the same: Clifford owed his sister nothing, for hers was a Gift-love, "that love which moves a [person] to work and plan and save for the future

---

22. Ibid., 78, 93, 89, 94. Emphasis added.
23. Ibid., 128, 127, 193. Emphasis added.
24. Lewis, *The Four Loves*, 23.
25. Hawthorne, *The House of the Seven Gables*, 98, 120, 100. Emphasis added.

well-being of his family . . . ," expecting and probably never receiving, anything in return. "Divine Gift-love," Lewis says, "is *wholly disinterested* [the same term used by Hawthorne] and *desires what is simply best for the beloved.*"[26]

Hawthorne's novel illustrates the truth of Lewis's conclusion about affection vis-à-vis the other loves: "Affection, besides being a love itself, can enter into the other loves and colour them all through and become the very medium in which from day to day they operate."[27] Such is the case with affection and friendship (*philia*), the latter based, as Lewis puts it, on some insight or interest not shared by others. "Friendship arises out of mere Companionship when two or more of the companions discover that they have in common some insight or interest or even taste which the others do not share and which, till that moment, each believed to be his own unique treasure (or burden). The typical expression of opening Friendship would be something like, 'What? You too? I thought I was the only one.'"[28] When young Holgrave meets the elderly Hepzibah, what initially might be a form of affection soon appears to become friendship: "*Are we not friends?*" the young artist asks, and when he attempts to pay her for the biscuits she gives him, she says, "A Pyncheon must not . . . receive money for a morsel of bread *from her only friend.*"[29]

Friendship, according to Lewis, is the least natural of loves, the least instinctive, the least organic, the least biological, the least gregarious, the least necessary, the least jealous, the least inquisitive but the most exclusive, the most spiritual. These characteristics are borne out in the developing friendship between Clifford and Phoebe, most notably in their mutual interest in and taste for the garden, for flowers, for reading, for music. As the narrator says, "What [Clifford] needed was the love of a very few [exclusiveness]; not the admiration, or even the respect, of the unknown many." Not only did Clifford delight in Phoebe's reading to him, but he received great pleasure from the sight and fragrance of flowers: ". . . Clifford's enjoyment was accompanied with a perception of life, character, and individuality that made him love these blossoms of the garden, as if they

---

26. Lewis, *The Four Loves*, 1, 128. Emphasis added.

27. Ibid., 34. Lewis remarked in a letter that Dickens "is the great author on mere *affection* (*storge*). only he & Tolstoi (another great favorite of mine) really deal with it. Of course his error lies in thinking it will do instead of Agape" (Letter of 23 January 1954, *The Collected Letters of C. S. Lewis*, III, 413).

28. Lewis, *The Four Loves*, 65.

29. Hawthorne, *The House of the Seven Gables*, 45, 46. Emphasis added.

were endowed with sentiment and intelligence."[30] On a Sunday morning after Phoebe goes off to church, Clifford experiences a "delightful reverence for God, and kindly affection for his human brethren." Hepzibah, recognizing that they are "scarcely friends with Him above," longs "to kneel down among the people, and be reconciled with God and man at once."[31] Hepzibah's perception of their relationship with "Him above," is ambiguous, for "*scarcely* friends" could mean "not quite," "barely," "hardly," "only just," or "probably not," even "certainly not." Lewis also pondered "friendship" with God. Though he describes friendship as "the most spiritual of loves," even "angelic," he wonders "why Scripture uses Friendship so rarely as an image of the highest love," concluding that "it is already, in actual fact, too spiritual to be a good symbol of Spiritual things . . . ; we might mistake the symbol for the thing symbolized."[32] Hawthorne's elderly fictional siblings, resolving to attend church, put on the best of their old-fashioned garments, but get no farther than their threshold, for they felt that "the eye of their Father seemed to be withdrawn, and gave them no encouragement"; they shrank back into the dark hallway of the accursed house. ". . . What other dungeon is so dark as one's own heart?" the narrator asks. "What jailer so inexorable as one's self!"[33] Sadly, Hepzibah and Clifford feel that they are "scarcely friends" with God, and Lewis does not develop the point about divine friendship, though Yahweh called Abraham "the friend of God" (James 2:23), and Jesus told his followers that he no longer called them slaves but friends, for they were his friends if they did what he commanded them to do (John 15:15, 14).

Phoebe and Holgrave develop friendship in their mutual concern for Hepzibah and Clifford: ". . . They almost daily met and talked together, in *a kind, friendly, and what seemed to be a familiar way* . . . Holgrave "took *a certain kind of interest in Hepzibah and her brother*, and Phoebe herself. He studied them attentively, and allowed no slightest circumstance of their individualities to escape him. He was *ready to do them whatever good he might*," though "he never exactly made common cause with them, nor gave any reliable evidence that he loved them better in proportion as he knew them more." As Phoebe remains puzzled, vexed, and distrustful, feeling the artist is holding something back, Holgrave pleads, "Then *let us part friends*!

---

30. Ibid., 272, 132.
31. Ibid., 150–51.
32. Lewis, *The Four Loves*, 87–88.
33. Hawthorne, *The House of the Seven Gables*, 150–51.

Four Loves and Seven Gables: The Four Love *and* The House of the Seven Gables

... Or, if not friends, let us part before you entirely hate me. You, who love everybody else in the world!"[34] Friendship, as Lewis says, is ambivalent; it can be a school of virtue or a school of vice, for "it makes good men better and bad men worse."[35] One might argue that Holgrave is a not-so-good man made considerably better.

Lewis argues that "when the two people who thus discover that they are on the same secret road are of different sexes, the friendship which arises between them will very easily pass ... into erotic love ... ; what begins as Friendship in both may become also Eros," "that state which we call 'being in love.'"[36] Eros, Lewis says, is the most god-like, the most mortal, potentially the most fickle, potentially the most idolatrous of the loves. There is ample evidence that the *philia* of Holgrave and Phoebe is, in fact, transformed into *eros*. The two, in the arbor of the Pyncheon garden at sunset, experience the commonplace characteristics being "transfigured by *a charm of romance*." The artist, sounding rather like Lewis, speaks of "a sense of second youth, *gushing out of the heart's joy at being in love* ..." Beguiled by Phoebe's silent charm and attentiveness, the artist "poured himself out into another self ... [note Lewis's citation of Charles Williams: "Love you? I *am* you."[37]]; the young man's earnestness and heightened color might have led you to suppose *that he was making love to the young girl!*" Later, in the gloom of the accursed house of death, Holgrave pours out his feelings for the maiden: "Phoebe, you crossed the threshold; and hope, warmth, and joy came in with you! The black moment became at once a blissful one. It must not pass without *the spoken word. I love you!*" Phoebe replies, "How can you *love a simple girl like me?*" Holgrave's response echoes Hawthorne's words to his beloved Sophia: "You are my only possibility of happiness! ... I have no faith in it, except as you bestow it on me!" The artist asks Phoebe point-blank, "*Do you love me? ... If we love one another,* the moment has room for nothing more. Let us pause upon it and be satisfied. *Do you love me, Phoebe?*" Phoebe replies, "You look into my heart ... *You know I love you!*" The narrator concludes, "... the descendant of the legendary wizard ... had thrown *Love's web of sorcery* ... [over] the village maiden."[38]

34. Ibid., 156, 157, 193. Emphasis added.
35. Lewis, *The Four Loves*, 80.
36. Ibid., 67, 73, 91.
37. Ibid., 95.
38. Hawthorne, *The House of the Seven Gables*, 188, 190, 161–62, 266, 267, 277. Emphasis added.

Part IV: Companion Pieces

The erotic love of Phoebe and Holgrave is etched in greater relief by its ironic contrast to the lack of such love in the lives of Hepzibah and Clifford. Hepzibah "had never had a lover—poor thing, how could she?—nor ever knew, by her own experience, what love technically means." Similarly, Clifford "had never quaffed the cup of passionate love, and knew that it was now too late." Ironically, among the organ grinder's mechanical figures, "a lover saluted his mistress on her lips"—but when the music abruptly ceased, "the lover was none the happier for the maiden's granted kiss!"[39] The music of erotic love has long since ceased for the two Pyncheon siblings. Lewis would likely reiterate that they have "reached the state at which nothing is more needed than a roar of old-fashioned laughter, for "sensible lovers"—or anachronous, would-be lovers—laugh.[40]

Lewis referred often to the interrelatedness or mixture of the four loves. In a letter he noted, "The splitting up of love into four species, I agree, is a trifle excessive. I *did* admit that Affection mixes with all the other sorts, and they would not for any length of time be much fun without it. And I think I shall have to admit that one aspect of Eros—the absorbed appreciative love—is found also in young friendship . . . 'Charity' is often used in spiritual writers to mean man's love for God, and I agree that this is like Eros, or can be."[41] Again, he said, "Eros won't do without Agape."[42] In another letter he contrasted Agape and Eros: ". . . Agape is selfless and Eros self-regarding . . . Agape [is] God active coming to man passive and Eros [is] man by desire ascending to God qua passive object of desire . . ." but then he wonders if the contrast is "really so sharp."[43]

One might argue that Lewis's chapter on "Charity" (*Agape*) is the weakest in the book, both for its use of the outmoded term "charity," which has taken on pejorative connotations, and because it seems to lack focus and precise development of the concept. He does note that this highest form of love is Divine Gift-love that comes by Grace—it is "Love Himself working in a man . . . , wholly disinterested and [desiring] what is simply best for the beloved."[44] It is altruistic (from the Latin *alter*, "another"), an unselfish concern for the welfare of others, though Lewis does not use this

---

39. Ibid., 34, 127, 145–46. Emphasis added.
40. Lewis, *The Four Loves*, 98, 100.
41. Lewis, Letter of 30 June 1962, *The Collected Letters of C. S. Lewis*, III, 1354.
42. Ibid., Letter of 6 March 1942, II, 513.
43. Ibid., Letter of 8 January 1935, II, 153.
44. Lewis, *The Four Loves*, 128.

Four Loves and Seven Gables: The Four Love *and* The House of the Seven Gables

term. One might well ask, in view of the role of the three other loves, if there is any evidence of *Agape* (*Caritas*) in Hawthorne's novel.

Shortly after Phoebe proclaims her love for Holgrave—"You know I love you"—the narrator's summary lends a spiritual quality to their love, perhaps suggesting its transformation into *Agape*: "It was in this hour, so full of doubt and awe, that *the one miracle was wrought* without which every human existence is a blank. The bliss which makes all things *true, beautiful, and holy* shone around this youth and maiden. They were conscious of nothing sad nor old. They *transfigured the earth, and made it Eden again, and themselves the two first dwellers in it* ... At such a crisis, *there is no death; for immortality is revealed anew*, and embraces everything in *its hallowed atmosphere*."[45] Note the key terms, all denoting or connoting a spiritual, numinous experience: "miracle," "true, beautiful, and holy," "transfigured," "made it Eden again," "no death," "immortality," "hallowed atmosphere." This miraculous transformation of their earth into a prelapsarian Eden, through divine love and grace, hearkens back to Hawthorne's story "The New Adam and Eve" (1843), in which a couple find themselves in a post-apocalyptic, wasted, and deserted world. They wander sequentially into a fashionable dry goods store, a church, a court of justice, a prison, a mansion on Beacon Street in Boston, a bank, a jewelry shop, the library at Harvard, and Mount Auburn Cemetery. Choosing nature over human artifice, they seek to discover what sort of world it is and why they have been sent there. The new Eve concludes, as Phoebe undoubtedly would, "Why? to love one another ... Is that not employment enough?" The new Adam responds, as Holgrave undoubtedly would, "Truly is it."[46]

Hawthorne provides further evidence for concluding that Phoebe manifests and evokes Agape in those about her. For example, the venerable Uncle Venner asserts, "I never knew a human creature do her work so much like one of God's angels as this child Phoebe does!" The narrator adds, "There was *a spiritual quality in Phoebe's activity*," for with grace she transformed the mundane into the charming. "The life of the long and busy day—spent in occupations that might so easily have taken a squalid and ugly aspect—*has been made pleasant, and even lovely, by the spontaneous grace* with which these homely duties seemed to bloom out of her character; so that labor, while she dealt with it, *had the easy and flexible charm of play. Angels do not toil, but let their good works grow out of them*, and so did

---

45. Hawthorne, *The House of the Seven Gables*, 267. Emphasis added.
46. Hawthorne, "The New Adam and Eve," *The Complete Short Stories of Nathaniel Hawthorne*, 335.

Part IV: Companion Pieces

Phoebe." "In her aspect *there was a familiar gladness, and a holiness that you could play with, and yet reverence it as much as ever. She was like a prayer, offered up in the homeliest beauty of one's mother tongue* . . . ; [in short, she was] *a religion in herself, warm, simple, true, with a substance that could walk on earth, and a spirit that was capable of heaven.*"[47]

Some modern readers of the novel, perhaps many of them not believing in divine grace or the redemptive power of love, have found it difficult to take the ending of the novel seriously, considering it facile, unconvincing, contrived. For example, Agnes McNeill Donohue accuses Phoebe of being "innocent and rather mindless" and Hawthorne of having "manufactured a clumsy *deus ex machina* ending which violated his theme and implicit intention."[48] Other critics have offered demurs about the incredible rapidity of Holgrave's transformation from political radicalism to avowed conservatism. Hyatt H. Waggoner concludes that "with a Phoebe who is both too good to be believed and too quickly symbolic in her goodness, a Holgrave who is much more interesting on a thematic level than he is convincing as a created character, and a marriage that comes too suddenly and may seem a mere contrivance, so that we have as much trouble believing in the love as we do in the lovers, it is not very surprising that many readers have failed to be convinced of the validity of the hope Hawthorne proffers in his ending. It is hard to believe that love will save us if we cannot believe in *the* love that is supposed to have saved the Pyncheons and the Maules."[49]

It may be true that "the garden of the country estate, built by the cursed blood money of the serpent Judge Pyncheon, is only tempting Phoebe-Eve and Holgrave-Maule-Adam to another ineluctable Fall."[50] Or perhaps, like the New Adam and Eve, in the story of that name, these two might live by the "law of love," for "in the course of the world's lifetime, every remedy was tried for the cure [of sin] and its extirpation except the single one, the flower that grew in heaven and was sovereign for all the miseries of earth. Man never had attempted to cure sin by Love!"[51]

---

47. Hawthorne, *The House of the Seven Gables*, 77, 78, 149–50. Emphasis added.

48. Donohue, *Hawthorne: Calvin's Ironic Stepchild*, 83, 76. *Deus ex machina,* "god from a machine," refers to Greek drama, when a "god" appeared, lowered from a "machine" to extricate characters from a seemingly impossible situation, hence any improbable, forced, contrived resolution of a dramatic or fictional situation.

49. Waggoner, *Hawthorne: A Critical Study*, 187.

50. Donohue, *Hawthorne: Calvin's Ironic Stepchild*, 94.

51. Hawthorne, "The New Adam and Eve," *The Complete Short Stories of Nathaniel*

Four Loves and Seven Gables: The Four Love *and* The House of the Seven Gables

In their New Eden, can they, perhaps like Lewis's Tor and Tinidril, resist temptation and see sin "cured" by Love Himself?

The narrator of Hawthorne's novel, it should be reiterated, adds that "it is a truth (and it would be a very sad one but for the higher hopes which it suggests), that no great mistake, whether acted or endured, in our mortal sphere, is ever really set right," echoing the "moral" Hawthorne provides in his Preface: "the truth . . . that the wrongdoing of one generation lives into successive ones, and, divesting itself of every temporary advantage, becomes a pure and uncontrollable mischief..."[52] This truth would be very sad indeed were it not for "the higher hopes"—the sunshine, the joy, the hope, the visible sign of Divine Grace, which Phoebe represents.

Perhaps the demurs about Hawthorne's depiction of Phoebe, Holgrave, and their courtship and marriage are best addressed by Lewis. Near the conclusion of *The Four Loves* he writes: "The invitation to turn our natural loves into Charity is never lacking. It is provided by those frictions and frustrations that meet us in all of them; unmistakable evidence that (natural) love is not going to be 'enough'—unmistakable, unless we are blinded by egotism . . . In everyone, and of course in ourselves, there is that which requires forbearance, tolerance, forgiveness. The necessity of practicing these virtues first sets us, forces us, upon the attempt to turn—more strictly, to let God turn—our love into Charity. These frets and rubs are beneficial. It may even be that where there are fewest of them the conversion of natural love is most difficult."[53] Readers of Hawthorne's novel who have as much difficulty believing in the love as they do in the lovers would do well to weigh carefully the "frictions and frustrations," the "frets and rubs" of Holgrave, as well as those of Hawthorne and their own—and the role of Phoebe as the visible sign of Divine Grace, transforming the natural loves into the higher form of Love Himself.

Hawthorne, 331.

52. Hawthorne, *The House of the Seven Gables*, 272, viii.
53. Lewis, *The Four Loves*, 135–36.

Conclusion: Baptized Imaginations

HAD THEY BEEN ABLE to meet in Oxford or in Salem, Nat Hawthorne and Jack Lewis would surely have enthusiastically and perhaps even heatedly discussed their common interests. How would the two, virtual cousins in their proclivities and evidentiary brothers in the faith, have assessed and reacted to each other's work? It is to be hoped that this study has provided some answers to this question. It has attempted to examine the lives and writings of these two exemplary authors, focusing on numerous affinities, such as their similar worldviews and the "Ultimates" which they both pondered, their backgrounds and lifestyles, their mutual themes, their characterization, and four sets of companion pieces. Examination of these affinities, which have not heretofore been studied together, provides mutual illumination of the two writers and their work.

Central to the work of both writers is the imagination, which clearly occupied the attention of each. For example, Lewis, in acknowledging his indebtedness to his "master," George MacDonald, said of his discovery of the novel *Phantastes*, "What it actually did to me was to convert, even to baptize . . . my imagination."[1] But what is a "converted" and "baptized" imagination? Note how the statement brings together or converges faith and art, suggesting a radical change, an analogy of the salvation experience, death to an old way of life and rebirth to a new kind of life, identification with the death and resurrection of Jesus Christ, obedience, and the first step of discipleship.

Lewis referred often to the imagination, as, for example, in his essay "Bluspels and Flalansferes: A Semantic Nightmare": "For me, reason is the natural organ of truth; but imagination is the organ of meaning. Imagination, producing new metaphors or revivifying old, is not the cause of truth, but its condition."[2] Similarly, in a letter to Dorothy Sayers,

---

1. Lewis, Preface, *George MacDonald: 365 Readings*, xxxiii.
2. Lewis, "Bluspels and Flalansferes: A Semantic Nightmare," *Selected Literary*

Conclusion: Baptized Imaginations

Lewis referred to the "image-making faculty, the 'mind's eye' (also its nose, ear, etc.) wh. ought to be called imagination if we literary meddlers hadn't spoiled that word for its plain sense."[3] In another letter he stated, "The true exercise of imagination, in my view, is (a) To help us to understand other people (b) To respond to, and, some of us, to produce, art."[4] In other letters Lewis referred to a "pure and unadulterated imagination," "true imagination," and "richness of imagination" (attributed to Charles Williams), but also to "poverty of imagination," to "poor imagination," and, in two different letters, to the need of "mouth-wash for the imagination," in both cases prescribing significant works of literature to be read.

The imagination was also important to Hawthorne, as one would expect of a putative Romantic writer. Whereas Lewis spoke of a "converted" and "baptized" imagination, Hawthorne spoke of keeping "a sane imagination." In a letter to Sophia, included also as an entry in his Notebook, he warned of artificial means, such as opium, to achieve a vision of the spiritual: "What delusion can be more lamentable and mischievous than to mistake the physical and material for the spiritual. What so miserable as to lose the soul's true, though hidden, knowledge and consciousness of heaven, in the mist of an earth-born vision ... Keep thy imagination sane—that is one of the truest conditions of communion with Heaven."[5] Not only is the imagination of one of his characters, Leonard Doane, in "Alice Doane's Appeal," not "sane," but this young man has "a diseased imagination." The narrator speaks of the need "to assist the imagination in appealing to the heart,"[6] just as Lewis recognized that "a story is only imagining out loud."[7]

The imagination, therefore, converted and baptized, kept sane, kept healthy and disinfected by intermittent cleansing with the "mouthwash" of significant reading, will serve its purpose as the organ of meaning, producing new metaphors and revivifying the old. Imagination is central

Essays, 265.

3. Lewis, Letter of 14 December 1955, *The Collected Letters of C. S. Lewis*, III, 683.
4. Ibid., Letter of 3 June 1956, 759.
5. Hawthorne, *Selected Letters of Nathaniel Hawthorne*, 96. Cf. *The American Note-Books*, 309.
6. Hawthorne, "Alice Doane's Appeal," *The Collected Short Stories of Nathaniel Hawthorne*, 564. Similarly, the imagination of Gottfried Wolfgang, in Washington Irving's story "The Adventure of the German Student," is "diseased," he being "too much of a theorist not to be tainted by the liberal doctrines of the day" (*Tales of a Traveller*, 67, 74).
7. Lewis, Letter of 2 March 1955, *The Collected Letters of C. S. Lewis*, III, 576.

to the literary / aesthetic theories of both writers, a full discussion of which is beyond the scope of this study. Suffice it to say here that Hawthorne's famous dictum about writing a Romance rather than a Novel would seem applicable as well to Lewis's fiction. The Romance, according to Hawthorne, allows greater latitude, presenting truths of the human heart according to the writer's own choosing and creation, whereas the Novel requires "a very minute fidelity, not merely to the possible, but to the probable and ordinary course of man's experience"[8] Similarly, in his Preface to *The Blithedale Romance* Hawthorne expressed his concern "to establish a theatre, a little removed from the highway of ordinary travel, where the creatures of his brain may play their phantasmagorical antics, without exposing them to too close a comparison with the actual events of real lives."[9] In like manner, he said he wrote *The Marble Faun* as "a fanciful story," with no attempt to depict "a portraiture of Italian manners and character," but only to present "a sort of poetic or fairy precinct, where actualities would not be so terribly insisted upon . . ."[10]

Lewis would certainly have concurred with the distinctions Hawthorne was making. For example, he said, "The effort to force such stories [literary fantasies] into a radically realistic theory of literature seems to me perverse . . . Clearly . . . if we are such radical realists as to hold that all good fiction must have truth to life, we shall have to take one or other of two lines"—that "the only good fictions are those which belong to the second type . . . , fictions of which we can say without reservation 'Life is like this'. . . Or else we shall have to argue that stories such as that of Oedipus, stories of the exceptional and atypical (and therefore remarkable) are also true to life."[11] "The dangerous fantasy" (or Romance), Lewis said, "is always superficially realistic."[12]

Hyatt H. Waggoner has argued that much of the negative criticism of Hawthorne's *The House of the Seven Gables* arises from reading it as a Novel rather than as a Romance, which it purported to be: ". . . It should be clear that it is only on this 'novelistic' level that the work fails, if it does. As a mythopoetic fiction, it is one of the greatest works in American

---

8. Hawthorne, Preface, *The House of the Seven Gables*, vii.

9. Hawthorne, Preface, *The Blithedale Romance*, 38.

10. Hawthorne, Preface, *The Marble Faun*, 2-3.

11. Lewis, "On Realisms," *An Experiment in Criticism*, 66, 63-64.

12. Lewis, "On Three Ways of Writing for Children," *Of Other Worlds: Essays and Stories*, 30.

literature."[13] The same could be said of Hawthorne's other novels and of Lewis's Space Trilogy, the Narnia Chronicles, *The Great Divorce*, *The Screwtape Letters*, and *Till We Have Faces*. As Henry James argued, the reader must "grant the artist his subject, his idea, his *donnee* . . . , [the] starting point . . . I have the standard, the pitch; I have no right to tamper with your flute and then criticize your music."[14] Unfortunately, all too many critics of Hawthorne's fiction and Lewis's have been tampering with their respective flutes and then criticizing their music.

In addition to the need for further discussion of the literary / aesthetic views of Hawthorne vis-à-vis those of Lewis, there is the need for an extensive, detailed examination of humor and its role in the work of the two writers.[15] As this study has briefly demonstrated, especially in chapter 11, Hawthorne and Lewis made effective use of satire, but they both also used irony, whimsy, and numerous other forms of humor, including the first three of Screwtape's causes of human laughter—Joy, Fun, the Joke Proper, and Flippancy. There is truth in Screwtape's assertion that "Humour is for them [humans] the all-consoling and (mark this) the all-excusing, grace of life."[16] Or as Lewis expressed it directly himself, "Humor involves a sense of proportion and a power of seeing yourself from the outside."[17]

Hawthorne's use of humor is no less exemplary. Herman Melville, in his review of Hawthorne's *Mosses from an Old Manse*, offered this high praise: "What a wild moonlight of contemplative humor bathes that Old Manse!—the rich and rare distillment of a spicy and slowly oozing heart. No rollicking rudeness, no gross fun fed on fat dinners, and bred in the lees of wine—but a humor so spiritually gentle, so high, so deep, and yet so richly relishable, that it were hardly inappropriate in an angel! It is the very religion of mirth."[18] Arlin Turner has said, "The humor in Hawthorne's works is not often singled out for comment, but even though a lesser element, it appears in some form on virtually every page he wrote . . . His pages abound in examples of contrast, incongruity, irony, and an

---

13. Waggoner, *Hawthorne: A Critical Study*, 187.
14. James, "The Art of Fiction," *The Future of the Novel*, 17-18.
15. See Terry Lindvall's *Surprised by Laughter*, Nashville, 1996.
16. Lewis, *The Screwtape Letters*, 55.
17. Ibid., Preface, ix.
18. Melville, "Hawthorne and His Mosses," *Herman Melville*. Edited by R. W. B. Lewis, 40.

unobtrusive but none the less effective humor."[19] A comprehensive study of humor and its role in the entire canons of Hawthorne and Lewis would be a major contribution to the criticism of each.

Still another needed study is an extensive examination of the attitudes toward women and the role of women in the canons of both Hawthorne and Lewis. Hawthorne, for example, was sometimes intemperate in his comments about women writers: "All women, as authors, are feeble and tiresome. I wish they were forbidden to write, on having their faces deeply scarified with an oyster-shell."[20] In a letter to William Ticknor, he remarked, "America is now wholly given over to a d-----d mob of scribbling women, and I should have no chance of success while the public taste is occupied with their trash—and should be ashamed of myself if I did succeed."[21] Similarly, in his essay on Anne Hutchinson he expressed concern that "the ink-stained Amazons will expel their rivals by actual pressure, and petticoats wave triumphantly over all the field."[22]

It may be difficult to imagine Hawthorne being intimidated, browbeat—or book-beat—by anyone, male or female, especially in view of such strong female characters as Hester, Phoebe, Hilda, and Zenobia. Hester counseled wronged and wounded women who came to her, assuring them "of her firm belief, that, at some brighter period, when the world should have grown ripe for it, in Heaven's own time, a new truth would be revealed, in order to establish the whole relation between man and woman on a surer ground of mutual happiness."[23] Coverdale also speaks of such a brighter period, of Heaven's own time: ". . . in the better order of things, Heaven grant that the ministry of souls may be left in charge of women! The gates of the Blessed City will be thronged with the multitude that enter in, when that day comes! The task belongs to woman. God meant it for her. He has endowed her with the religious sentiment in its utmost depth and purity, refined from that gross, intellectual alloy, with which every masculine theologian—save only One, who merely veiled Himself in mortal and masculine shape, but was, in truth, divine—has been prone to mingle it."[24] Hawthorne clearly affirms the truth of the Incarnation, which Lewis

19. Turner, *Nathaniel Hawthorne: An Introduction and Interpretation*, 118, 120.
20. Wineapple, *Hawthorne: A Life*, 282.
21. Mellow, *Nathaniel Hawthorne in His Times*, 456.
22. Hawthorne, "Mrs. Hutchinson," *Miscellanies: Biographical and Other Sketches and Letters*, 2.
23. Hawthorne, *The Scarlet Letter*, 239.
24. Hawthorne, *The Blithedale Romance*, 127.

called "The Grand Miracle,"[25] and the truth of the divinity of Christ. Some currently might accuse Hawthorne of stereotyping both the female—deep, pure, refined religious sentiment—and the male—gross, intellectual alloy. It is Zenobia who eloquently argues against female oppression. When Coverdale asserts that feminine creatures "are always happier than male creatures," Zenobia replies, "Did you ever see a happy woman in your life? . . . How can she be happy, after discovering that fate has assigned her but only one single event, which she must contrive to make the substance of her whole life? A man has his choice of innumerable events."[26]

Lewis also depicted strong, positive female characters, such as Lucy Pevensie, Sarah Smith, Queen Tinidril, Jane Studdock, Psyche and Orual. Kath Filmer, however, has concluded that "there is something a little unpleasant about the way Lewis portrays women in his fiction . . . —they are either saints or sluts." Filmer goes on to speak of "Lewis's unrelenting animosity towards women," accusing him of blatant misogyny.[27] Lewis would likely disagree with Hawthorne's Coverdale and his eloquent plea for a woman to preside at the ministry of souls at the gate of the Blessed City, for he argued against priestesses in the church, objecting to a woman representing God to humans, for the Father in the Incarnation took a male form and, in the Person of Jesus, is the Bridegroom, not the Bride, and concluding that "God Himself has taught us how to speak of Him."[28] Yet Lewis in a letter stated that "there ought spiritually to be a man in every woman and a woman in every man. And how horrid the ones who haven't got it are. I can't bear a 'man's man' or a 'woman's woman.'"[29] What would Hawthorne say to Lewis, and vice-versa?

Exercising a baptized imagination, one might envision a Tuesday morning in The Rabbit Room of The Eagle and Child (Bird and Baby) pub at 49 St. Giles, Oxford. Present at this weekly meeting of the Inklings are Jack Lewis, Warnie Lewis, Owen Barfield, J. R. R. Tolkien, Charles Williams, "Hugo" Dyson, "Humphrey" Havard, Nevill Coghill, John Wain, Charles Wrenn, and Lord David Cecil. Huddled around the coal fire in the little back room, all enjoy a pint or two of bitters (strongly

---

25. Lewis, "The Grand Miracle," *God in the Dock: Essays on Theology and Ethics*, 80-88.

26. Hawthorne, *The Blithedale Romance*, 80.

27. Filmer, *The Fiction of C. S. Lewis: Mask and Mirror*, 88, 95, 99.

28. Lewis, "Priestesses in the Church?" *God in the Dock: Essays on Theology and Ethics*, 237.

29. Lewis, Letter of 10 January 1952, *The Collected Letters of C. S. Lewis*, III, 158.

Part IV: Companion Pieces

hopped ale). Jack introduces their guest, the Foreign Consul at Liverpool, and requests that he read from his current work in progress, *The House of the Seven Gables*. During the reading, Lewis may be heard whispering to Tolkien, "Isn't it a pity that such a genius should be a beastly American?"

Bibliography

Abel, Darrel. *The Moral Picturesque: Studies in Hawthorne's Fiction*. West Lafayette: Purdue University Press, 1988.
Apuleius, Lucius. *The Golden Ass*. Translated by Robert Graves. New York: Penguin, 1980.
Augustine. *City of God*. Translated by Gerald G. Walsh. Garden City: Image Books, Doubleday, 1958.
———. *The Enchiridion on Faith, Hope and Love*. Washington, D. C.: Regnery, 2002.
———. *Of True Religion*. Translated by J. H. S. Burleigh. Chicago: Henry Regnery, 1959.
Baldwin, James. *Go Tell It on the Mountain*. New York: Modern Library, 1995.
Bell, James Stuart and Anthony Palmer Dawson, Compilers. *From the Library of C. S. Lewis: Selections from Writers Who Influenced His Spiritual Journey*. Colorado Springs: Waterbrook Press, 2004.
Berkhof, Louis. *Systematic Theology*. Carlisle: Banner of Truth Trust, 1998.
Blake, William. *The Complete Poems*, Edited by Alicia Ostriker. New York: Penguin, 1977.
Bloom, Harold. *The Anxiety of Influence: A Theory of Poetry*. New York: Oxford University Press, 1973.
———. *The Anatomy of Influence: Literature as a Way of Life*. New Haven: Yale University Press, 2011.
Bodkin, Maud. *Archetypal Patterns in Poetry: Psychological Studies of Imagination*. London: Oxford University Press, 1965.
Boyer, Paul and Stephen Nissenbaum. *Salem-Village Witchcraft: A Documentary Record of Local Conflict in Colonial New England*. Amherst: University of Massachusetts, 1971.
Brooks, Gwendolyn. *Selected Poems*. New York: Harper & Row, 1963.
Bunyan, John. *The Pilgrim's Progress*. Edited by Roger Sharrock. Baltimore: Penguin, 1965.
———. *The Pilgrim's Progress and Grace Abounding*. Edited by James Thorpe. Boston: Houghton Mifflin, 1969.
Burson, Scott R. and Jerry L. Walls. *C. S. Lewis and Francis Schaeffer*. Downers Grove: InterVarsity Press, 1998.
Calvin, John. *Institutes of the Christian Religion*. Translated by John Beveridge. Grand Rapids: Eerdmans, 1975.
Campbell, Joseph. *The Hero with a Thousand Faces*. Princeton: Princeton University Press, 1973.

Bibliography

———. and Henry Morton Robinson. *A Skeleton Key to Finnegans Wake*. New York: Harcourt, Brace, 1944.

Cantwell, Robert. *Nathaniel Hawthorne: The American Years*. New York: Octagon Books, 1971.

Canwell, Diane and Jonathan Sutherland. *Witches of the World*. Edison, N.J.: Chartwell Books, 2007.

Carpenter, Humphrey. *The Inklings: C. S. Lewis, J.R.R. Tolkien, Charles Williams, and Their Friends*. New York: Ballantine, 1978.

Charnock, Stephen. *The Existence and Attributes of God*. Grand Rapids: Baker, 2000.

Cirlot, J. E. *A Dictionary of Symbols*, Translated by Jack Sage. New York: Barnes and Noble, 1995.

Colacurcio, Michael J. *The Province of Piety: Moral History in Hawthorne's Early Tales*. Durham: Duke University Press, 1995.

Crowley, J. Donald, Editor. *Nathaniel Hawthorne: A Collection of Criticism*. New York: McGraw-Hill, 1975.

Curtius, Ernst R. *European Literature and the Latin Middle Ages*. Translated by William R. Trask. New York: Pantheon, 1953.

Deadly Sins. New York: William Morrow, 1993.

Demos, John. *Entertaining Satan: Witchcraft and the Culture of Early New England*. New York: Oxford University Press, 2004.

de Rougemont, Dennis. *Love in the Western World*. Translated by Montgomery Belgion. San Francisco: Harper and Row, 1974.

Donohue, Agnes McNeill. *Hawthorne: Calvin's Ironic Stepchild*. Kent: Kent State University Press, 1985.

Downing, David C. *C. S. Lewis's Journey to Faith: The Most Reluctant Convert*. Downers Grove: InterVarsity Press, 2002.

Duriez, Colin. *The C. S. Lewis Encyclopedia*. Edison, N. J.: Inspirational Press, 2003.

———. *Tolkien and C. S. Lewis: The Gift of Friendship*. Mahwah, N. J.: HiddenSpring, 2003.

Elder, Marjorie J. *Nathaniel Hawthorne: Transcendental Symbolist*. Athens: Ohio University Press, 1969.

Eliot, T. S. *The Complete Poems and Plays*. New York: Harcourt, Brace, 1952.

Emerson, Edward Waldo. *The Early Years of the Saturday Club, 1855–1870*. New York: Norton, 1918.

Emerson, Ralph Waldo. *Selected Writings of Ralph Waldo Emerson*, Edited by Brooks Atkinson. New York: Random House Modern Library, 1950.

Euripedes. *Bacchae*. Translated by David Franklin. New York: Cambridge University Press, 2007.

Faulkner, William. *The Portable Faulkner*, Edited by Malcolm Cowley. New York: Viking, 1975.

Fick, Leonard J. *The Light Beyond: A Study of Hawthorne's Theology*. Westminster, Maryland: Newman Press, 1955.

Filmer, Kath. *The Fiction of C. S. Lewis: Mask and Mirror*. New York: St. Martin's, 1993.

Flaubert, Gustave. *Madame Bovary*. New York: Holt, Rinehart and Winston, 1960.

Fleming, Ian. Editor. *The Seven Deadly Sins*. New York: William Morrow, 1962.

Fogle, Richard Harter. *Hawthorne's Fiction: The Light & the Dark*. Norman: University of Oklahoma Press, 1975.

Frye, Northrop. *Anatomy of Criticism*. Princeton: Princeton University Press, 1973.

Bibliography

Glover, Donald E. *C. S. Lewis: The Art of Enchantment*. Athens: Ohio University Press, 1981.
Golding, William. *Lord of the Flies*. New York: Capricorn Books, 1959.
Grahame, Kenneth. *The Wind in the Willows*. New York: Scribner's, 1961.
Green, Roger Lancelyn and Walter Hooper. *C. S. Lewis: A Biography*. New York: Harcourt Brace Jovanovich, 1976.
Griffin, William. *Clive Staples Lewis: A Dramatic Life*. San Francisco: Harper & Row, 1986.
Hannay, Margaret Patterson. *C. S. Lewis*. New York: Frederick Ungar, 1981.
Hansen, Chadwick. *Witchcraft at Salem*. New York: George Braziller, 1969.
Hawthorne, Nathaniel. *The American Notebooks*. Edited by Claude M. Simpson. Columbus: Ohio State University Press, 1972.
———. *The Blithedale Romance*. New York: Bedford Books, 1996.
———. *The Complete Short Stories of Nathaniel Hawthorne*. Garden City, New York: Hanover House, 1959.
———. *The English Notebooks*. Edited by Randall Stewart. New York: Russell & Russell, 1962.
———. *The English Notebooks, 1856–1860*. Edited by Thomas Woodson & Bill Ellis. Columbus: Ohio State University Press, 1997.
———. *French and Italian Notebooks*. Newcastle upon Tyne: Cambridge Scholars, 2008.
———. *Grandfather's Chair*. New York: Hurst & Co., 1840.
———. *The House of the Seven Gables*. New York: Signet Classic, 2001.
———. *The Marble Faun*. New York: Penguin Books, 1990.
———. *Miscellanies: Biographical and Other Sketches and Letters*. New York: Houghton, Mifflin, 1900.
———. *Mosses from an Old Manse*. New York: Houghton, Mifflin, 1900.
———. *Our Old Home*. Boston: Houghton, Mifflin, 1900.
———. *Passages from The American Note-Books*. New York: Houghton, Mifflin, 1900.
———. *The Scarlet Letter*. New York: Bantam Books, 1986.
———. *Selected Letters of Nathaniel Hawthorne*. Edited by Joel Myerson. Columbus: Ohio State University Press, 2002.
———. *Twice-Told Tales*. New York: Houghton, Mifflin, 1900.
———. *A Wonder-Book for Girls and Boys and Tanglewood Tales*. New York: Houghton, Mifflin, 1900.
Hill, Frances. *A Delusion of Satan: The Full Story of the Salem Witch Trials*. New York: Da Capo Press, 1997.
Hodge, Charles. *Systematic Theology*. Edited by Edward N. Gross. Phillipsburg, N. J.: Presbyterian and Reformed, 1997.
Hoeltje, Hubert H. *Inward Sky: The Mind and Heart of Nathaniel Hawthorne*. Durham: Duke University Press, 1962.
Hooper, Walter. *C. S. Lewis: A Companion and Guide*. San Francisco: HarperCollins, 1996.
Hughes, Pennethorne. *Witchcraft*. Baltimore: Penguin, 1865.
Hulme, T. E. *Speculations: Essays on Humanism and the Philosophy of Art*. London: Routledge and Kegan Paul, 1960.
Irving, Washington. *Tales of a Traveller*. New York: G. P. Putnam's Sons, n.d.

Bibliography

James, Henry. *The Future of the Novel: Essays on the Art of Fiction*. Edited by Leon Edel. New York: Vintage Books, 1956.

———. *Hawthorne*. Ithaca: Great Seal Books of Cornell University Press, 1963.

Joyce, James. *A Portrait of the Artist as a Young Man*. New York: Viking, 1967.

———. *Finnegans Wake*. New York: Viking, 1975.

Jung, Carl. *Archetypes of the Collective Unconscious*. Princeton: Bollingen, 1990.

Kaplan, Fred. *The Singular Mark Twain: A Biography*. New York: Doubleday, 2003.

Kehl, D. G. "The Cosmocrats: Diabolism in Modern Literature," *Demon Possession*. Edited by John Warwick Montgomery. Minneapolis: Bethany, 1976.

Kreeft, Peter. *C. S. Lewis: A Critical Essay*. Grand Rapids: Eerdmans, 1969.

Levin, David. Editor. *What Happened in Salem?* New York: Harcourt, Brace, 1960.

Lewis, C. S. *The Abolition of Man*. New York: Collier Books of Macmillan, 1986.

———. *The Allegory of Love*. New York: Oxford University Press, 1965.

———. *All My Roads Before Me: The Diary of C. S. Lewis*. Edited by Walter Hooper. San Diego: Harcourt Brace Jovanovich, 1991.

———. *Christian Reflections*. Edited by Walter Hooper. Grand Rapids: Eerdmans, 1967.

———. *The Collected Letters of C. S. Lewis*, Volume I. Edited by Walter Hooper. San Francisco: HarperCollins, 2004.

———. *The Collected Letters of C. S. Lewis*, Volume II. Edited by Walter Hooper. San Francisco: HarperCollins, 2004.

———. *The Collected Letters of C. S. Lewis*, Volume III. Edited by Walter Hooper. San Francisco: HarperCollins, 2007.

———. *The Discarded Image: An Introduction to Medieval and Renaissance Literature*. New York: Cambridge University Press, 1970.

———. *English Literature in the Sixteenth Century Excluding Drama*. New York: Oxford University Press, 1954.

———. *An Experiment in Criticism*. New York: Cambridge University Press, 1965.

———. *The Four Loves*. San Diego: Harvest Book of Harcourt, Inc. 1991.

———. *God in the Dock: Essays on Theology and Ethics*. Edited by Walter Hooper. Grand Rapids: William B. Eerdmans, 1985.

———. *The Great Divorce*. San Francisco: HarperCollins, 2001.

———. *A Grief Observed*. New York: Bantam, 1976.

———. *The Horse and His Boy*. New York: Collier Books of Macmillan, 1972.

———. *The Last Battle*. New York: Collier Books of Macmillan, 1972.

———. *Letters to an American Lady*. Edited by Clyde S. Kilby. Grand Rapids: William B. Eerdmans, 1969.

———. *Letters to Children*. Edited by Lyle W. Dorsett and Marjorie Lamp Mead. New York: Macmillan, 1985.

———. *Letters to Malcolm: Chiefly on Prayer*. San Diego: Harvest Book of Harcourt, 1964.

———. *The Lion, the Witch and the Wardrobe*. New York: HarperCollins, 1994.

———. *The Magician's Nephew*. New York: Collier Books of Macmillan, 1972.

———. *Mere Christianity*. San Francisco: HarperCollins, 2001.

———. *Miracles: A Preliminary Study*. New York: Collier Books of Macmillan, 1978.

———. *Of Other Worlds: Essays and Stories*. Edited by Walter Hooper. New York: Harvest Books of Harcourt Brace Jovanovich, 1975.

———. *On Stories and Other Essays on Literature.* Edited by Walter Hooper. New York: Harcourt Brace Jovanovich, 1982.
———. *Out of the Silent Planet.* New York: Macmillan, 1965.
———. *Perelandra.* New York: Collier Books of Macmillan, 1965.
——— and E. M. W. Tillyard. *A Personal Heresy: A Controversy.* London: Oxford University Press, 1965.
———. *The Pilgrim's Regress.* New York: Bantam Books, 1981.
———. *A Preface to Paradise Lost.* New York: Oxford University Press, 1961.
———. *Present Concerns.* Edited by Walter Hooper. San Diego: Harcourt Brace Jovanovich, 1987.
———. *Prince Caspian.* New York: Collier Books of Macmillan, 1972.
———. *The Problem of Pain.* New York: Collier Books of Macmillan, 1986.
———. *Reflections on the Psalms.* New York: Harcourt, Brace & World, 1958.
———. *The Screwtape Letters with Screwtape Proposes a Toast.* San Francisco: HarperCollins, 2001.
———. *Screwtape Proposes a Toast and Other Pieces.* London: Fontana Books, 1965.
———. *Selected Literary Essays.* Edited by Walter Hooper. New York: Cambridge University Press, 1980.
———. *The Silver Chair.* New York: Collier Books of Macmillan, 1972.
———. *Surprised by Joy.* New York: Harcourt, Brace and Co., 1955.
———. *That Hideous Strength.* New York: Scribner, 1996.
———. *The Voyage of the "Dawn Treader".* New York: Collier Books of Macmillan, 1972.
———. *The Weight of Glory and Other Addresses.* Grand Rapids: Eerdmans, 1965.
———. *They Stand Together: The Letters of C. S. Lewis to Arthur Greeves.* Edited by Walter Hooper. New York: Macmillan, 1979.
———. *Till We Have Faces: A Myth Retold.* San Diego: Harvest Book of Harcourt, Inc., 1980.
Lindvall, Terry. *Surprised by Laughter.* Nashville: Thomas Nelson, 1996.
MacDonald, George. *George MacDonald: 365 Readings.* Edited by C. S. Lewis. New York: Collier Books of Macmillan, 1986.
———. *Phantastes.* New York: Ballantine Books, 1970.
———. *Unspoken Sermons.* London: Alexander Strahan, 1867.
MacSwain, Robert and Michael Ward, Editors. *The Cambridge Companion to C. S. Lewis.* New York: Cambridge University Press, 2010.
Male, Roy R. *Hawthorne's Tragic Vision.* New York: Norton, 1964.
Martin, Thomas L., Editor. *Reading the Classics with C. S. Lewis.* Grand Rapids: Baker Academic, 2000.
Martindale, Wayne and Jerry Root, Editors. *The Quotable Lewis.* Wheaton: Tyndale, 1989.
Mather, Cotton. *Cotton Mather on Witchcraft: The Wonders of the Invisible World.* New York: Dorset Press, 1991.
Mellow, James R. *Nathaniel Hawthorne in His Times.* Boston: Houghton, Mifflin, 1982.
Meltzer, Milton. *Nathaniel Hawthorne: A Biography.* Minneapolis: Twenty-First Century Books, 2007.
Melville, Herman. *Herman Melville: Stories, Poems, and Letters.* Edited by R. W. B. Lewis. New York: Dell, 1962.
———. *Moby Dick.* New York: Random House Modern Library, 1950.

Bibliography

Miller, Edwin Haviland. *Salem Is My Dwelling Place: A Life of Nathaniel Hawthorne*. Iowa City: University of Iowa Press, 1991.

Miller, Ryder W. Editor. *From Narnia to a Space Odyssey: The War of Ideas Between Arthur C. Clarke and C. S. Lewis*. New York: ibooks, 2003.

Milton, John. *The Portable Milton*. Edited by Douglas Bush. New York: Viking, 1962.

Moore, Margaret B. *The Salem World of Nathaniel Hawthorne*. Columbia: University of Missouri Press, 2001.

Morris, Lloyd. *The Rebellious Puritan: Portrait of Mr. Hawthorne*. New York: Harcourt, Brace, 1927.

Myers, Doris T. *C. S. Lewis in Context*. Kent: Kent State University Press, 1994.

Neumann, Erich. *Amor and Psyche: The Psychic Development of the Feminine, A Commentary on the Tale by Apuleius*. Translated by Ralph Manheim. Princeton: Princeton University Press, 1973.

Nicholl, Armand M. *The Question of God: C. S. Lewis and Sigmund Freud Debate God, Love, Sex, and the Meaning of Life*. New York: Free Press, 2002.

Norton, Mary Beth. *In the Devil's Snare: The Salem Witchcraft Crisis of 1692*. New York: Knopf, 2002.

Otto, Rudolph. *The Idea of the Holy*. New York: Oxford University Press, 1958.

Otto, Walter. *Dinonysus: Myth and Cult*. Translated by Robert B. Palmer. Bloomington: Indiana University Press, 1965.

Piper, Wendy. *Misfits and Marble Fauns: Religion and Romance in Hawthorne and O'Connor*. Macon: Mercer University Press, 2011.

Poe, Edgar Allan. *Edgar Allan Poe: Representative Selections*. New York: Hill and Wang, 1966.

———. *Poe: A Collection of Critical Essays*. Edited by Robert Regan. Englewood Cliffs: Prentice-Hall, 1967.

Powers, Ron. *Mark Twain: A Life*. New York: Free Press, 2005.

Prose, Francine. *Caravaggio: Painter of Miracles*. New York: Harper Perennial, 2010.

Raglan, Lord. *The Hero: A Study in Tradition, Myth, and Drama*. New York: Meridian New American Library, 1979.

Reed, Gerard. *C. S. Lewis Explores Vice and Virtue*. Kansas City: Beacon Hill, 2001.

Sayer, George. *Jack: C. S. Lewis and His Times*. San Francisco: Harper & Row, 1988.

Schakel, Peter J., Editor. *The Longing for a Form: Essays on the Fiction of C. S. Lewis*. Grand Rapids: Baker, 1979.

Schimmel, Solomon. *The Seven Deadly Sins*. New York: Oxford University Press, 1997.

Settle, Mary Lee. *I, Roger Williams: A Fragment of an Autobiography*. New York: Norton, 2001.

Shelley, Percy Bysshe. *Selected Poetry and Prose*. Edited by Kenneth Neill Cameron. New York: Holt, Rinehart and Winston, 1960.

Singer, Isaac Bashevis. *Satan in Goray*. New York: Avon, 1971.

Smith, David E. *John Bunyan in America*. Bloomington: Indiana University Press, 1966.

Spenser, Edmund. *Edmund Spenser's Poetry*. Edited by Hugh Maclean. New York: Norton, 1968.

Starkey, Marion L. *The Devil in Massachusetts: A Modern Enquiry into the Salem Witch Trials*. Garden City: Doubleday, 1961.

Stewart, Randall. *American Literature and Christian Doctrine*. Baton Rouge: Louisiana State University Press, 1958.

———. *Nathaniel Hawthorne: A Biography*. New Haven: Yale University Press, 1948.

Bibliography

Strong, Augustus H. *Systematic Theology*. Valley Forge: Judson Press, 1907.
Sugg, Richard P., Editor. *Jungian Literary Criticism*. Evanston: Northwestern University Press, 1992.
Summers, Montague. *The History of Witchcraft*. New York: Barnes & Noble, 1993.
Thackeray, W. M. *Vanity Fair*. New York: Random House Modern Library, 1950.
Thiessen, Henry Clarence. *Introductory Lectures in Systematic Theology*. Grand Rapids: Eerdmans, 1963.
Tolkien, J. R. R. *The Fellowship of the Ring*. New York: Del Rey, 2012.
Turner, Arlin. *Nathaniel Hawthorne: A Biography*. New York: Oxford University Press, 1980.
———. *Nathaniel Hawthorne: An Introduction and Interpretation*. New York: Holt, Rinehart and Winston, 1961.
Twain, Mark. *Life on the Mississippi*. New York: Signet Classic, 2001.
Tyler, Anne. "Still Just Writing," *The Writer on Her Work: Contemporary Women Writers Reflect on Their Art and Situation*. Edited by Janet Sternburg. New York: Norton, 2000.
Updike, John. *The Centaur*. New York: Fawcett Columbine, 1996.
Van Doren, Mark. *Nathaniel Hawthorne: A Critical Biography*. New York: Viking, 1966.
Wagenknecht, Edward. *Nathaniel Hawthorne: The Man, His Tales and Romances*. New York: Continuum, 1989.
Waggoner, Hyatt H. *Hawthorne: A Critical Study*. Cambridge: Belknap Press, 1963.
———. *The Presence of Hawthorne*. Baton Rouge: Louisiana State University Press, 1981.
Ward, Michael, "The Church in C. S. Lewis," *C. S. Lewis and the Church: Essays in Honour of Walter Hooper*. Edited by Judith Wolfe and B. N. Wolfe. London: T. and T. Clark, 2011.
White, William Luther. *The Image of Man in C. S. Lewis*. London: Hodder and Stoughton, 1970.
Williams, Charles. *Witchcraft*. Cleveland: Meridian Books, 1968.
Wilson, A. N. *C. S. Lewis: A Biography*. New York: Norton, 1990.
Wineapple, Brenda. *Hawthorne: A Life*. New York: Knopf, 2003.
Wood, James Playsted. *The Unpardonable Sin: The Life of Nathaniel Hawthorne*. New York: Pantheon Books, 1970.

Index

Abel, Darrel, *The Moral Picturesque: Studies in Hawthorne's Fiction*, 3n, 71, 104, 146
Abolition of Man, The (Lewis), 76, 152
Addison & Steele, *The Spectator*, 31
agape (altruistic gift-love), 208–11
Ahab, Captain, 67n
Alcott, Bronson, 38
"Alice Doan's Appeal" (Hawthorne), 108–9, 124, 125, 213
allegory, 183–97, 183 (definitions)
Allegory of Love: A Study in Medieval Tradition,, The (Lewis), 19, 183–84.
Allingham, William, 39
All My Road Before Me: The Diary (Lewis), 5, 177
American Notebooks, The (Hawthorne), 7, 19n, 34, 38, 67, 68, 70, 82, 89, 104, 114, 119, 127, 135, 151, 152, 167, 187, 189, 200, 202, 213n
Androscoggin Loo Club, 39
anima naturaliter Christiana ("soul by nature Christian"), 182
Apollyon, 194
apostate, apostasy, 91, 135–36, 141
Apuleius, Lucius, *Metamorphoses, or The Golden Ass*, 59, 176, 178, 182n
Aquinas, Thomas, 156
archetype, 113–14
Aristotle, 103
Aslan, 29. 50, 98, 104, 115

Augustine, *Enchiridion on Faith, Hope, and Love*, 155; *Of True Religion*, 156; *The City of God*, 156
Aylmer, 21, 66–67, 71, 88, 172

Bacchus, 54–56, 154
Baglioni, Pietro, 69
Baldwin, James, *Go Tell It on the Mountain*, 121n
Baptism, 32
Barfield, Owen, xi, 5–6, 37–38, 74, 217
Baum, Frank, Wizard of Oz, 110
Baxter, Richard, 171
Beatrice, 68–69, 70
Beelzebub, 119, 194
Bell, John Stuart, *From the Library of C. S. Lewis: Selections from Writers Who Influenced His Spiritual Journey*, xi
belles-lettres, 157, 165
Bellamy, Edward, *Looking Backward*, 192
Bellingham, Governor, 143, 144
Berkhof, Louis, *Systematic Theology*, 90
Bernard, St. of Clairvaux, *On Loving God*, 201n
"Birthmark, The" (Hawthorne), 21, 66–67, 84
Black Humor, 138
Blake, William, *Songs of Innocence* and *Songs of Experience*, 161
Blithedale Romance, The (Hawthorne), 6, 60n, 82, 88, 112, 144n, 167–82, 187, 214, 216, 217

227

Index

Bloom, Harold, xii, 116–17n
"Bluspels and Flalansferes: A Semantic Nightmare" (Lewis), 212–13
Bodkin, Maud, *Archetypal Patterns in Poetry: Psychological Studies of Imagination*, 113n
Boxen: The Imaginary World of the Young (Lewis), 33
Brand, Ethan, 7, 28, 72, 77, 88, 91, 120, 128, 172
Bridge, Horatio, 38–39
Bright, Henry A., 39
Broad, Mr., 137, 190
Bronte, Emily, *Wuthering Heights*, 199n
Brook Farm, 6. 18, 39n, 172
Brodhead, Richard, 163
Brooks, Gwendolyn, *Selected Poems*, 175n
Bunyan, John, 18, 92–93, 137, 183; *The Pilgrim's Progress*, 30–31, 72, 92, 183–97; *Grace Abounding to the Chief of Sinners*, 92n
Bush, Douglas, 65
Byron, Lord, *Childe Harold's Pilgrimage*, 31

Cacaphodel, Dr., 69–70, 71, 104
Calvin, John, Calvinism, 3, 16–17, 73, 81, 91, 123, 132n, 155n, 163
Campbell, Joseph, *The Hero with a Thousand Faces*, 50
Campbell, Joseph and Henry Morton Robinson, *A Skeleton Key to Finnegan's Wake*, 157
Carpenter, Humphrey, *The Inklings: C. S. Lewis, J. R. R. Tolkien, Charles Williams and Their Friends*, 38n
Carrier, Martha, 109
Carroll, Lewis, *Alice in Wonderland*, 192
"Celestial Railroad, The" (Hawthorne), 11, 18n, 27, 137, 183–97
Channing, William Ellery, 17, 38
Characterization, 103–47
Charnack, Stephen, *The Existence and Attributes of God*, 155–56n

Chaucer, Geoffrey, 31, 192
Chesterton, G. K., xi
Chillingworth, Roger, 7, 28, 70–71, 72–74, 78, 88, 92, 96, 104, 120, 143, 144–46, 186
Christian, 189–97
Christian Reflections (Lewis), 15n, 22
"Christmas Banquet, The" (Hawthorne), 141
Chronicles of Narnia, The, (Lewis), 29, 32, 49, 183, 184, 215
Church, Church attendance, 12–15
Circe, 113
Cirlot, J. E, *A Dictionary of Symbols*, 58, 117
Clarke, Arthur C, *2001: A Space Odyssey*, 75–76, 78n
clerics, clergymen, 135, 189
Clifford, 20–21, 186, 200–211
Coghill, Neville, 38, 217
Colacurcio, Michael J., *The Province of Piety: Moral History in Hawthorne's Early Tales*, 3n, 13
Coleridge, Samuel Taylor, 32, 37
Confession, (definition) 95, Hawthorne, 95–97, Lewis, 97–99, 145, 146
Conversion, 9–10, 17, 165n, 189
Coverdale, Miles, 169–82, 187, 216, 217
C. S. Lewis Letters to Children, 29
Crowley, Donald, *Nathaniel Hawthorne: A Collection of Criticism*, 164
Cupid and Psyche, 59, 176–78
"Custom House, The" Introduction to *The Scarlet Letter* (Hawthorne), 32, 124

Dance, the Great, 158
Dante, 5, 31, 62
Davidman, Joy, xi, 59, 176
Deadly Sins (seven), 87
Depravity, 7–8, Lewis's rejection of Total, 86, 123
de Rougemont, Denis, *Love in the Western World*, 201
deus ex machina, 210

228

Index

Devil, Satan, 83–84, 106, 114–21, 153n, 162
"Devil in Manuscript, The" (Hawthorne), 119–20
Devine, Dick, 74–75
Dickinson, Emily, 13n
Dimmesdale, Arthur, 72–73, 96, 111, 120, 126, 143–47, 163, 165
Dionysus, 55, 154
Discarded Image, The: An introduction to Medieval and Renaissance Literature (Lewis), 47n
Disney, Walt, 110
Divinity of Christ, 217
Donatello, 62–63, 160–64
Donne, John, 201n, 215
Donnee, 63
Donohue, Agnes McNeill, *Calvin's Ironic Stepchild*, 3 n, 91, 124, 145–46, 163–64, 172, 210
Doppelganger, 108
Downing, David C. *C. S. Lewis's Journey to Faith: The Most Reluctant Convert*, 9n
"Dr. Heidegger's Experiment" (Hawthorne), 70
Dyson, Hugo, 9, 38, 217

Eagle & Child (Bird & Baby), 38, 217
"Earth's Holocaust" (Hawthorne), 6n, 20
Edmund (Pevensie), 98, 114–15, 165
Edwards, Jonathan, 6
"Egotism; or, The Bosom Serpent" (Hawthorne), 84, 87
Egotism, 87–88
Elder, Marjorie J., *Nathaniel Hawthorne: Transcendental Symbolist*, 104n
Eliot, T. S., xi, 110
Emerson, Edward Waldo, *The Early Years of the Saturday Club*, 40
Emerson, Ralph Waldo, x n, 4, 18–19, 38, 39, 103
"Endicott and the Red Cross" (Hawthorne), 127, 142
English Literature in the Sixteenth Century (Lewis), 20n, 132

English Notebooks, The (Hawthorne), 4–5, 23, 31, 41–42, 117, 124
Enlightenment, Mr., 88, 191
eros (romantic love), 207–8
Eternity, 20–22, 171
"Ethan Brand" (Hawthorne), 26, 28, 72, 88–91, 120, 186
Euripides, *Bacchus*, 55, 57
Evangelist, 194
Experiment in Criticism, An (Lewis), 48, 133, 214

face (seeking), 181
faith, 94, 126, 128, 132, 163, 200
Faith Brown, 104, 109, 128
Faithful, 194
Fall of Man, 82, 86, 157–64
Famous Old People (Hawthorne), 32
"Fancy's Show Box" (Hawthorne), 8, 94
Faulkner, William, ix n., 6n, 199
Faust, 120, 174
"Feathertop: A Moralized Legend" (Hawthorne), 110
Felix Culpa ("fortunate fall"), 95n, 151–66
Feverstone, Lord, 88, 138
Fick, Leonard, *The Light Beyond: A Study of Hawthorne's Theology*, 3n, 134, 164–65
Fields, James T, 185
Filmer, Kath, *The Fiction of C. S. Lewis: Mask and Mirror*, 217
Fitzgerald, F. Scott, 70n
Flaubert, Gustave, *Madame Bovary*, 138n
Flavel, John, 171
Fleming, Ian, *The Seven Deadly Sins*, 87n
Fogle, Richard Harter, *Hawthorne's Fiction: The Light & the Dark* 184–185
forgiveness, 87, 97, 163
Four Loves, The (Lewis), 36, 39, 40, 198–211
Franklin, David, 57
French and Italian Notebooks, The (Hawthorne), 95

Index

Freud, Sigmund, xi, 190
Frye, Northrop, *Anatomy of Criticism*, 113–14,
Fuller, Margaret, 38

"Gentle Boy, The" (Hawthorne), 126–27
George MacDonald: 365 Readings (Lewis), 212
Georgiana, 66, 69, 70
"Ghost of Doctor Harris, The" (Hawthorne), 140
Giovanni, 69
Glover, Donald E., *C. S. Lewis: The Art of Enchantment*, 47n,
God in the Dock (Lewis), 15, 61, 88, 118, 217
Goethe, xii
Goodman Brown, 91, 94, 120, 128, 131, 141
Goody Cl;oyse, 83, 109, 120
Gothicism, Gothic fiction, ix, 199n, 200
Grace, 93, 95, 132, 159, 165–66, 200, 202, 211
Grahame, Kenneth, *The Wind in the Willows*, 48n
"Grand Miracle, The" (Lewis), 217
Grandfather's Chair: A History for Youth (Hawthorne), 32, 124
Graves, Robert, 59n
"Great Carbuncle, The" (Hawthorne), 69
Great Divorce, The (Lewis), 28–29, 53, 70, 93, 97, 116, 119, 135, 137n, 151, 166, 192, 215
Green, Roger Lancelyn, 49, 61
Greeves, Arthur, ix-x, 9, 18, 30–31, 61, 115n, 133, 153, 159, 187, 188, 198
Grief Observed, A. (Lewis), 17, 36
Griffin, William, *Clive Staples Lewis: A Dramatic Life*, 19n, 41
Grimm, Jakob and Wilhelm, 49n
guilt, 94, 144

Halfways, Mr., 104

"Hall of Fantasy, The" (Hawthorne), 186n
Harwood, Cecil, 37
"Haunted Quack, The", 72n
Havard, Humphrey, 38, 217
Hawthorne, Nathaniel, U. S. Consul in Liverpool, 4, Transcendental Club, 6, 18; the heart, 6, 7; church and church attendance, 11–13, 15, mother Elizabeth (death of), 34–35–36, sister Elizabeth, 38; view of the English and England, 40
Hawthorne, Sophia (Peabody (wife, Dove), 3, 8–9, 17, 20, 31, 35, 163, 189, 200, 213
heart, 6, 7, 10–11, 213
Heaven, 24–27, 34–36, 98, 106, 122, 135, 163, 210, 213, 216
Heidegger, Dr., 71
Hell, 26–29, 98, 106, 121, 130, 135, 190
Hepzibah, 186, 201–11
Herbert, George, 18
hero, 50
Hesed (lovingkindness, faithfulness), 59n
Hester (Prynne), 72–77, 94, 96, 110–11, 120, 125–27, 143, 145, 146, 153–54, 163, 216
Hibbins, Mistress, 7, 110–11
Hilda, 95, 160–66, 216
Hoeltje, Hubert H., *Inward Sky: The Mind and Heart of Nathaniel Hawthorne*, xii n, 3n, 68
Hodge, Charles, *Systematic Theology*, 90
Holgrave, 206–11
Hollingsworth, 88, 112, 169–82
"Hollow of the Three Hills, The" (Hawthorne), 108, 110
Holmes, Oliver Wendell, 39
Hooper, Father, 94, 141, 144, 165–82
Hooper, Walter, 24, 49, 88
hope, 24, 200
Hopeful, 193–97
Horse and His Boy, The (Lewis), 32

230

Index

House of the Seven Gables, The (Hawthorne), ix, 20-21, 74, 82-84, 93, 111-12, 119, 186-87, 198-211, 214, 218
"Howe's Masquerade" (Hawthorne), 141
hubris, 88
Hulme, T. E., *Speculations: Essays on Humanism and the Philosophy of Art*, 82
humor, 215-16
Hutchinson, Anne, 216
Huxley, Thomas Henry, 17

idée fixe, monomania, 171
Ignorance, 193-97
imagination, 32, 212-18
Incarnation, 61, 158, 159, 176 ("the grand miracle"), 216-17
Inklings, xi, 38
"Intelligence Office, The" (Hawthorne), 152
Irving, Washington, x n, 33, 213n

James, Henry, x n, xi, 63, 103 n, 106, 124, 215
John, 193-97
Johnson, Samuel, 18; *The Idler*, 31
joy, serious business of heaven, 24, 200
Joyce, James, *A Portrait of the Artist as a Young Man*, 22n; *Finnegan's Wake*, 157
Jung, Carl, *Archetypes of the Collective Unconscious*, 113

Kant, 18
Kaplan, Fred, *The Singular Mark Twain: A Biography*, 134n
Keats. John, 31, 192
Kenyon, 62, 82, 160-63
Kilby, Clyde S., *The Christian World of C. S. Lewis*, 130, 182
Kreeft, Peter, *C. S. Lewis: A Critical Essay*, 105

"Lady Eleanore's Mantle" (Hawthorne), 140

Langland, William, 192
Last Battle, The (Lewis), 19n, 32, 178n
Letters to an American Lady (Lewis), 76
Letters to Children (Lewis), 33
Letters to Malcolm: Chiefly on Prayer (Lewis), 26, 85, 166, 181
Lewis, C. S., admiration for Hawthorne, ix-x, church and church attendance, 13-14-15; conversion, 17; mother Flora (death of), 34-35-36, wife (Joy Davidman), 35; view of the English and England, 41-43
Lewis, Warner (Brother Warnie), ix, 37, 38, 217
Liberty Tree (Hawthorne), 32
Lindvall, Terry, *Surprised by Laughter*, 215n
Lion, the Witch, and the Wardrobe, The (Lewis), 32, 51, 56, 98, 113, 114-15, 165n
litotes, 143 n
London, Jack, x n,
Longfellow, Henry Wadsworth, x n, 39
Lowell, James Russell, 39
Lucy Pevensie, 53-55, 70, 152, 217
Luther, Martin, 131

MacDonald, George, xi; 18, 28-29, 119, 151; *Sir Gibbie*, 10; *Phantastes*, 31, 199n, 212
Magician's Nephew, The (Lewis), 32, 51, 85, 115, 116
"Main Street" (Hawthorne), 125
Male, Roy R. *Hawthorne's Tragic Vision*, xii, 68, 110, 164
"Man of Adamant, The" (Hawthorne), 127-28
Marble Faun, The (Transformation) (Hawthorne), x, 22-23, 62, 74, 82, 95, 96, 151-66, 187, 214
Marchen, 49
Marion E. Wade Center, Wheaton College, xi, 19n, 74n, 167, 200
Martin, Thomas, *Reading the Classics with C. S. Lewis*, xi

231

Index

Mather, Cotton, 124, 125n
Maule, Matthew (curse), 84, 112, 199–211
"Maypole of Merry Mount, The" (Hawthorne), 129–30
Mellow, James R., *Nathaniel Hawthorne in His Times*, 16n, 89, 186, 189, 200, 216
Meltzer, Milton, *Nathaniel Hawthorne: A Biography*, 62
Melville, Herman, xn, 4, 47n, 67n, 69, 81, 115, 185, 215
mercy, 94, 96, 143, 145
Mere Christianity, (Lewis), 11, 21, 23–24, 72, 85, 87, 112, 113, 117–18, 135, 158, 160
metonymy, 202n
Milton, John, *Paradise Lost*, 31, 116, 119n, 156–57, 162
"Minister's Black Veil, The" (Lewis), 60n, 94, 144, 165n, 167–82
Miracles (Lewis), 22n, 29, 56
Miriam, 82, 160–63
Miscellanies: Biographical and Other Sketches and Letters (Hawthorne), 216
Molech, 27
Molineux, Robin, 7–8, 141
Moore, Margaret B., *The Salem World of Nathaniel Hawthorne*, 3n, 12n
More, Sir Thomas, 131
Morrow, William, *Deadly Sins*, 87n
Mosses from an Old Manse (Hawthorne), 19, 188, 215
Mother Kirk, 137, 197
"Mrs. Hutchinson" (Hawthorne), 216
"multiple choice techniquef" (Hawthorne), 147
"My Kinsman, Major Molineux" (Hawthorne), 8, 120, 141, 165
myth, 47 ff., 61, 176, 183

Narnia Chronicles, The (Lewis), see *Chronicles of Narnia*
Navy Club, 39
Neo-Angular, Mr., 136, 190

Neumann, Erich, *Amor and Psyche: The Psychic Development of the Feminine*, 59n
"New Adam and Eve, The" (Hawthorne), 82, 209
numinous, 48n,

O'Connor, Flannery, 66
Of Other Worlds: Essays & Stories (Lewis), 33, 51, 61, 214
"Old Manse, The" (Hawthorne), 18–19, 140
O'Neill, Eugene, 199
Oreibasia, 54
original sin, 67, 81, 106, 123
Orual, 60, 169–82, 217
Otto, Rudolph, *The Idea of the Holy*, 48n
Otto, Walter, *Dionysus: Myth and Cult*, 55
Our Old Home (Hawthorne), 40, 42, 134
Out of the Silent Planet, 74–75, 86
Ovid, *the Art of Love*, 201n
Owen, John, 171
oxymoron, 145n

parody, 192
"Passages from a Relinquished Work" (Hawthorne), 141
Patmore, Coventry, *The Rod, the Root and the Flower*, 36
Pearl, 73–74, 96, 104, 110–11, 120, 125, 145
Pegasus, 53, 166
penance, 96, 99
penitence, 94, 96, 99
Perelandra (Lewis), 37, 58, 74, 76–78, 86, 95n, 97, 121, 151–66
Personal Heresy, The (Lewis), 50
philia (friendship), 205–7
philosophical idealism, 19
Phoebe, 83, 119, 198–211, 216
Pilgrim's Regress, The (Lewis), 23, 130, 136, 137n, 183–97
Piper, Wendy, *Misfits and Marble Fauns, Religion and Romance in Hawthorne and O'Connor*, 66, 68

Index

Plato, Platonism, 19, 20n
Poe, Edgar Allan, ix, x n, 27, 170n, 199
Pole, Jill, 57
Pope, Alexander, 31, 41n
Pot-8-O Club, 39
Powers, Ron, *Mark Twain: A Life*, 134n
prayer, 12, 171
Preface to Paradise Lost, A (Lewis), 116–17, 157, 162
pride, 86, "the great sin" (Lewis), 145
"Priestesses in the Church" (Lewis), 217
Prince Caspian (Lewis), 32, 51, 54, 56, 116
Priscilla, 173–82
Problem of Pain, The (Lewis), 7, 11, 24, 26, 28, 48n, 86, 158
Prose, Francine, *Caravaggio, Painter of Miracles*, 55n
Providence, 115, 160, 164, 189
Prunapismia, 104
Psyche, 169–82, 217
Puddleglum, 57
Puritan, Puritanism, 3, 7–8, 31, 73, 81, 95, 96, 106, 123–30, 141, 145, 154, 160–63, 171, 185, 189
Pynchon, 7, 84, 88, 112, 119, 186, 198–211

Raglan, Lord, *The Hero*, 50
Ransom, Elwin, 58, 65, 74, 77–79, 90–92, 97, 104, 121, 152, 153, 158–59
"Rappacccini's Daughter" (Hawthorne), 82
Rappaccini, Giacomo, 7, 68, 71, 88, 172
redemption, 8, 11, 159, 166, 174
Reed, Gerard, *C. S. Lewis Explores Vice and Virtue*, 87n
Reepicheep, 29
Reflections on the Psalms (Lewis), 36
Refrigerium, 151
regeneration, 9, 10
remez, 186
repentance, 8, 74, 91, 96, 99

Resurrection, 135, 157
Robin Molineux, 120
"Roger Malvin's Burial" (Hawthorne), 165n
roman a clef, 172n
Romance vis-à-vis Novel, 105–6, 214
Romanticism, 31, 191

salvation, 9
Satan, see Devil
satire, 190, 215
Saturday Club (Boston), 39
Sayer, George, *Jack: C. S. Lewis and His Times*, 17, 30, 37
Sayers, Dorothy, 213
Scarlet Letter, The, (Hawthorne), x, 28, 32, 71–74, 93–96, 107–8, 110–11, 120, 124, 125, 127, 143, 144, 147, 154, 163, 165, 186, 200, 216
Schaeffer, Francis, xi
Schimmel, Solomon, *The Seven Deadly Sins*, 87n
Science, Scientism, 64–80, 153
Science Fiction, 105
Scott, Sir Walter, 31
Screwtape Letters, The (Lewis), 10, 22, 28, 121–22, 139, 215
Screwtape Proposes a Toast and Other Pieces (Lewis), 65, 117n, 118, 119n
Screwtape, 10, 22, 27, 72, 88, 104, 116, 117n, 121, 122, 131, 139, 155
Scrubb, Eustace, 52, 57, 88, 98, 165
Sehnsucht, 189
Selected Literary Essays (Lewis), 20n, 31n, 114, 132, 188, 197
Septimius Felton (Hawthorne), 72n
Settle, Mary Lee, *I, Roger Williams, A Fragment of Autobiography*, 142n
"Seven Vagabonds, The" (Hawthorne), 142
Shakespeare, William, 30, 186
Shelley, Percy Bysshe, 31, 173
Silenus, 55
Silver Chair, The (Lewis), 32, 51, 57, 115
sin, 81–99, defined by Lewis, 85, 155, 163

Index

Singer, Isaac Bashevis, *Satan in Goray*, 121n
Slough of Despond, 195
Smith, David E., *John Bunyan in America*, 193
Smith, Sarah, 217
Smooth-it-away, Mr., 88, 104, 184, 190, 194
Sophia Peabody (see Hawthorne, Mrs.)
Sovereignty of God, 147, 164
Space Trilogy (Lewis), 184, 215
spectral evidence (witchcraft), 107
Stendhal (Marie-Henri Beyle), *On Love*, 201n
Spenser, Edmund, *Faerie Queene*, 30–31, 156, 186
Stevens, Wallace, 32
Steward, Keeper, 136
Stewart, Randall, *Nathaniel Hawthorne: A Biography*, 3 n, 6, 20 n, 66, 87, 200; *American Literature and Christian Doctrine*, 82, 123
storge (affection), 203–5
Strong, Augustus H., *Theology: A Compendium*, 90
Studdock, Jane and Mark, 79, 98–99, 165, 217
Sugg, Richard P., *Jungian Literary Criticism*, 113n
"Sunday at Home," (Hawthorne), 11–13, 17
Surprised by Joy, (Lewis), 9, 13–14, 34, 41, 130, 134
Swift, Jonathan, 41n
symbol, symbolism (sacramentalism), 114, 170, 184
synecdoche, 171

Tanglewood Tales for Girls and Boys (Hawthorne), 32, 49, 51
Tertullian, *Apologeticus*, 182n
That Hideous Strength (Lewis), 58–59, 65–66, 79, 86, 93, 98, 137–39, 152, 165n, 199
Theism, 5, 9, 17, 19

They Stand Together: The Letters of C. S. Lewis to Arthur Greeves, x n, 133, 167, 198
Thiessen, Henry Clarence, *Introductory Lectures in Systematic Theology*, 90
Thoreau, Henry David, 38
Ticknor, William, 216
Till We Have Faces: A Myth "Retold" (Lewis), 59, 60n, 113n, 144n, 154, 167–82, 215
time, 20–23, 200
Tinidril, Queen, 78, 152, 154, 158, 160, 211, 217
Tophet, 27
Tolkien, J. R. R., xi, 9, 38, 74, 185, *The Fellowship of the Ring*, 217, 218
Tor, King, 78, 211
total depravity, 7
Traherne, Thomas, 20
Transcendentalism, 3, 6, 18–19, 103, 189, 195
Transformation (Hawthorne), x
Trinitarianism, 17
Turkish Delight, 114
Turner, Arlin, *Hawthorne: A Biography*, 62; *Nathaniel Hawthorne: An Introduction and Interpretation*, 164, 185, 186, 215–16
Twain, Mark, 70n, 103n, 133–34, 192
Twice-Told Tales (Hawthorne), 11, 17
Tyler, Anne, 33

Unitarianism, 3, 11, 17–19
Unpardoned Sin, 81, 88, Hawthorne's view, 89, theologians' views, 90–91, Lewis's view, 92–93, 128
Updike, John, *The Centaur*, 176n

Van Doren, Mark, *Nathaniel Hawthorne: A Critical Biography*, 108, 172, 197
Vanity Fair, 195–96
veil, 167–82
Virtue, Mr., 184
"Vision of John Bunyan, The" (Lewis), 188, 197

Voyage of the "Dawn Treader," The (Lewis), 29, 32, 52, 53, 70, 88, 98, 152, 165n

Wagenknecht, Edward, *Nathaniel Hawthorne: The Man, His Tales and Romances*, 66, 94, 125n, 146
Wain, John, 38
Waggoner, Hyatt H., *Hawthorne: A Critical Study*, ix n., 3n, 8, 16, 63, 82, 123, 146, 163, 165n, 174–75, 190, 192, 210, 214–15; *The Presence of Hawthorne* 11n, 19n
Ward, Michael, 135
Warren, Austin, 30–31
Warren, Robert Penn, ix n.
Watson, Thomas, 171
Weight of Glory, The (Lewis), 23
Westervelt, 173–82
Weston, Edward Rolles, Westonism, 74–77, 80, 85, 88, 91–93, 97, 120–21, 153, 158–59
Whipsnade Zoo, 9
White, William Luther, *The Image of Man in C. S. Lewis*, 105–6
"White Old Maid, The" (Hawthorne), 140–41
Williams, Charles, *Witchcraft*, 107
Whittier, John Greenleaf, 39
Wilde, Oscar, 40
Williams, Charles, xi, 10, 38, 207, 213, 217
Williams, Roger, 142–43
Wilson, A. N. *C. S. Lewis: A Biography*, 41
Wilson, Rev. John, 143
Wineapple, Brenda, *Hawthorne: A Life*, 16n, 38, 89n, 124, 172, 216
Winthrop, Governor, 142, 143
Wisdom, Mr., 137
witches, witchcraft, 106 ff.
Wonder-Book for Girls and Boys, A (Hawthorne), 32, 48, 49n, 51–52
Wordsworth, William, 31, 37
Worldly-Wiseman, Mr., 184, 193
worldviews, 16–29
Wormwood, 104, 121, 131, 139

"Young Goodman Brown" (Hawthorne), 83–84, 91, 94, 109, 120, 128, 141

Zenobia, 169–82, 216–17

www.ingramcontent.com/pod-product-compliance
Lightning Source LLC
Chambersburg PA
CBHW052102230426
43662CB00036B/1756